MYTHIC ASTROLOGY APPLIED

MYTHIC ASTROLOGY APPLIED

PERSONAL HEALING THROUGH THE PLANETS

ARIELLE GUTTMAN & KENNETH JOHNSON

ECHO POINT BOOKS & MEDIA, LLC
Brattleboro, Vermont

Published by Echo Point Books & Media
Brattleboro, Vermont
www.EchoPointBooks.com

All rights reserved.
Neither this work nor any portions thereof may be reproduced, stored in a retrieval system, or transmitted in any capacity without written permission from the publisher.

Copyright © 2004, 2019 by Arielle Guttman & Kenneth Johnson

Mythic Astrology Applied
ISBN: 978-1-63561-778-8 (paperback)

Interior design by Kate Thomssen

Cover design by Alicia Brown

Cover images: *front*—horoscope wheel with signs of zodiac, by Studio_3321, courtesy of shutterstock; *spine*— illustration of an ancient greek background pattern, eps10 vector, by phoelixDE, courtesy of shutterstock

Also by Arielle Guttman and Kenneth Johnson

Mythic Astrology Applied: Personal Healing Through the Planets

Other Books by Arielle Guttman

Astro-Compatibility

The Astro *Carto* Graphy Book of Maps (co-authored with Jim Lewis)

Venus Star Rising: A New Cosmology for the 21st Century

Other Books by Kenneth Johnson

The Pyramid of Time: A Guide to the Mayan Calendar

The Grail Castle: Male Myths and Mysteries in the Celtic Tradition
  (co-authored with Marguerite Elsbeth)

DEDICATION

I'd like to dedicate this book to the spirit of Chiron, who figured so prominently in its making, from start to finish. As we began the writing of this volume, I was experiencing my once-in-a-lifetime Chiron Return upon turning fifty. The first chapter to come forth was not the first chapter given here—no, indeed it was the gifted centaur himself who would guide me to write the very first piece—the chapter on Chiron. As we are nearing the final printout, my coauthor, Ken, is turning fifty and experiencing his Chiron Return, and wouldn't you know it, his final contribution to the piece was to include more ideas on the magical centaur.

It was also at my Chiron Return that an old companion reappeared in my life—a magical and capricious free-spirited healing presence much like Chiron himself—who supported me in many ways, assisting me in the entire conception, research, and writing of this piece. It is to him, Joseph, that I give great thanks for all the love, laughter, and healing he has brought me.

It is in the spirit of Chiron, the magical healer/teacher, that we offer the contents herein to you, the reader. If astrology can do anything, it can be an effective tool in the human healing process. And this was something at which our wise little centaur excelled.

Arielle Guttman
April 12, 2002

CONTENTS

Acknowlegments . . . x

Preface . . . xi

PART I
ASTROLOGY, PSYCHOLOGY, AND MYTH

Chapter 1
Astrology and the Gods   3

Chapter 2
The Gods Must Be Crazy   21

Chapter 3
Planetary Healing   43

Chapter 4
The Healing Power of Dreams   57

PART II
THE INNER PLANETS

Chapter 5
The Sun: God of Light and Life   79

Chapter 6
The Moon: Ruler of the Night   91

Chapter 7
Mercury: Messenger of the Gods   103

Chapter 8
Venus: Goddess of Love   115

Chapter 9
Gaia: Mother Earth   127

Chapter 10
Mars: God of War   135

PART III
THE ASTEROIDS

Chapter 11
An Introduction to the Asteroids   149

Chapter 12
Ceres: Goddess of the Harvest   161

Chapter 13
Pallas Athene: Wisdom's Warrior   171

Chapter 14
Juno: Goddess of Sacred Union   181

Chapter 15
Vesta: Goddess of Hearth and Home   193

Chapter 16
Lilith: Dark Goddess of the Night   203

PART IV
THE PLANETS BEYOND

Chapter 17
Jupiter: King of the Gods   217

Chapter 18
Saturn: Lord of Time   229

Chapter 19
Chiron: Teacher and Healer   241

Chapter 20
Uranus: Maker of Worlds   251

Chapter 21
Neptune: Ecstasy and Dreams   263

Chapter 22
Pluto: Lord of the Underworld   275

Appendix I: The Minor Asteroids . . . 285
Appendix II: Planetary Archetypes . . . 295
Bibliography . . . 299
Index . . . 305

CHARTS

Lotte Lenya . . . 28
Kurt Weill . . . 30
Sigmund Freud . . . 32
Carl Jung . . . 34
Carl Jung's 1912 Solar Return Chart . . . 37
Hillary Rodham Clinton . . . 156

ACKNOWLEDGMENTS

This book would not have been possible without the help and encouragement of my partner, Joseph, to whom I am greatly indebted. To Kenneth Johnson, who always weaves our ideas and words together in a seamless patch and whose writing and understanding of both subjects—astrology and myth—is phenomenal. To the library and staff at Pacifica Institute in Carpinteria, and to the library and staff at St. John's College, Santa Fe, wherein reside priceless classical collections that helped greatly in the preparation of this manuscript. To Greece and its landscape, and to the voices of the Olympians, both past and present, who always clarify and communicate their wisdom. To the people of the Center in Galaxidi, particularly Ariadne Koumari Sanford, whose warm welcome and superb understanding of life became my teacher. To the many great astrologers—students and teachers alike—colleagues and clients alike—who teach me something new each time I consult a chart. To Stephanie Clement, editors, and others at Llewellyn who have read the manuscript and taken it forward to see it in print. And to that mysterious stranger who took my hand and guided me into Athens thirty years ago, pointing my way to the road called Astrology while we strolled around Athene's ruins at the Parthenon. As a result of that brief meeting, the course of my life was forever changed.

Arielle Guttman
January 2004

PREFACE

Mythic Astrology: Archetypal Powers in the Horoscope was published by Llewellyn in 1993. The enthusiastic reception it received from both the astrological community and from many people outside of astrology was quite gratifying. It is being re-released by Llewellyn with a new title, *Mythic Astrology: Internalizing the Planets,* in early 2004. Along with it comes a second volume of mythic astrology called *Mythic Astrology Applied.* Many have asked, Why a second volume? What does it contain that the other does not?

In the first volume, we delved into the history of astrology to some extent by offering correlations to the objects in the sky (planets, asteroids, etc.) and the zodiac itself in terms of how did our ancient predecessors think about them and what is the connection between the planet and the god or the zodiac sign and the goddess. It focuses on the link between the ancient understanding of the sky and its stories and how those interpretations are used in today's astrological knowledge.

In this volume, we seek to take it a step further. In chapters 2 and 3 we speak about planetary healing, and in chapter 4 we engage in a lengthy discussion about dreams. What does all that have to do with astrology? you might ask. By planetary healing, we mean the healing of the planets within each of us who may be adversely affecting people who are influenced by them, and we also mean planetary healing without—in the sense that when the person is healed, a ripple effect occurs and it spreads around the world. Planetary healing, then, is good for the individual, it is good for the community in which one lives, and it is good for the earth itself.

Dreams are messages from the unconscious, often portrayed in symbolism. In the ancient world, myths and stories were relayed that told of the hero or heroine of the story dreaming something profound, usually a message from the gods, in one form or another. Here, we attempt to translate these dream images into an astrological and mythological language, by looking at the deeper symbols contained in the landscape of the dream. We offer these gods and goddesses to you by way of the planets and asteroids that are contained in our own horoscopes, symbolizing what lies planted in the interior landscape of the psyche.

If astrology is good at determining character, and character determines fate, we'd like to offer a deeper look at the players who operate within us, whether they be conscious or not. Invoking these planetary characters within us can be helpful in our search to know ourselves, heal ourselves, and understand where we are going in life. The sections we have devoted to each planet for invocation can be a great help in achieving this end. Enjoy the journey!

Arielle Guttman
January 2004

Part I

ASTROLOGY, PSYCHOLOGY, AND MYTH

CHAPTER 1

ASTROLOGY AND THE GODS

Anyone who has ever delved into the art of astrology, whether deeply or not, has heard phrases like "Mars in Capricorn" or "Jupiter in the Fourth House." This might give you the impression that the planets, like Mars and Jupiter, are characters in a drama, and that when we speak of them as being in "Capricorn" or "the Fourth House" or wherever, it is just as if we were to say "Joan is in Pennsylvania" or "Derek is at his brother's house."

In fact, this impression is correct. The planets are characters or actors in a drama, and the drama is you—your life, your consciousness, your spirit. As part of your life drama, they may choose to occupy a certain sign or a certain house, but it is the planets themselves who are the actors, the personalities.

But who are they, really? All we have to do is consider their names, and the answer suggests itself very easily: they are the goddesses and gods of ancient Greek and Roman mythology. Jupiter, for example, is the planet of abundance, just as Jupiter or Zeus, the king of the Olympian gods, was a "giver of gifts." Venus is the planet of love, and of course the goddess Venus or Aphrodite was the ancient goddess of love and desire. But this is to state the case in a very basic, even simplistic way.

The goddesses and gods who gave their names to the astrological planets have a long ancestry—and it doesn't actually begin in Greece itself. There is a common misconception among casual observers of history that the framework of our Western world was entirely originated by the Greeks. But the Greeks did not invent the planetary deities; the mythic background of astrology came originally from Sumer and Babylon.

During the past century, whole libraries from ancient Sumer and Babylon have been uncovered. Stacks and stacks of cuneiform tablets have been translated by scholars. Thousands of inscriptions record the omen literature of the era. Esoteric writings, ritual texts, lamentations, medical recipes, dream books, texts to counter witchcraft, lists of auspicious days, and so on fill these ancient tablets.

Anu was the god of heaven. His son Enlil was the god of earth. These were not separate domains, but instead two parts of the same domain. Earth was not lesser than heaven. There was an interdependence and complementary relationship between the two, and the omens or messages could clearly be seen as coming from one or the other realm. From them and their interplay, the West has inherited much of the body of its astrological mythology—the names and details changing but the stories remaining relatively similar.

Though many may speculate that astrology is much older, the first written proof of its usage dates from the seventh century BCE and was found in King Ashurbanipal's library in Assyria. Here we find predictions that dealt with matters affecting the entire country and its rulers, such as war and peace, plagues and famines, floods and droughts, etc. The world's oldest astrology book, the *Enuma Anu Enlil,* was the chief astrological/astronomical text of the time. Astrological divination was its chief concern. The kings of ancient Babylon required two things from their astrologers. First, it was necessary to predict, with some precision, the occurrence of eclipses. Second, the moment the moon appeared as a crescent sliver each month in the night sky was extremely important, because it was at this moment that the Babylonian calendar month began.[1] From the actual observable appearance in the sky of moons, eclipses, stars, and planets, stories began to unfold. It was not enough simply to observe a crescent moon in Taurus; the stars that the two horns of the moon pointed to were equally important. And if the moon contained a halo, that was another omen.

The planets as we know them today originated as the goddesses and gods of Sumer and Babylon. Matched with their Greek counterparts and given Greek and Latin names, they remain with us even today. Many—perhaps most—of them bore names that have become distant and unfamiliar to us. There was Anu the supreme sky god, his sons Enlil and Enki (who were sworn rivals), and then Ninhursag, Marduk, Ishkur, Nannar, Ninurta, Inanna, Nabu, Utu, and Nergal. Some of the members of this divine family got along great together; others absolutely hated each other. Sound familiar? We might recognize these deities as having some similarities both in character and function to the later twelve Olympians of the Greek system. The important point here, however, is that as astrology developed in the observatories of ancient Babylon, it was these early deities for whom the planets were named, and who were recognized as having a nature and function similar to the planet with which they were linked.[2]

Babylonian Deity	Planet
Sin	The Moon
Shamash	The Sun
Ishtar	Venus
Ninurta	Saturn
Nergal	Mars
Marduk	Jupiter
Nabu	Mercury

Mesopotamian astrology was concerned primarily with politics, matters of state, and the fortunes of kings. It was not especially concerned with ordinary individuals and their daily problems. There is no evidence that personal horoscopes were calculated much before about 409 BC. In fact, it was the astrologers of Greek-speaking Egypt who, in the first centuries before the Christian era, transformed Babylonian astrology into the personal and individuated art form that it is today. In these same centuries, Babylonian astrology also traveled to Persia and India, where it influenced older forms of indigenous astrology. The astrologers of this "classical" period were still focused upon the observable sky, and they evolved interpretive tools that made use of their observations.

Some of these tools have, unfortunately, been forgotten. One of the most important was called planetary *sect*. Sect was determined simply by whether one was born during the daylight hours when the sun ruled the sky, or at night when the lunar force was dominant.[3] Planets were linked with the Sun and Moon, Sol and Luna, according to their nature. There were variations upon the central theme. For example, one could be born at night, under Luna's power, even when Luna was not visible. (For this to occur, the Moon would have to be in its dark phase, very close to the Sun.) And for those instances when the Sun was right on the local horizon, just rising or setting, one had to be there to determine its true position.

There are very few civilizations upon this planet that did not deem astrology essential to its very existence all the way back through recorded history. Astrologers have always been priests and priestesses who kept the myths and traditions of their people.

The Greeks did not invent the planetary goddesses and gods. All the same, it is Greek mythology that forms the most important foundation for the planetary archetypes of Western astrology. Not only is it at the foundation of Western civilization itself, Greek myth constitutes a highly sophisticated and poetically detailed worldview that has sustained, entertained, educated, and informed our thinking for the past 3,500 years. The Greek poets were master storytellers. There's probably still not a book in print that can surpass the tales told by Homer in *The Iliad* and *The Odyssey*, though if one were to curl up with Gilgamesh's heroic journeys and adventuresome tales for summer beach reading, one might find something just as exciting as any current bestseller. Gilgamesh, for those who haven't met the gentleman, is the hero of a Babylonian poem bearing the same name—a very old story indeed, for it has its roots in ancient Sumer.[4] Here, already, we find some of the planetary deities—notably Ishtar—storming across the page. Here we find the symbolism of the four fixed signs of the zodiac already fully developed as Ishtar's lion (Leo), her bull (Taurus), the scorpion men who guard the mountain passes to the Otherworld (Scorpio), and the fabulous Utnapishtim, Keeper of the Waters of Life (Aquarius) and survivor of a Great Flood much older than the one in the Bible. Though Gilgamesh's tales were told 6,000 years ago, a good Hollywood screenwriter could no doubt turn it into an epic blockbuster (for a few hundred million dollars).

But despite astrology's Mesopotamian origins and Greek florescence, the names we give to the planets today are Latin. The Romans had their own tribal myths that greatly resembled those of Greece (and in fact the two cultures are linguistically related), but tended to adopt the Greek versions of the stories in their entirety after Greece was conquered by Rome. They tampered but little with the images and symbolism that the Greeks wrote, sung, talked about, and painted on thousands of temple walls, frescoes, friezes, and vases. They just changed the names—Greek Zeus was now Roman Jupiter; Greek Aphrodite was now Roman Venus. And that's where our planetary names originate—imported from Mount Olympus by way of Rome. (The following list includes asteroids and contemporary astrological factors as well as the traditional ones.)

Greek	Roman
Apollo	Sun (Sol)
Artemis	Moon (Luna)
Gaia	Earth (Terra)
Hermes	Mercury
Aphrodite	Venus
Ares	Mars
Zeus	Jupiter (Jove)
Cronus	Saturn
Ouranos	Uranus
Poseidon	Neptune
Hades	Pluto
Demeter	Ceres
Athene	Pallas
Hera	Juno
Hestia	Vesta

The appropriation of one culture's religion by another is something that is oft repeated in almost every civilization. When one civilization overtakes another, whether by conquest or cultural absorption, it sometimes seeks to eradicate the other culture's religion entirely. There are countless examples all over the world: Greek temples built upon the sites of former Goddess shrines, Christian cathedrals built over Pagan worship sites, Spanish missions built next to an Indian pueblo's sacred kivas, and the like.

And yet one civilization often adopts the other's gods peacefully, though usually with significant changes. In many cases this is a true integration of religious traditions between the conqueror and the conquered. In ancient Ireland, the deities of the Indo-European Celtic tribes were clearly merged with and influenced by the older religion of the megalith builders. In Brazil, the gods of the African slaves have impacted and influenced the religious attitude of the entire culture. We may be seeing another such phenomenon in America today, as the Japan it conquered during World War II continues to influence Americans through its religious traditions such as Zen and other Buddhist or

Taoist traditions that the Japanese themselves had inherited from the older civilization of China.

In the case of Greece and Rome, the adoption of Greek deities by the Romans was more than peaceful—the Romans were eager to experience the more sophisticated culture of conquered Greece, and eagerly embraced her gods. And because Western civilization as a whole derives directly from the break-up of the old Roman Empire, the deities of the Greeks have become the common inheritance of our entire civilization, something all of us hold in common in the deepest recesses of the soul.

By the twentieth century, astrology had all but been removed from the sky. On the one hand, precision of mathematical calculations made the calculation of planetary motion much easier for astrologers, first with astrolabes, then with calculators, and finally with computers. But at what price? In a sense, we have lost the real feeling and imagery of what the sky looks like at the magical moment of creation or birth, with their accompanying stories. Next time you're in the desert, under a clear night sky, you might notice that a luminescent Venus is setting in the western sky while a brilliant Jupiter might be rising in the east through the horns of the bull. Further, a two-thirds full moon is up overhead. That is the way to the magic of the birth moment.

Nothing else shows this magic of existence with the crystal clarity of astrology.

ASTROLOGY AS A MYTHIC LANGUAGE

It is the premise of our earlier book, *Mythic Astrology: Archetypal Powers in the Horoscope*, that the identification between planets and ancient deities is more than just a vague, generalized kind of identification—it is specific and deep, and it opens windows of understanding upon the planets that cannot be opened in any other way.[5] These windows of understanding are important because they help to make it clear that astrology is indeed a mythic language.

But what do we mean by the term *mythic language*? Many people are accustomed to thinking of the word "myth" as referring to a mere fairy tale or, at worst, a fabrication, an "untrue story." But this is to misunderstand the very nature of mythology itself. The stories we call myths are, in fact, the wisdom tales and spiritual truths of ancient religions, the religions of our own ancestors as well as of people in widely scattered regions of the globe. As such, myths convey to us, in story form, the deepest and most profound truths of the human psyche, and of our shared human experience. This is why it is important to understand that astrology is a mythic language, and that it contains the same universal truths about the human soul that are to be found in all the world's great mythologies.

It is even more important because of the simple fact that most of us are no longer aware of the rich, profound world of myth. The Western world has been progressively turning away from myth ever since the advent of Christianity, and the so-called "scientific revolution" of the past 200 years has very nearly destroyed our mythic sensibilities altogether. Astrology is one of the few remaining ways in which we still touch the mythic dimension of life. Through astrology, people living in urban apartment buildings, rural farmsteads, or middle-American trailer parks know that Jupiter is the planet of abundance and Venus the planet of love. They may not know that Jupiter's abundant nature reflects his status as "king of the gods" and they may not know the lore and legends surrounding the goddess Aphrodite, whose myths provide us with the inner meaning of the planet Venus. But because of astrology, they too are speaking a mythic language.

PSYCHOLOGY AND MYTH

For centuries, then, astrology was the last remaining "mythic language" to be widely known and practiced in the Western world. But in recent years, psychology has also discovered the world of myth.

It began with Carl Jung. One of the founders of psychology, Jung broke with his mentor, Sigmund Freud, in 1912. The two great thinkers had reached a point of fundamental disagreement about the nature of the human psyche. Freud saw the unconscious minds of human beings as a chaotic and dark receptacle of primitive sexual urges; and, as a scientist, he took a dim view of all religious and psychic phenomena, preferring to see these elements of human nature simply as another aspect of sex, neurosis, and repression. Jung, on the other hand, believed that the unconscious world discovered by Freud was only the tip of a great iceberg. Beyond the primitive sexual unconscious perceived by his mentor, Jung perceived an even greater ocean of the unconscious mind, one shared by all human beings and one that was mystical and magical rather than troubled and neurotic. He called it the *collective unconscious*.

According to Jung, the collective unconscious was a vast ocean of dreams, images, and symbols, shared by all of us. From this limitless symbolic ocean arose all the myths and stories, legends and lore that have given meaning and delight to humankind ever since the beginning. To Jung, then, such stories and myths were not mere fairy tales, silly bedtime stories for children; they were, in fact, the repository of all the wisdom and meaning that lead us onward towards wholeness, joy, or "enlightenment."

To Jung, the characters who appear in myths and legends were figures filled with power and great inner meaning; he called such figures *archetypes,* using a word coined by the Greek philosopher Plato to refer to "a divine idea in the mind of the infinite." Therefore, a magician in a fairy tale, such as the Celtic Merlin, is not just a colorful character with a staff and a white beard; he is the archetype of the Wise Old Man, and like wise old men in hundreds of other tales, he symbolizes wisdom and knowledge. The mysterious and otherworldly lovers who appear in so many European legends featuring young women are not just fictional creations; they represent the *animus* within every woman, the masculine half of her own soul; this is why the young women in such fairy tales inevitably win through to wisdom and wholeness after mastering their relationship with this turbulent character.

Joseph Campbell often said: "A dream is a private myth; a myth is a public dream."[6] Just as archetypes appear in the "public dream" of mythology and folklore, they also appear in the "private myth" of our own dreams and fantasies. Each one of us contains all the archetypes common to humanity as a whole; the Anima, Animus, Wise Old Man, and Divine Child walk through our dreams every night, and appear in our fantasies and our aspirations, even if we do not know them by name. Because of this, it is dangerously narrow-minded and incomplete to imagine, as Freud did, that the human unconscious is just a turbulent sexual soup. Although this aspect of the unconscious does exist for most of us, it is by no means the whole story, or even the most important part of the story; the deeper meaning of our unconscious lives is to be found in the world of the archetypes.

Jung also believed that the goddesses and gods of all the old mythologies were also archetypes—in fact, Plato (who served as an inspiration for much of Jung's work) had stated as much in very explicit terms. This means that each one of us contains, within our own unconscious being, all the deities of ancient times—the shining female figure who comes to us in a dream to teach us may well be the same archetype the Greeks called Athene, while the wild and hairy man-beast at the nervous edges of our awareness is more than likely old Pan himself, the goat-footed god of "panic."

As we have seen, the planets that astrologers use to chart the course of the human psyche are, in fact, none other than the goddesses and gods of Greek and Roman mythology. So Jungian psychology, like astrology, believes that all the old deities reside within us. In fact, Jungian psychology and astrology seem to be made for each other, a "marriage made in heaven."

But that is not quite the end of the story. Jung himself believed that all the archetypes within us sought naturally to unite together into a oneness, a whole, a unified field of consciousness. A student of alchemy, Jung saw the quest for the Philosophers' Stone, which turns lead into gold, as the quest for such a unity of consciousness. He even had a name for the archetype of wholeness: the Self. He believed that the Hindu concept of the atman, which also refers to a higher or divine Self, was the same thing; and he believed that Christ was the symbol of the Self for Western civilization.

Over the years, however, some of Jung's students and followers came to disagree with him. These new thinkers are sometimes called neo-Jungians, although a better term (and the one that they prefer) is *archetypal psychologists*. Let us spend some time becoming familiar with their opinions, because, as we shall see, astrology is a form of archetypal psychology. How do we know this? Because the archetypal psychologists themselves are telling us so.

For most of us, the most familiar names among the archetypal psychologists are Jean Shinoda Bolen and James Hillman. Bolen's best-selling books *Goddesses in Everywoman* and *Gods in Everyman* introduced readers to the idea that the old Greek goddesses and gods dwell within all of us as archetypes.[7]

Bolen's vision of archetypal psychology, as set forth in her books, became best-sellers in the 1980s, during the same years when Joseph Campbell was also emerging into the public consciousness with his numerous books and his renowned series of interviews with Bill Moyers.[8] For a while there was even a lingo that developed among Bolen's readers, who, convening at conferences and seminars, replaced the old "What's your sign?" with "Who's your Goddess?" as a way of meeting and identifying people. It was a refreshing way of reframing ourselves as well as an excellent way to meet the goddesses and gods of Greece—and go home with them or not. The limitation of this type of thinking, however, is that when taken to extremes it quickly becomes as restrictive as reducing an individual to her or his astrological Sun sign. As we shall explore in the next chapter, we all contain all the Goddesses and Gods within us, all the time.

The principal philosopher of the archetypal psychology movement is James Hillman, who has stirred up a great deal of controversy with his unorthodox views on psychology. As we go on, we will examine some of those controversies, because they have just as much importance to the practice of astrology as to the practice of psychology. But first, let us start at the point where Hillman parts company with Jung, just as Jung once parted company with Freud.

According to Hillman, Jung's idea of a unified Self reflects his deep study of Hinduism and his strong background in Christianity (Jung's father was a minister). Hillman believes that this concept was not part of the old Greek worldview that gave birth to Plato's notion of the archetypes. Instead, the original Pagan idea behind archetypal psychology was more concerned with psychological diversity—a recognition of all the divine forces within us, each one appreciated for itself rather than simply as an element to be bent, blended, or coaxed into some "unified" Self.[9]

In ancient Greek psychology, those states of consciousness that we now describe as "madness" or "mental illness," as well as those that we describe as "bliss," "divine ecstasy," and "inspiration," were all said to come to us "from the gods." To travel beyond our "madnesses" and produce and sustain the bliss and inspiration that is our true heritage is, in the ancient or Pagan sense, a process of appeasing some of our own inner gods while nurturing others.

Some people may feel that such a notion is close to branding everyone as a "multiple personality," or at least creating an inner climate of the soul that is somewhat like the chaos of a subway rush hour. But it may just as easily be seen as a dance. In fact, we are constantly creating the divine dance of the Gods within our own psyches, and in the old Pagan sense of things a "life well lived" was a life spent in dancing gracefully along with the divine flow—dancing with wisdom and with humor, whether the Gods (the planets) should choose, in their capricious way, to bless or curse us. Hillman suspects that our own lives might be happier were we simply to accept them as a strange, chaotic, but ultimately ecstatic dance rather than fussing too much about Oneness, or "integration," or any of the other disciplines that seek to resolve the polytheistic richness of the human psyche into a homogenized whole.[10]

This, of course, is very close to the ancient worldview of astrology, and Hillman himself says that astrology is an early form of archetypal psychology. If Jung's psychology opened the door to a "divine marriage" between astrology and psychology, the door lies even more widely open when we consider the overtly Pagan sensibilities of the archetypal psychologists.

ASTROLOGY AND PSYCHOLOGY

If Jungian or archetypal psychology combined with astrology constitutes a "marriage made in heaven," it is certainly not the first time that astrologers and psychologists have attempted such a marriage. As a matter of fact, astrologers have been speaking the language of contemporary psychology and doing much the same work as psychologists for at least thirty years now. Many astrologers are, in fact, licensed psychotherapists in their own right.

The basic idea behind psychotherapy is that we talk about our problems until they become clear to us—until we recognize the source and meaning of our problem or "complex." In becoming consciously aware of our issues, we become better equipped to deal with them, because awareness is the first step towards action.

A psychotherapist may see our problems, issues, or "complexes" in any number of ways, depending on her or his training and orientation. A classical Freudian psychotherapist (there are very few of these left) might see things in terms of repressed sexual feelings, while more contemporary psychologists would focus on issues surrounding dysfunctional family structures, interrelationships, and so on. A therapist with a background in recovery therapy sees dysfunction as a kind of illness, and seeks to heal the illness through the "twelve steps" common to all recovery therapies. A Jungian or archetypal psychologist sees issues and complexes in terms of the archetypes or Goddesses and Gods within us.

But despite all these different (and sometimes contradictory) ways of looking at the human psyche, all psychologists share one thing in common: they all strive to make us more aware of the issues and problems that disturb our potential for happiness, and, by making us more aware, they hopefully make us stronger.

The astrologer does precisely the same thing, using her or his own model of the psyche. This model is based on the planets and their positions in the signs of the zodiac and the houses of the horoscope, and their interactions with each other, whether harmonious or otherwise. Complexes and issues are seen in terms of the archetypes (or deities) represented by the planets. The astrologer makes the client more aware of these issues, and, hopefully, gives the client some material with which to heal the problem.

It is because of this essential similarity between astrology and psychotherapy that so many astrologers have become interested in psychology. Numerous books have been written to link the astrological model with various kinds of psychological models, from transactional analysis to Freud to recovery therapy. And many of these experiments in astrological thinking have great value.

Nevertheless, astrologers and psychotherapists alike are generally content simply to talk to their clients. We should remember that psychotherapy was originally referred to (somewhat sarcastically) as the *talking cure*. Many astrologers, just like many therapists, are proficient at the art of "talk therapy" and are able to help their clients tremendously.

But is talk always enough?

Some of the archetypal psychologists have wondered if we need something more than mere words in order to touch the soul at its deepest level. And, in fact, from Jung's time onwards they have given a great deal of attention to techniques such as *active imagination*, in which clients use guided imagery to journey to deeper levels of the self and contact the Goddesses and Gods who dwell there.

A technique like this may seem to be closely allied with astrology. Why not use active imagination to visit the planetary archetypes within us?

Indeed, why not? And yet the majority of astrologers never use such techniques. Nor do they make use of their clients' dreams, despite the fact that our dreams are another "road" to the planetary archetypes within.

To some, such techniques may seem more akin to magic than to "rational" forms of psychology. And perhaps it is closely linked to the old magical arts. This may disturb some astrologers (or astrological students) who, for years, have labored to remove astrology from its old magical context and link it with modern science. And yet a truly scientific proof for astrology remains elusive. Meanwhile, the last thirty years have seen a disillusionment with science itself, and a deepening respect for spiritual practices and disciplines that, years ago, would have been criticized as "magic." At a recent world congress of astrologers, the keynote speaker was Thomas Moore, author of the best-selling *Care of the Soul* and *Soul Mates*.[11] He asked the body of astrologers in attendance to consider focusing less on making astrology statistically accurate to please the scientific community and on trying to psychologize astrology in order to gain more academic credibility. Instead, he suggested that astrologers honor their ancient legacy of Pagan worship and magic; seen in that context, astrology still constitutes one of the best and most well-defined oracular systems in place.

This vision has powerful implications for our own time. As we are thrust into a new millennium in which technology seems to overtake every aspect of daily life, with computers, modems, and cell phones practically strapped to our bodies like appendages, we must look to nature to resolve our dilemmas and polarize our extremes. Here we find the archetypal mother and father of all the gods, Gaia and Uranus, at work in our own time. As we enter a technological Aquarian age (ruled by Uranus), the natural mythic polarity must necessarily be Gaia (Earth, nature, Taurus, simplicity). So why not forge a union between the most Uranian of divinatory systems—astrology—and the ancient sense of oneness with nature by looking back to our Hellenistic and Renaissance forebears to see what wisdom their approach contained?

If astrology embodies a frame of references that originated from correspondences between heavenly bodies (each assigned to a god) appearing in the sky and the actual events on earth as recorded in the Babylonian lists of omens, then we must examine those correspondences. What are the natures (desires, impulses, whims) of those planets/gods? And if we are predestined to act in certain ways at a prescribed time, how then can we best handle that occurrence?

There is an underlying assumption by practitioners of astrology that character is fate, or that character is destiny. What better way to determine one's destiny or fate than to examine character as revealed by one's stars? Recently, Hillman has written and spoken about the force of character as it relates to age, and the force of character as a distinctly missing ingredient from our culture. He asserts that character has pretty much been relegated to the domain of the palmists and astrologers.[12] Going all the way back to Heraclitus, he tells us: "Character is our guardian daimon and our fate."[13]

If astrology is successful at revealing character and ultimately predicting fate, then what part does "mythic" astrology play? If there's anything the current paradigm shift and pending age change is producing, it's the idea that storytelling, imagery, mythology, visualization, and right-brained methods of achieving understanding are at a peak rebirth. Astrology has usually been taught through means of learning a language. First, one learns the alphabet (Aries, Taurus, Gemini, etc.). Then one develops keywords, sentences, and lists of ingredients that make up a Taurus or a Gemini type. It's a great way for computer technicians and engineers to learn, but totally incomprehensible to those with visually oriented processes. Myths are stories. Like the arts, drama, and music of any culture, myth provides a way of understanding that opens up a universal language, a poetry of the cosmos through a simple story.

Learning in ancient times was through storytelling and imagery. Why do we keep uncovering so many cave paintings and petroglyphs along the way? Our predecessors were attempting to preserve something of their knowledge and information that would withstand the challenges of the elements and the ravishments of war. Some modern thinkers actually believe that once we began to use our brains for reading and writing, we lost essential attributes of communicating with one another through shared visions, dreams, and telepathy.

In this book, we shall examine a number of ways in which the planetary archetypes within us can be contacted, worked with, and brought into harmony. You don't need to be an astrologer to practice these techniques or gain from them. In fact, you don't really need to know anything about astrology at all. You can simply start with the images themselves—the dreams and imaginative pictures you share with all other living human beings. You can allow those dreams and images to lead you to your inner planetary deities and, later, to the horoscope itself.

But before we examine the techniques of healing, let us try to learn more about how archetypes become troubled, and why the Gods are in need of our help.

---

1. Baigent, Michael, *The Omens of Babylon: Astrology and Ancient Mesopotamia* (London: Penguin-Arkana, 1994).

2. Ibid.
3. Hand, Robert, *Night & Day: Planetary Sect in Astrology* (Reston, VA: ARHAT, 1995).
4. Sandars, N. K., trans., *The Epic of Gilgamesh* (London: Penguin, 1988).
5. Guttman, Ariel, and Kenneth Johnson, *Mythic Astrology: Archetypal Powers in the Horoscope* (St. Paul, MN: Llewellyn Publications, 1993).
6. Campbell, Joseph, with Bill Moyers, *The Power of Myth* (New York: Doubleday, 1988) 40.
7. Bolen, Jean Shinoda, *Goddesses in Everywoman* (New York: Harper & Row, 1984); *Gods in Everyman* (New York: Harper & Row, 1989).
8. Campbell & Moyers, op.cit.
9. Hillman, James, *A Blue Fire* (New York: Perennial, 1991).
10. Ibid.
11. Moore, Thomas, *Care of the Soul* (New York: Harper Collins, 1992); *Soul Mates* (New York: Harper Perennial, 1994).
12. Hillman, James, *The Force of Character and the Lasting Life* (New York: Random House, 1999).
13. Hillman, James, *The Dream and the Underworld* (New York: Harper and Row, 1979).

CHAPTER 2

THE GODS MUST BE CRAZY

It may give us a sense of strength and empowerment to realize that our own psyche is a kind of Mt. Olympus, home of goddesses, gods, and heroic archetypal figures. But lest we allow ourselves to become too grandiose about our divine heritage, let it be stated at the very outset that we are not often aware of the divine figures within us until they become annoyed with us and start to "act up."

If we have a background in any one of the numerous psychologies that compete with each other on today's market, we are probably used to thinking of a psychological complex in terms of some issue with absent Daddy, unfeeling Mommy, or the host of other relatives and siblings who inhabit the current psychological landscape. The notion put forth by Jungians and other archetypal psychologists—that a complex is based primarily upon the inharmonious or just plain cranky actions of one of our inner deities—may seem more than a bit strange to us. But this is precisely how our ancestors thought of it.

In Homer's *Iliad,* the great heroes of the Greeks have a habit of taking beautiful young girls captive as slaves. (Not a very politically correct thing to do by today's standards, but let's just let that one go for the moment and continue to the main point.) The hero Achilles takes a fancy to one of King Agamemnon's captive slave girls and simply steals her. Since Agamemnon is the commander of all the Greek forces and Achilles the most celebrated warrior, this throws the whole Greek army into a major snit and brings the Trojan War temporarily to a halt. Eventually Achilles is forced to return the girl and apologize publicly, but his only real apology consists of his claim that he was possessed by some deity who impelled him to steal her.

In other words, he simply shrugs his shoulders and says: "I couldn't help myself: Some god made me do it."[1]

Some modern forms of psychology may brand this as a form of denial, but Achilles' attitude was essentially the attitude of ancient Greek psychology in general. It is also, to a certain degree, the attitude of contemporary archetypal psychology. There are, of course, some important differences: for example, ancient Greek psychology gives little recognition to the parental or family complexes that form the background of most contemporary psychology, while archetypal psychologists look for these issues in the behavior of the archetypes themselves (though it must be admitted that they are less concerned with Mommy and Daddy than, for instance, the Freudians).

But how does this process happen? How do the Gods become active in our lives? And why do they choose to reach us principally when they are troubled?

Look at it this way. The Goddesses and Gods may be regarded as more than human, larger than life. Their blasts of thunder and storm, tempests of rage, and turbulent love affairs all mark them as forces of nature, actresses and actors on a vast, primordial stage. They do things on a grand scale, as befits the conduct of deities.

This primordial grandeur is present within each and every one of us, but for the most part we remain unaware of it. We go on about our ordinary lives without much concern for the "mythic dimension" that lies within. We certainly don't think of ourselves as Homeric heroes, stormy goddesses, or divine figures. And for the most part, our inner deities may be content to remain sleeping in our unconscious—or, deeper still, in the collective unconscious that links us with all of humanity. They may feel no particular compulsion to swim up through the depths and make themselves known to our ordinary waking consciousness.

Unless, of course, they really need to.

Many or most of us—perhaps all of us—contain within our souls one or two of these deities who are of primary importance, who form the cornerstones and foundations of our personalities. In Afrocentric traditions like Candomble or Voudoun, such a deity is called "the master of your head," meaning that the particular deity is the master or primary determinant of your personal consciousness. In such traditions, there are religious specialists who are skilled at identifying such a deity and, through ritual and initiation, bringing the worshipper into harmony with her or his master of the head. Here in the Western world, we no longer possess such specialists; although it is here that the astrologer may be of great help. The astrologer sees these inner deities in terms of planets, signs, and other astrological themes. The astrologer is, in many ways, very competent to identify the master of your head by directing your attention to the planet (or planets) that plays the largest role in your life, and that sets the tone for your personality.

This may well be the planet that is giving you the most trouble.

As we begin to grow psychologically, we begin to take more and more control over our true nature, our real individuality. When we grow strong enough in terms of our self-knowing—or, as the Jungians call it, our *individuation*—we may begin to seem a little bit larger than life as well. At such a time, the

Goddess or God—and planet—who best represents our emerging individuality may very well awaken. In most cases, such a figure awakens when we are at a time of crisis—when our individuality or sense of self faces a challenge and when we are called upon to be ourselves in a powerful and dramatic way.

Astrologers may be of help here, too, for the astrologer is also trained to identify the times at which such transitional challenges may occur, and to identify the planets—and hence the archetypes—that are involved.

So here we are, trying to gain greater knowledge of ourselves, trying with such passion and intensity that the waters of the unconscious begin to stir, the underground volcanoes in our souls begin to erupt, and a divine figure blasts up out of the depths and says: "I am the master here! Pay attention to me!"

And so the archetype begins to play its role as an actor upon the stage of our ordinary lives. But in most cases our lives are still just that—ordinary—and we are not equipped to play host to a powerful divinity. We are not prepared for blasts of thunder and storm, tempests of rage, turbulent love affairs, or the other activities of these forces of nature. We are not prepared for our homes and workplaces to become a vast, primordial stage upon which wild deities perform.

So when we first meet the Gods, it seems as if they're crazy.

Let us illustrate this point with an example from recent artistic history. In the late 1920s, just before Hitler's rise to power, Germany went through a great explosion of artistic creativity during the last days of the Weimar Republic. This was the era of the great Expressionistic silent movies and the great Berlin cabaret shows. The most renowned writers on the cabaret scene were playwright Bertolt Brecht and his musical partner, the composer Kurt Weill. Weill was married to a remarkable cabaret singer by the name of Lotte Lenya. Though not conventionally beautiful, Lotte was highly erotic, and, as a former prostitute, she was also sometimes rather daring. Her stage routines with black fishnet stockings, a top hat, and high heels were deliberately provocative and helped to set the sexual tone of the era.

Now, the fact that Lotte Lenya more or less defined the erotic sensibilities of her time should make it clear to us that she was strongly under the influence of the archetype of Aphrodite, the goddess of love. Astrologers know this goddess under her Roman and planetary name as Venus. So we don't even need to look at Lotte's horoscope to figure out that she was dominated by the planet Venus. Her Venus was so powerful that it influenced the world around her: it was an archetypal rather than a merely personal Venus, and quite obviously formed the cornerstone of her personality.

Many astrologers prefer to look at Venus as a planet of marriage. This is quite an ancient tradition, but—as we argued in our earlier book—it is not correct. Venus was never regarded as the goddess of marriage[2]—that honor went to Juno, and when young women were married in ancient Greece and Rome, they actually surrendered all their pretty things (their Venus gear) to the temple of Venus or Aphrodite, to symbolize that they had left her behind and gone over to the world of Hera or Juno instead.

Actually, Venus was the goddess of purely erotic love, which, to the ancients, was a very different thing than married love. Venus was an archetype of sexual freedom, for she chose her numerous lovers entirely according to her own whim, and was generally uninterested in whether her choices were socially appropriate or even reasonable. She simply did whatever she wanted with whomever she pleased.

We might suspect that a Venus woman would have some difficulties in an ordinary marriage situation, but in many cases the Venus woman will succeed in bringing her freestyle eroticism under control and channeling it into the confines of an intimate married relationship. However, if Venus is too strong or too wild, then she may begin to "act out," and things may begin to get a bit crazy. And all the poor Venus girl will be able to say is: "The goddess made me do it."

Let's get back to Kurt and Lotte. If we look at the stories about Venus, we can see that although she had countless love affairs, she had four major relationships in her life.[3] One of these was her husband, Vulcan (Greek: Hephaestus). This god, who was lame and ugly and spent all his time working as the divine blacksmith, seems like an unlikely mate for the goddess of love, but it was Jupiter (Greek: Zeus), the king of the gods, who arranged their marriage, so they didn't have much to say about it. So here we have a talented but brooding and inarticulate man, not very attractive, mated to a wild, erotic love goddess. It is interesting to note how often this kind of a match occurs in real life.

Venus' other "stable" relationships (which is not a great choice of words in her case) were with Adonis, whom she adored, though it was short-lived; with Mars, the war god, her "passionate" lover; and with Mercury, the clever god of communications and the mind, who was also the "captain of the nymphs" and who appreciated a woman simply for her sexual prowess without getting attached to her at all (which made him a rather appropriate partner for Venus, who had the same instincts).

But in this case we are mostly concerned with Vulcan, because Kurt Weill was a Vulcan type. (No, we're not talking about a planet here, and in fact, many people take on the characteristics of archetypes and deities that are not part of our astrological sky, but we will take up this question later in the book.) The more Lotte flirted and cavorted on the stage, the more her quiet, inarticulate husband (a thin fellow with thick glasses) turned inward towards his writing. Sometimes the results were brilliant—anyone who sees Lotte Lenya singing the Brecht-Weill ballad "Pirate Jenny" from the old German film version of *The Threepenny Opera* will witness a performance so powerful it brings chills to the spine.

But despite their archetypal power, the two were not happy as a couple, and soon Lotte's controlling Venus began to act up in style, compelling her into an endless series of casual sexual affairs. But if the Goddess was crazy, so was the God—Weill turned even more deeply inward, ignoring his wife's obvious infidelities in favor of more and more writing.

The Gods made them do it.

We have been unable to obtain exact birth times for either Lotte or Kurt, but even a quick look at the day of Lotte Lenya's birth reveals the source of her out-of-control Venusian behavior.

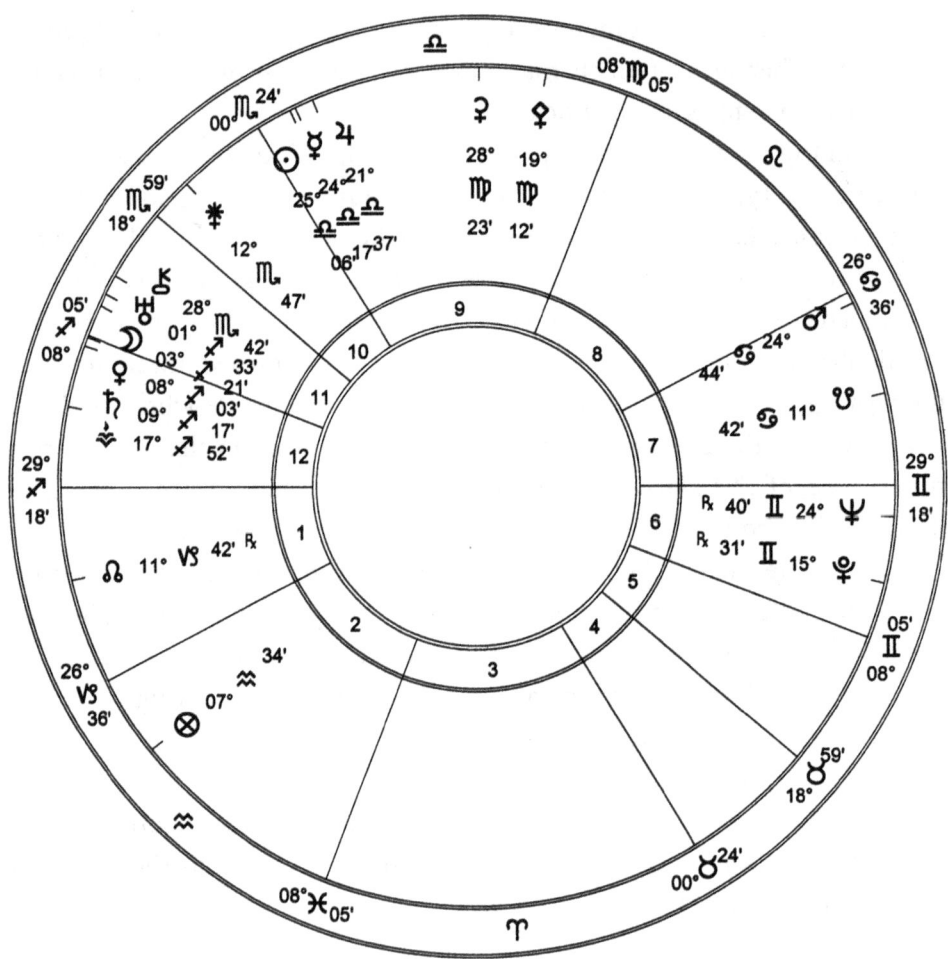

LOTTE LENYA
October 18, 1898 / 12:00:00 PM CET / Vienna, Austria
Koch Houses

Lotte Lenya's Venus is in Sagittarius, which in most cases would not be considered a particularly erotic or even "feminine" Venus. Ordinarily such a Venus might be regarded as a sign of independence, of emotional detachment, and of a temperament that is more interested in personal freedom than relationships. Note that Venus is also conjunct the Moon, so that two of the most powerful feminine archetypes combine into one to create a distinctly feminine—although somewhat strong-willed and free-spirited—personality.

But what is especially important to our own theme is that Venus and the Moon are hemmed in on each side by Saturn and Uranus, and they are opposed by Pluto. With the opposite poles of limitation (Saturn) and freedom (Uranus) exerting equal force, Venus and the Moon are placed under tremendous pressure. Imagine that you have a small rubber ball in your hands, and that you are squeezing it as hard as you can. Eventually it will shoot out of your grasp and into the air. This is precisely what happened to Lotte Lenya's Moon-Venus conjunction. Caught between powerful opposing forces, the Goddess was forced out of the unconscious and onto the stage of Lotte's waking life—in fact, the experience was so powerful that it became archetypal and forced itself onto the stage of the world at large.

Beneath the rather obvious Saturn-Uranus conflict, the conjunction of Moon and Venus is further fueled by the vast underground power of Pluto, which often shows collective (i.e., archetypal) forces much greater than any individual. Lotte Lenya's very public Venus was colored by the freedom of Sagittarius, the provocative androgyny of Uranus, the pessimistic but licentious darkness of Saturn, and powered by the dark, somewhat perverse force of Pluto—which was discovered in the same year that *The Threepenny Opera* was filmed, and which heralded the rise of the Plutonian Third Reich that rose on Weimar's overstressed ashes. Lotte Lenya's rare blend of archetypes was perfectly suited to make her one of the living symbols of the cabaret era's desperate, decadent, but supremely creative moment in history.

Those of you who are familiar with mythology may remember that Venus' husband, Vulcan or Hephaestus, the god of the forge, was a lame and altogether unattractive fellow, and that he buried himself in his creative work while his wife flaunted her amorous escapades all over Mt. Olympus. Of course, Vulcan was a magnificent craftsman, and his work was so fine that it was literally magical. His introverted focus on his artistry was responsible for a great deal of beauty in the world, but his soul was filled with resentment towards his faithless wife. One story tells us that he even trapped her with her lover Mars in a magical net and hoisted her up so that all the gods might witness her shame, but for the most part he was far too inarticulate to raise his voice in protest.

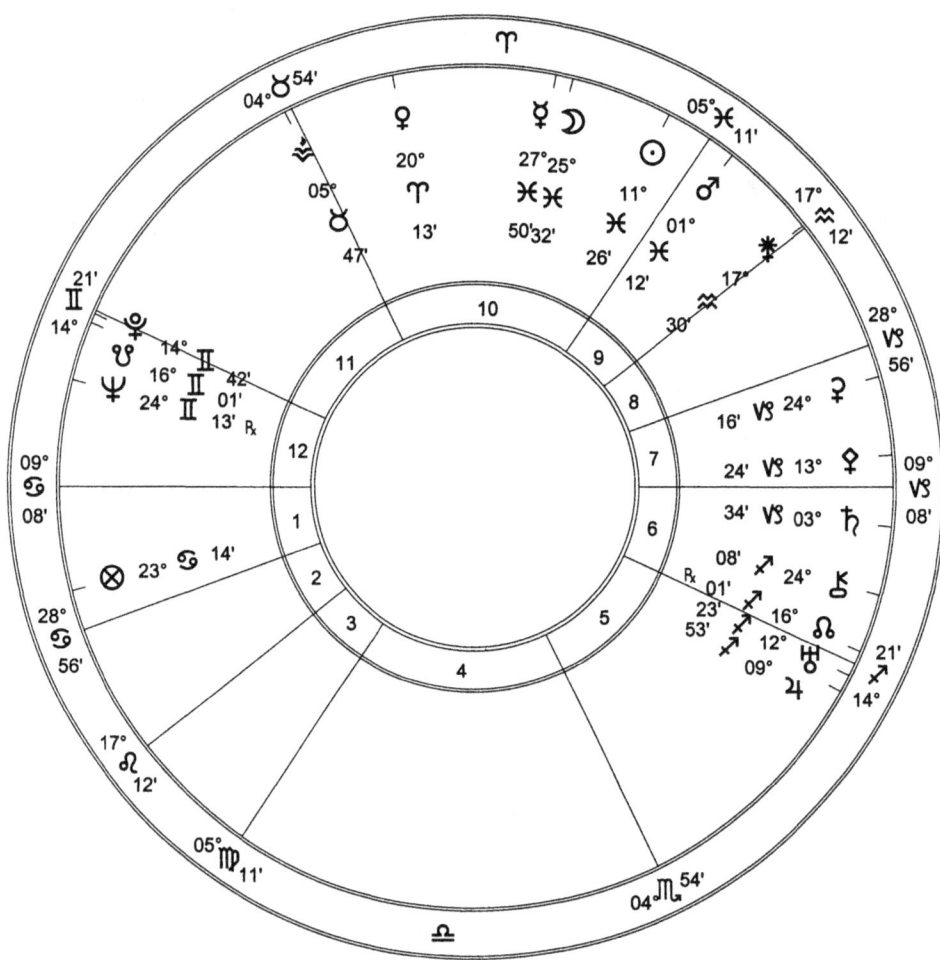

KURT WEILL
March 2, 1900 / 12:00:00 PM CET / Dessau, Germany
Koch Houses

Kurt Weill's horoscope reveals a supremely introverted personality, as we might expect from an individual whose life was dominated by the archetype of Vulcan. There is a way to plot Vulcan in the horoscope, using various astrological programs. The astrology software program Solar Fire places Vulcan at 14° Pisces, very close to his Sun at 11° Pisces (Vulcan is never very far from the Sun).[4] What is truly illuminating is that this position of Vulcan, along with the Sun, becomes the focal point of a T-square, a very sensitive placement and the activating principle of his life—involving Jupiter, Pluto, Uranus, and the lunar nodes in his chart. Note also that the position of the Black Moon Lilith is in exact opposition to his natal Sun, also part of this T-square (actually making it a grand mutable cross). There is no doubt the role that Lilith played out in his life was portrayed indeed by Lotte (read more on Lilith in a later chapter in this volume). The opposition of Pluto in Gemini to a Saturn-Uranus conjunction in Sagittarius may have impelled Lotte Lenya towards the stage, but a similar combination in her husband's chart had a very different effect. In Kurt Weill's case, the opposition of Pluto to Uranus (he was two years younger than Lotte, and Saturn had already moved on, though wild and crazy Uranus remained in Sagittarius) exerts its archetypal force on an incredible cluster of planets in the sign Pisces.

Whenever a planet stands at a ninety-degree angle from either side of an opposition, we call it a T-square, and it symbolizes enormous pressure. In this case no fewer than four planets stand midway between the Uranus-Pluto opposition—the Sun, Moon, Mercury, and Mars are all in Pisces. Pisces is a moody, introverted sign, and Weill had a temperament to match. Like Vulcan, he may also have considered himself somewhat unlovely or unlovable. In the shining and glittery world of the Weimar cabarets, he was a quiet man with thick glasses, a Jewish intellectual, the son of a rabbi. He remained immersed in the great Piscean ocean of the unconscious, bonded to his piano like Vulcan to his forge, responding in true Piscean fashion to the enormous collective pressures brought to bear upon him by producing some of the greatest music of his time. How did he feel about his wife's unfaithful romps through the demimonde of Berlin's cabaret scene? Like a true Vulcan, Weill was too inarticulate to even comment on the matter.

Of course, sometimes the crazy-making tendencies of our inner gods can have a positive impact on our lives. In the previous chapter, we mentioned the split that occurred between Sigmund Freud and Carl Jung. When we examine the astrological charts of both men, their parting of the ways seems not only logical but inevitable.[5]

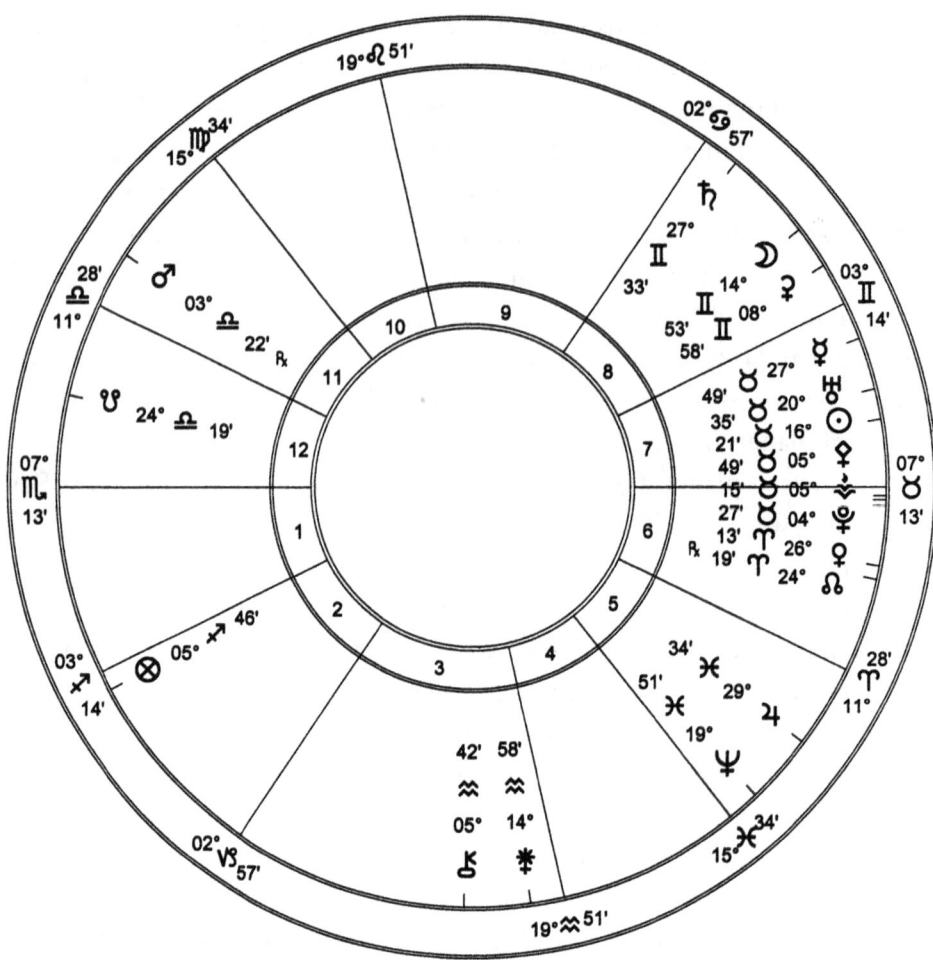

SIGMUND FREUD
May 6, 1856 / 6:30:00 PM LMT / Friedberg, Germany
Koch Houses

Freud, as it turns out, was born with the Sun in Taurus. His Taurus Sun is accompanied by a stellium of five other planets in the same sign. In addition, he has Scorpio rising. The earth is always assumed to be opposite the Sun, so it too appears in Scorpio. With such a strong Taurus/Scorpio polarity, it is no wonder that Freudian theories of oral gratification, over-active libido, Oedipal complexes, and fixations framed his worldview. It is a view that is comfortable and highly instinctual to this polarity's expression. If we use traditional medieval rulerships, it is Mars rather than Pluto that rules Scorpio and thus his entire horoscope (the ruler of the Ascendant was traditionally regarded as the ruler of the whole chart). Freud's Mars stands alone in the eastern half of the chart with few connections to other planets. It is in its sign of detriment and is retrograde. When we remember that Mars, in ancient astrology, was the planet most associated with raw lust and "licentiousness," it is easy to see that Mars was the "angry god" who was acting up in Freud's life and urging him onward with its crazy-making power. If we take Pluto as the ruler of Scorpio, we may note that this planet is close to Freud's Descendant, the point in his chart that rules relationships. Is it any wonder that he perceived human relationships in terms of their dark, underworld side? Poor Venus is in the troubled Sixth House and in her sign of detriment, so there is little sense of love and beauty to brighten Freud's dark portrait of human nature.

34   *The Gods Must Be Crazy*

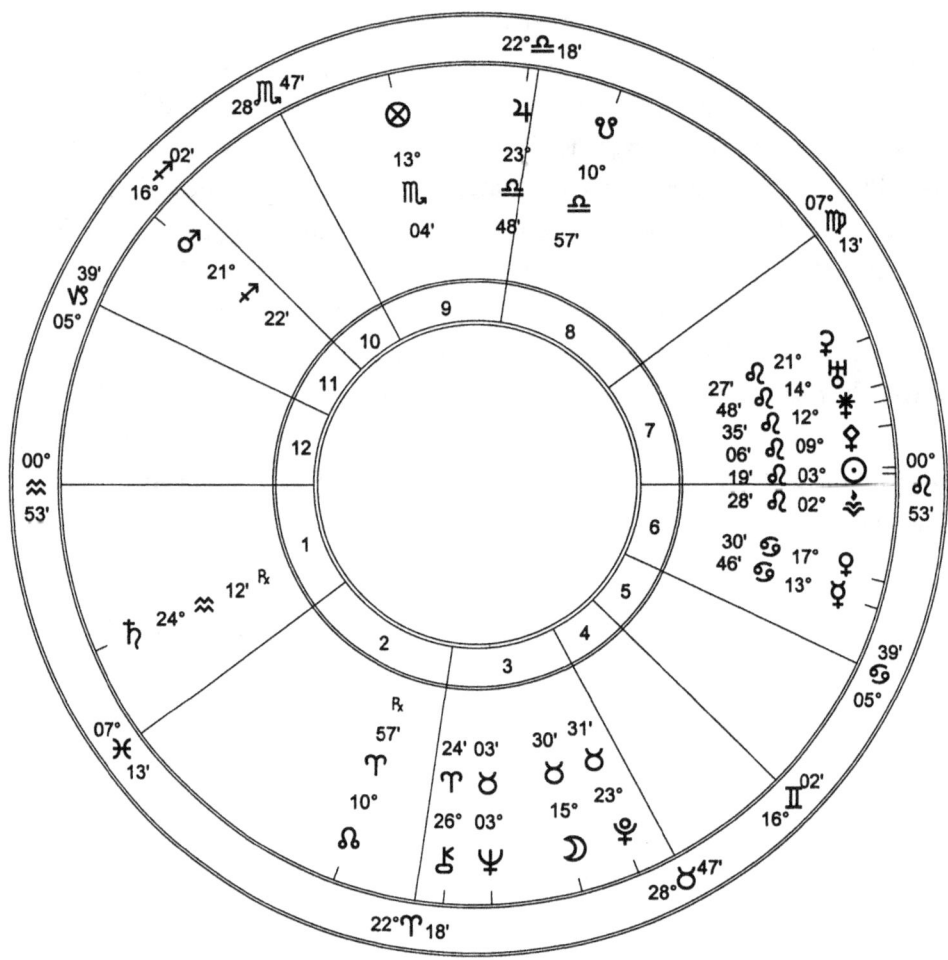

CARL JUNG
July 26, 1875 / 7:30:00 PM LMT / Kesswil, Switzerland
Koch Houses

Jung, on the other hand, had a Leo Sun with five other planets in Leo. In addition, he was Aquarius rising (and because he had the Sun in Leo, his earth appears in Aquarius). Terms like *individuation,* the *collective unconscious,* and even *archetype* reflect a Leo/Aquarius viewpoint. His ultimate theory involves the eventual integration to wholeness, which he defines as The Self—how Leo indeed!

If Freud's ruling Mars was troubled, Jung's ruling Saturn (the old ruler of Aquarius) was very positively placed. It is in its own sign (Aquarius) and rising in the First House—a very potent spot indeed. It connects with Jupiter and Mars in a very positive way—by trine and sextile, thus allowing it to play a grounding role in Jung's life. It is interesting to note that he called his ideas "depth psychology," and that Jung's Pluto was conjunct his exalted Moon in the quintessentially psychological Fourth House, which, as the nadir, is the "deepest" point in the chart, anciently called the angle of earth because it connects us to everything beneath the surface of our lives—notably the ancestral stream of consciousness that Jung redefined as "the collective unconscious."

Now, differences in theory aside, these two men have strikingly similar charts in terms of essential astrological principles of chart delineation: the same western hemispheric emphasis, a similar overall chart pattern, both Seventh House fixed Suns conjunct the asteroid Pallas and planet Uranus (glowing intellect and paradigm-shifting ideas), and the lunar nodes in the same sign (they were born nineteen years apart, a full nodal and eclipse cycle). But the primary tension in their relatedness or synastry is the number of 90° squares between the fixed earth and water signs in Freud's chart and the fixed fire and air signs in Jung's chart. The 90° aspect in astrology—the square—can signify a great degree of tension leading to a splitting off and denial of one side for the mostly unconscious psyche, or a resolution leading to a new way of living for the more integrated psyche.

If one believes that a person will take an entire lifetime to fulfill their destiny, and that one's destiny is written in the birth chart at the moment they are born (the character equals fate argument), then these different personalities, or rather expressions of a personality, will manifest accordingly at various junctures in life. And when might we predict that these would occur? Most of us mortals are not gifted with the Athene-like ability to be born fully grown, totally aware, and ready to tackle life's work instantly. It takes an entire lifetime for all of the different nuances of the birth chart to manifest. To determine timing, astrology uses a variety of calculations that advance the planets forward according to one's age, variously called *directions, transits,* and *progressions*. The razor-sharp precision or synchronicity with which events can occur for an individual when seen against these transits continues to baffle highly educated, academic minds.

Jung tells us: "... in 1912 my book *Wandlungen und Symbole der Libido* was published, and my friendship with Freud came to an end. From then on, I had to make my way alone."[6] Now, let's not forget that both of these men had Seventh House Suns and no doubt rejoiced upon finding each other initially. But

Jung was Aquarius rising with a Leo Sun. Would it have been his destiny to stay in a professional relationship that wasn't working and that placed severe restrictions and limitations on his own intellectual freedom and expression? The choice he made to split with Freud was the most difficult decision he had to make, but he did have to make it.

Though the friendship came to a screeching halt in 1912, the separation and frustration had been building since 1910. At the beginning of the developmental tension that would ultimately lead to the split between these two great thinkers, there occurred a Saturn-Uranus square (April 1910). Though we are not given a specific date of the actual split, we might look to the overall transits of 1912 to see what comes up. Beginning in February, Uranus began to transit the sign of Aquarius, opposing Jung's stellium in Leo and squaring Freud's stellium in Taurus. That same year, Saturn was in Taurus, transiting Freud's stellium in Taurus and squaring Jung's stellium in Leo. By May of that year, Saturn had reached 22° Taurus and Uranus had reached 3° Aquarius, so that for Freud's 1912 solar return, Uranus was stationary at 3° Aquarius (square natal Pluto) and Saturn was at 22° Taurus, conjunct natal Sun and Uranus. By the time of Jung's solar return in late July, Saturn had entered Gemini and was forming a trine with transiting Uranus in Aquarius. Uranus was opposite Jung's Sun, but Saturn was sextiling it. As split as he had initially felt by the separation with his former mentor, it was now clear that this break was the next necessary step and would prove to be the road to Jung's own individuation process.

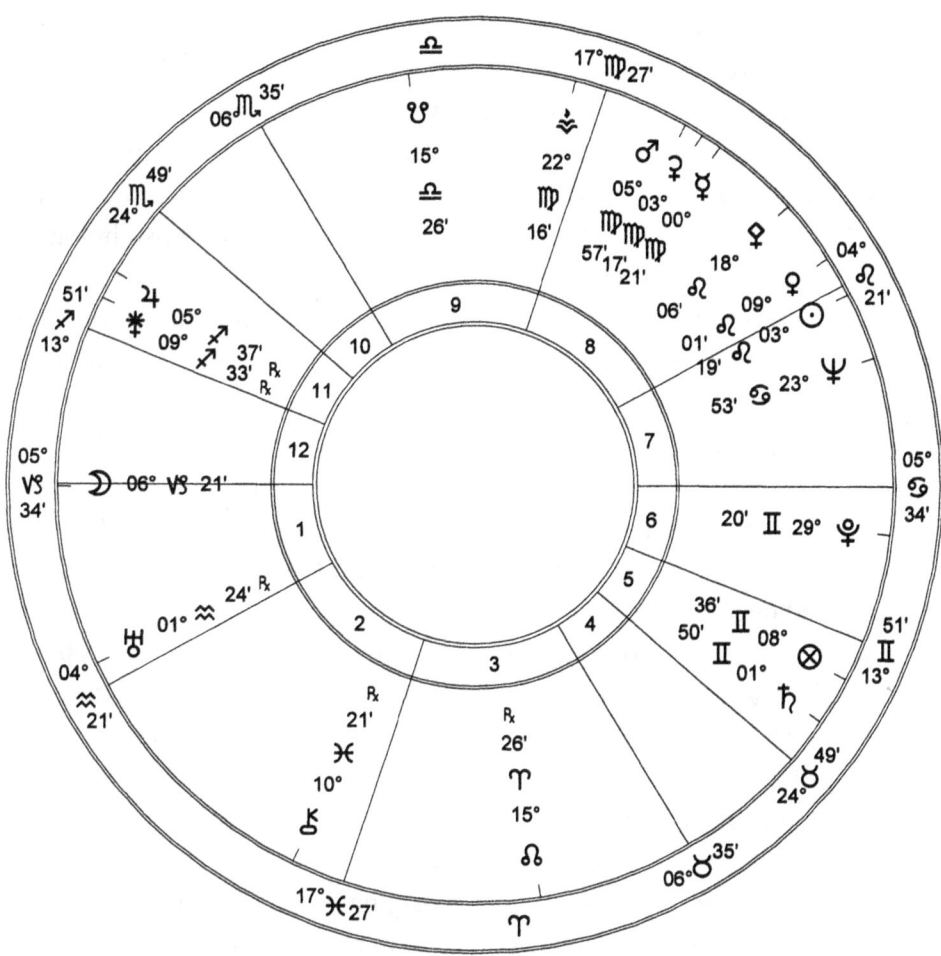

CARL JUNG'S 1912 SOLAR RETURN CHART
July 26, 1912 / 7:30:00 PM LMT / Kesswil, Switzerland
Koch Houses

Now, we know from astrology that Saturn represents tradition and structure, and Uranus represents a sudden, unpredictable change of direction in one's life. Mythic astrology further reveals that when we examine the planets Saturn and Uranus a bit closer, we find they are connected to the Greek deities Cronus and Ouranos. This was a father/son pair, the son ultimately casting out the father by removing his genitals (generative power). A strong mythological archetype for Uranus is Prometheus, who stole fire from the gods to give to mankind. He was subsequently punished for such an act.

We could look at both of these myths as pertinent to the Freud/Jung union and its resulting dissolution. While Jung may have initially gotten his fire (inspiration and ideas) from Freud's work, it was his personal vision, treatment, and transformation of it that clearly became his own. In addition, the son (Jung) cast out many of his father's (Freud's) ideas, especially the fixation on libido, incest, and related themes to account for every psychological disorder, as Freud had so stressed. Jung often saw Freud as a father figure and related conversations and interactions with him as relevant to his relationship with his own father. It is clear from the transits that the split affected Freud much more intensely than Jung. Jung, like any son who forges a new path away from the father's house, would always be haunted by the fact that the father (figure) wasn't there any longer to guide, nourish, and bless the journey. Though Jung was thoroughly and totally convinced of his own ideas' relevance (Leo/Aquarius), the split between him and Freud was something that he anguished over for the rest of his life.

Jung may have been dominated by Saturn and Pluto, but during his break with Freud it was Uranus who stood up, flexed his muscles, and howled like a crazy god until Jung recognized his power and took action. The result was positive for humanity at large.

When an ordinary mortal was chosen by the Gods to embody some powerful destiny, the Greeks looked upon her or him as literally "mad," or, in their terminology, "manic." (The word *mania* originally signified possession by a god.) However, most types of madness or mania were considered to be positive rather than otherwise, as we learn from one of Plato's greatest dialogues, the *Phaedrus*.[7]

Plato claims that the Gods send us four different kinds of madness. The first is sent by Apollo, and brings us the gift of prophecy. Another is sent by Dionysus, and this is the only madness that Plato deems negative, for it refers not to the ecstasy of the Dionysian mystic rituals, but to mental imbalances stemming from family karma. Thereby it encompasses all the psychoses and schizoid states recognized by modern psychology. A third madness comes from the Muses, and this produces poetry, while a fourth is the erotic madness sent to us by Aphrodite, the madness that seizes our souls whenever we fall in love, and this, according to Plato, is the most divine madness or "mania" of them all, the one that brings us into direct communion with the One.

The astrologer will note that Plato's manias accord quite nicely with some of the astrological planets: the Sun (Apollo), the Moon (Muses), Neptune (Dionysus), and Venus (Aphrodite). Some of the implications are, in fact, rather fascinating for astrology. We may see the logic of looking to Venus for the details of a person's "love madness" or to the Moon for a "poetic temperament," but Plato may lead us to look, as did the ancient astrologers, to the Sun for the cause of the situation when an individual demonstrates prophetic gifts (or egomaniacally attempts to present himself as a prophet). And we might wish to examine the role of Neptune in cases of psychic or emotional dissociation, the Neptunian "meltdown" of the ego.

Of course, the field is not really limited to four planets or four kinds of archetypal possession. And despite what Plato says, the ancients knew this as well. What we call a "panic attack" was anciently regarded as possession by the god Pan. It was said that Pan loved to lie in wait in the forests of Arcadia, and then to leap out at unsuspecting human travelers with a great shout. This shout induced "panic" in its listeners. Since ancient times, Pan has been associated with the sign Capricorn, which is ruled by Saturn. Behind the gloomy visage of Saturn lies the feral and occasionally obscene god with the feet of a goat,[8] and Saturn will ordinarily be found to be the culprit in most cases of anxiety or panic attacks. The myth, however, also provides us with another window, and thereby with a solution: panic attacks occur when we are out of harmony with our inner wildness, our animal soul, as symbolized by the god Pan. Having lost contact with our feral side, we are easily thrown into a panic by the god's angry, primal roar, and only a living connection with nature and with our own naturalness can heal us again.

There is a theme developing here that may seem a bit unsettling to some people. As we mentioned earlier, an ordinary girl with an ordinary Venus might have been able to keep her erotic wildness under control and create a somewhat happy marriage. But it is the woman whose "Venus factor" is extremely powerful, who is in deep inner communion with the archetype of that particular goddess, who experiences the most difficulties.

Does this mean that the stronger the divine figures are within us, the more messed up our lives will be? And are we therefore better off if they keep to themselves, buried deep inside us, instead of pulling us towards an archetypal destiny that is (let's face it) downright uncomfortable?

It is true that a life lived according to the Gods is not as quiet or as peaceful as a life lived according to the rules. The Gods challenge us to go beyond the merely personal, to live life upon a grand scale, to become more than we are. We may choose not to answer such a challenge—to make use of psychotherapy or of astrology to persuade the Gods to go back to sleep and leave us alone.

For if we open ourselves to the powerful collective forces symbolized by the deities and the astrological planets, we may well appear mad—or at least a little bit eccentric—in the eyes of the world around us. Sometimes we may be mad indeed, and our lives may even be endangered. Like Lotte Lenya, Marilyn Monroe was possessed by the archetype of Venus-Aphrodite, but Marilyn's more fragile ego structure crumbled under the strain and brought her to a tragic early death. Jim Morrison believed that he was possessed by the god Dionysus, and spent his life in a continual bacchanal that ended in a bathtub in Paris at the age of twenty-seven.[9]

Now, many of you may say: "Of course I want to be larger than life and live out a grand destiny! Who wouldn't? But if I am archetypally empowered, do I also have to be archetypally miserable? Because that doesn't sound like fun."

In order to empower individuals with the magic of their inner deities and render their lives archetypally significant, while at the same time ensuring their health, happiness, and prosperity, the astrologers of Hellenistic, medieval, and Renaissance times made use of various techniques of *planetary healing*. These were meditative, psychological, and magical methods aimed at harmonizing the energies of the planets so that they might embody their fullest and most transcendent potential.

It is these methods that are the real subject of this book.

---

1. Dodds, E. R., *The Greeks and the Irrational* (Boston: Beacon Press, 1957).

2. Professional astrologers may have some difficulty with this one. In our earlier book, we argued that the asteroid Juno is more properly concerned with marriage. However, some astrologers do not use the major asteroids, while others feel that there should be more to it than this. In ancient astrology, the ruler of the Seventh House was always taken as a primary significator for marriage, and probably still should be. Also, one great difference between ancient Greece or Rome and our present Western society is that the ancients thought of marriage as a social contract, devoid of eroticism, while we tend to marry more for erotic or passionate reasons than anything else. This being the case, Venus, as the planet of passion and erotic love, definitely plays a role.

3. Bolen, Jean Shinoda, *Goddesses in Everywoman* (New York: Harper & Row, 1984).

4. Solar Fire Astrological Software® published by Astrolabe, Brewster, MA.

5. Among astrologers and followers of Jung, there appear to be several charts in circulation, with a resultant difference of a few degrees of zodiac rising. In some charts he is a very early degree of Aquarius rising, and in the other charts he is late Capricorn rising. In both cases, Saturn rules the chart (the Ascendant) and is placed in Aquarius, giving him the Aquarian expression noted.

6. Jung, Carl, *Memories, Dreams, Reflections*, recorded and edited by Aniela Jaffé, trans. from the German by Richard and Clara Winston (1963; reprint, New York: Vintage Books, 1989).

7. Plato, "Phaedrus," in *The Works of Plato* (New York: Modern Library, 1956) 263–332.

8. Ariel Guttman and Kenneth Johnson, *Mythic Astrology: Archetypal Powers in the Horoscope* (St. Paul, MN: Llewellyn Publications, 1993) 334–5.

9. Though Jim Morrison certainly seems to have been "possessed by an archetype," one wonders if he was mistaken as to its identity. The "big snake" who proclaimed himself "the lizard king" and enjoined his audience to "Follow me down!" seems in many ways to have been more Plutonian than Dionysian.

CHAPTER 3

PLANETARY HEALING

As we noted earlier, contemporary Western astrology is mostly "talk therapy." Astrologers place primary value on being good counselors. Like the psychotherapists upon whom they model themselves, they have become non-directive, and would prefer to be good listeners rather than take charge of their clients' lives.

If you were to go to an astrologer in India, the situation would be entirely different. Only about half of the actual session would be spent analyzing the planets in your horoscope and their effect upon your life. Instead, a great deal of time and energy would be given to the planetary remedies.

If a planet is sick, they fix it.

Every planet corresponds to many different things in nature. For example, each planet has its particular gemstone, and the Vedic astrologer may recommend that you wear a certain gemstone in order to strengthen a planet that is weak. If a malefic planet (in the West we no longer use such terms; we would say "challenging") is giving you trouble, you might be advised to obtain a special yantra or talisman that embodies that planet's energies, or to chant a special mantra related to the planet.

All of this may sound more like folk magic than astrology—at least as we are accustomed to thinking of astrology. But the fact is, all these techniques were once common practice in Western astrology, and they go back to the beginnings of the art—in Babylon and in Gnostic Egypt. Earlier, we quoted Thomas Moore to the effect that astrologers might do well to return to their Pagan and magical roots. In essence, astrologers were originally magicians, and we may have lost a great deal by laying down the mantle of the magus.

Magic itself was a kind of psychotherapy as well as a form of spiritual practice—the Western world's equivalent of yoga. James Hillman shows his awareness of this fact when he writes that Marsilio Ficino was one of the great "ancestors" of archetypal psychology.

Who was Marsilio Ficino? He was a medical doctor who lived in Florence during the early days of the Italian Renaissance; he served as personal physician to Lorenzo de Medici, the Florentine nobleman who acted as patron to some of the greatest of Renaissance artists, from Botticelli to Michelangelo. But Ficino was more than just a doctor. He was also an astrologer and a magician. As a scholar, he translated Plato's metaphysical works and also introduced the Renaissance world to the mystical Hermetic writings, which had been lost to Western Europe for centuries. He often lectured and taught in

Florence, and it is believed that the painter Botticelli was deeply influenced by his teachings, and that Ficino's doctrines are embodied in some of Botticelli's great works, such as the "Primavera" and "The Birth of Venus." As an astrologer, Ficino composed a book entitled *On Making Your Life Agree with the Heavens*. In this work, Ficino demonstrates that our common perception of medieval astrologers as negative fatalists is completely untrue. Ficino instructs us on methods of harmonizing the planetary Goddesses and Gods within us to create a wholeness of being and a sense of happiness, and he uses a wide number of different techniques in the process, including herbal remedies and the construction of magical talismans.

Sorcery? Indeed. And yet the archetypal psychologists recognize Ficino's talent and accept him as one of their own.

Perhaps it is time that astrologers did the same. Perhaps it is time that we cherished rather than denied our heritage in the art of magic and realized that the tribal shaman is the ancestor of the contemporary healer.

Today, "healing," i.e., the healthcare field, has become a phenomenon—indeed, it is a huge industry that offers thousands of both natural and pharmaceutical remedies to treat hundreds of different maladies. In this era of "self-help," people are becoming educated in countless ways to improve all aspects of their lives, whether the focus lies with external improvements and remedies (like feng shui) or with internal remedies such as we discuss herein. Our intent here is to delve into a very small portion of what is currently available by addressing practices and techniques that relate directly to our subject at hand—and that specifically utilize astrological, psychological, mythological, and archetypal awareness.

Medical astrology has probably been practiced since the beginning of the art. A wealthy heritage of texts, including those written by William Lilly, Nicholas Culpepper, and Marsilio Ficino, are still widely used and consulted. The Greeks assigned certain temperaments to certain signs, elements, and planets, and treatments were recommended accordingly. The air signs are sanguine (hot and moist); the fire signs are choleric (hot and dry); the earth signs are melancholic (cold and dry); and the water signs are phlegmatic (cold and moist).[1]

Hindu astrology has developed planetary remedies into a fine art. The birth chart is consulted in order to determine which planets are well placed and thus functioning optimally in the birth chart, and which ones are afflicted and therefore in need of remedies or cures. These remedial practices can be powerful healing rituals, invoking particular deities, chanting mantras (particularly when the Moon is in the proper *nakshatra*) wearing a particular gemstone, etc.[2]

Peter Lemesurier has given us an interesting thesis wherein the gods themselves are called into the healing process.[3] His idea is that although we might be inspired by the gods' magic, that very magic can also turn on us in terrible ways. His work is a testament to Jung's teaching that the unfinished business in our own psyches, when not made conscious, results in an inevitable and sometimes unenviable fate manifested in the outer world.

Examples most often show up in psychological disorders accompanied by symptoms of actual physical discomfort and illness. This manual of *theotherapy* gives us two lists. One list names the god or goddess. The other list names the symptoms. If you aren't sure which deity has control, you can look at your symptoms, and by process of elimination you can connect it to the deity. In determining which deity has seized you, you may now assess the nature, emotion, and attributes of that particular deity, thereby recognizing its proper function or dysfunction, as the case may be. For instance, *anorexic* turns out to be symptomatic of several goddesses, including Aphrodite, the Furies, Artemis, Daphne, Demeter, Niobe, and a few gods including Orpheus, Narcissus, and Midas. A further look at their stories will help elucidate how one might be dishonoring such a god.

GEMSTONES

One of the oldest planetary remedies involves the wearing of gemstones, which are believed to correspond to particular planets. But in order to understand this notion of correspondence, we must first understand an ancient idea called the *doctrine of signatures*.

In ancient thinking, everything in heaven and on earth was interconnected, bound together in a universal network of energy. The source of this connective network was the world of the archetypes.

We have already defined archetypes as "ideas in the mind of the infinite." The Gods themselves are archetypes, cosmic figures such as the Wise Old

Crone or the Divine Child, characters who live in the hearts and souls of all of us. But according to the doctrine of signatures, each archetype or universal "signature" has its resonance in every aspect of reality. That which appears as the Wise Old Man in the mind of the infinite may appear as the planet Saturn in the sky above, and its "signatures" within the human body are our knees and shins (Capricorn and Aquarius, the two Saturnian signs). And the same archetype has a resonance in the animal world, in the mineral kingdom, in color vibration and sound vibration—indeed, in everything.

The planetary gemstones are, of course, the corresponding signature of a planet in the mineral kingdom, and as such they carry the same archetypal energy and nuances as the planet itself. This sounds simple and easy, save for the fact that, among all the lists of planetary gemstones surviving from medieval and Renaissance times, no two are identical. For the most part, the only real common tone is that the gemstones tend to be the same color as the planet's correspondent color. Unfortunately, the planetary colors have also changed. Even archetypes are transformed over time.

Turning to India, we find a completely different situation. The planetary gemstones are established by tradition and are always the same. What is more, they are probably the same gems that were originally assigned to the planets in late Greek or Hellenistic times.

How do we know this? Let us take one example.

Ordinarily, the planet Mercury is assigned any number of different colors. There is something about its mutability that seems to spark a myriad of attributions among astrologers both ancient and modern. In India, however, Mercury is always green and its gem is always an emerald.

This may sound unreasonable to some Western astrologers who are accustomed to thinking of green in connection with Venus. And indeed, the connection between Venus and the color green has been around for a long time—Ficino assigns the two of them as correspondences, based largely upon the medieval and Renaissance concept of Venus as a goddess of the springtime (which, originally, she was not).

And yet Hellenistic astrologers may have followed contemporary Vedic practice and believed Mercury to be correspondent with the color green and the gemstone emerald. We know this because one of the great foundation texts of Western alchemy, dating from the late Hellenistic era, is entitled *The Emerald Tablet of Hermes*.

Rather than try to steer a course through a morass of medieval contradictions, we shall use the oldest and most traditional correspondences here, the Hellenistic and Vedic ones. Of course, the trans-Saturnian planets and asteroids do not appear in this list, which is limited to the seven "ancient" or visible planets.

Planet	Color	Gemstone
Sun	Red	Ruby
Moon	White	Pearl
Mercury	Green	Emerald
Venus	White	Diamond
Mars	Red	Red Coral
Jupiter	Yellow	Yellow Sapphire
Saturn	Blue	Blue Sapphire

Many of these gemstones are very expensive, and the average individual may say, with justifiable cynicism, that it would be very difficult to heal a planet that is causing financial problems by spending a whole other fortune on one of these gems. But as we shall see later in the book, there are less expensive substitutes for most of them.

In addition to gemstones, there were also corresponding metals for every planet, and these constitute an important part of the alchemical tradition. In Renaissance times, planetary talismans were often made of the correspondent metal.

Planet	Metal
Sun	Gold
Moon	Silver
Mercury	Quicksilver
Venus	Copper
Mars	Iron
Jupiter	Tin
Saturn	Lead

Before we move on to other kinds of planetary remedies, let us pass on a piece of practical wisdom from the contemporary Vedic tradition:

The vibration of gemstones simply increases the essential vibration of a planet. Therefore, gemstones should only be used to strengthen benevolent planets. Never try to use a gemstone to heal a difficult planet, since this is likely to simply increase the difficulties. Difficult planets need to be handled in a different way.

PRESCRIPTIONS FOR LIVING

Perhaps the most effective way to harmonize the energies of the planets is through changes in our lifestyle. Like gemstones and talismans, these "prescriptions for living" are likewise based upon the doctrine of signatures—although in this instance it is the correspondences within the human heart and soul that form our working material.

In India, for example, a person who is having difficulties with Saturn might be advised to take up the practice of hatha yoga—hatha is Saturn's own particular yoga, for Saturn corresponds to the joints and bone structure in the human body. By the same token, the energy of Venus or the Moon can be increased by the practice of bhakti yoga, the yoga of love and devotion, for these two planets are heart centered, and hence the yoga of love corresponds naturally to them.

These changes in our habits and attitudes tend to be the most powerful and effective of all planetary remedies. When we depend upon gemstones or talismans, we rely passively upon forces outside ourselves; when we reshape our lives and habits, we exercise our own will and volition.

In the Western tradition, Marsilio Ficino was perhaps the master of such prescriptions for living, and it is this aspect of his work that makes it valuable even now, 500 years later. He had a vast arsenal of correspondences at his disposal:[4]

> If you want your body and spirit to receive power from some limb of the world, for example the Sun, learn which are the Solar things among metals and stones, even more among plants, but among the animal world most of all, especially among men. . . . Solar things are all those that are called Heliotrope—because they are turned to the Sun—for example, gold and the color of gold, chrysolite, carbuncle, myrrh, incense, musk, amber, balsam, golden honey, aromatic calamus, saffron, spikenard, cinnamon, wood aloe,

and other aromatics, the Ram, the Hawk, the hen, the swan, the lion, the beetle, the crocodile, people who are golden-haired, curly-haired, sometimes bald-headed people, and the magnanimous.

After giving his readers an exhaustive list of things in nature that enhance the energy of a particular planet (in this case the Sun), he goes on to discuss the ways and means by which its energies may be most usefully harmonized and rendered into a positive force in our lives:[5]

So be sure you organize your Solar stuff carefully. Start making use of Solar things, with this one caution, however: be careful to avoid getting dried out under its heat.... Keep your movements here frequent and light, find suitable quiet, get air that is thin and serene and remote from heat and cold, and especially keep a happy disposition. It will not be Solar if it is not warm, subtle, and clear. You will make yourself subtle and clear if you avoid sadness and thick and dark things. Use things that are bright and cheerful, both inside and outside. Get plenty of light both day and night. Get rid of filth, dullness, and torpor. First and foremost, avoid darkness!

Similarly, he recommends walks in fields of flowers to nurture the Venus within us, and he insists that scholars (who are naturally under the influence of serious Saturn) should always spend a great deal of time in the sunlight (because the Sun is the natural opposite of Saturn, and therefore necessary in order to achieve balance between the two).

Unlike the gemstones and talismans, which are based upon ancient and medieval traditions and which therefore do not include "remedies" for the outer planets and asteroids, changes in lifestyle and prescriptions for living are improvisational, psychological, and open to inventiveness. Therefore they may be designed for any planet or heavenly body—including those yet to be discovered.

INVOCATION AND AWARENESS

Here is probably the most accessible of all the methods we have discussed. In the art and practice of astrology, awareness of planetary themes and cycles is the primary tool. On a daily, monthly, or yearly level, planets make passages from one sign to another, thus giving a certain sign ruler or planetary lord the emphasis of the moment.

Each and every day, solar energy reaches its zenith around the noon hour, just as every year its zenith is during the summer months and solstice. Similarly, lunar energy peaks during full moon periods. Venus is heightened twice a year when she is in her own domains of Taurus and Libra (and so on for the other planets) and when she turns retrograde, about every 584 days. When the outer planets change direction from direct to retrograde and back again, they are considered stationary for several weeks at a time. These stationary periods give great emphasis to the planet in question. Awareness is at its height then, because we are talking about and experiencing the nature of the particular planet all around us. At these times, invocation may not be necessary, but focused awareness is. The focused awareness that is tied in with an understanding of the archetype in all its potential can allow the best utilization of the planetary transit at hand. When the planet or ruling deity will not be making its presence felt for some time, invocation is more useful. At such times we might call on Jupiter or Venus or Ceres, much as a particular saint is prayed to for help in a certain arena, or how a particular animal spirit is called upon in shamanic work.

Furthering our awareness of these archetypal elements is useful in knowing how we unconsciously bring them into our sphere in everyday life. Next time you bring fresh flowers into your home, light a candle or incense, prepare and present a meal in a certain way, or even place certain objects in a particular way in your home or office or garage, you may have unknowingly brought forth Venus or Vesta or Ceres. The gods and goddesses like to be called upon. It is for this that they exist.

When we "invoke," we call upon divine energies; we make them present in our lives. Any prayer to the Gods—of whatever faith—is in this sense an invocation, and in fact the difference between a prayer and an invocation is a subtle one.

In some cultures, the Gods or archetypes are invoked through the use of sacred sound, and we shall not be incorrect if we assume that sound vibration, like everything else, has its magical correspondences in the doctrine of signatures. In India, for example, an astrologer may assign her or his client a particular mantra or chant that resonates with the vibration of the planet that is in need of strengthening or healing. Chanting the mantra places the client in a state of harmonious resonance with the planetary energy. In fact, mantras are often prescribed to deal with the more challenging or "malefic" planets. Unlike a gemstone, which simply channels the basic energy of the planet, whether favorable or unfavorable, a mantra automatically harmonizes the energy of any planet at its highest level because a mantra is based upon divine sound vibration—and in many spiritual traditions, including Hermetic philosophy and the Kabbalah, sound vibration is the primordial material from which the universe itself was fashioned.

Although the notion of planetary mantras may seem culturally specific to India, this is not really the case. Marsilio Ficino deeply enjoyed the so-called Orphic hymns, a group of mystical Greek poems dedicated to the ancient gods. Composing his own musical settings for these ancient hymns, Ficino matched them with specific planets and sang them to harmonize the energy of the planet in question.

In certain Kabbalistic traditions, the divine names of God—the chanting of which is a standard spiritual practice—also have planetary correspondences, and may be used in precisely the same way.

Ficino's Orphic hymns may seem just as culturally distant to us as a Hindu mantra—readers who are familiar with yoga or Eastern meditative techniques may wish to explore the idea of planetary mantras on their own, while Kabbalists may benefit from a study of the divine names. But for most of us, it may well be most useful to simply contact the planetary archetypes directly, by calling upon them, invoking them, dialoguing with them.

In contemporary archetypal psychology, which regards all the ancient deities as aspects of our own multivalent selves, this sort of direct contact with the archetypes is standard practice—although it is most often achieved through dreamwork and active imagination rather than through direct invocation, as we shall see in the next chapter. Nevertheless, the archetypal psychologists have sometimes been accused of introducing the worship of the Greek gods into the realm of serious psychology. To an astrologer—especially one who is deeply involved with myth—this may sound more like a compliment than an accusation.

In fact, the worship of the Goddesses and Gods was always a part of the ancient astrological tradition, both Babylonian and Hellenistic. We are accustomed—thanks to the influence of too many silly movies—to perceiving Greek religion in terms of a bunch of hairy men in tunics shouting "Great Zeus!" Or, if we have received our knowledge of Western history in the usual way—from writers bent upon proving that all human civilization is merely a series of highways and byways leading up to the triumph of Western science—

then we may even have been led to believe that the Greeks, the founders of Western scientific "rationalism," didn't really believe in their gods at all.

Ultimately, one becomes continually aware of the shifting tapestry of archetypal energies that informs each moment of our lives. In the constantly changing episodes and experiences of our daily lives we may perceive an infinite number of goddesses, gods, and planets eternally dancing and interacting. In time, we also learn to invoke or call upon the divine energies that exist in profusion all around us, and to involve them—the Gods—in our experience of the here and now.

For the purposes of this book, invocation can be accomplished simply through meditation. What we are referring to here is simply the inner process of establishing a deep connection with a planetary archetype. Whether one chooses to use pictures, images, or music in order to facilitate the meditation and establish the connection is entirely up to the individual. There are as many different ways of connecting as there are people who wish to connect.

Constant awareness, however, is perhaps the best way to connect with the planetary archetypes. When you get up in the morning and have a bowl of cereal, remember Ceres, the goddess of the grain. If you are male, then become aware of Mars while you shave, for Mars rules sharp objects made of metal. As you walk down the street and examine store windows, you will find a virtual panoply of planets. The bejeweled mannequin in the fashion store is an obvious Venus, while the store that sells computers, printers, and office products is the realm of Mercury. Every time advertisers try to lure you with words like *bigger* and *better*, they are appealing to the Jupiter within you. But if they use the word *faster*, they're back in the realm of Mercury, who is always in a hurry and prefers DSL to standard dial-up. After all, Mercury is the quickest planet, speeding around the Sun as fast as lightning. The athlete jogging down the block is Mars. The old man sitting in the park bench is Saturn.

This may sound like a peculiar way to go through life, but this practice of awareness is the best way to make astrology a deep and abiding part of you. It leads naturally to the kind of invocation that takes place in your soul, and that truly calls the energies of the planets to you.

If these kinds of remedies seem strange to our modern Western culture, then consider this. In an average thirty-minute segment of the nightly evening national news, the viewer is bombarded by at least ten minutes of paid advertisements by pharmaceutical companies hawking their latest remedies. Backed by millions of dollars, these multimillion-dollar drug dealers are promoting every kind and color of pill imaginable for whatever ails you. The "new purple pill" may stop heartburn, but they caution you that it may also promote stomach cramps, diarrhea, headache, dizziness, and a host of other maladies. The blue pill may be the answer for menopause, but warnings are issued forth that it may also cause skin eruptions, blood clots, and loss of appetite. This "legal" drug industry is highly touted by the schooled and licensed medical establishment, backed by insurance companies, making it affordable and accessible to all who qualify, and legislated by our Congress. In light of this, we may not find it that unreasonable to consult planets, recite mantras, and wear gems after all.

---

1. Crane, Joseph, *A Practical Guide to Traditional Astrology* (Reston, VA: ARHAT, 1997).

2. Johnsen, Linda, "Dealing with Disaster: The Vedic Approach," *The Mountain Astrologer* (June/July 1997).

3. Lemesurier, Peter, *The Healing of the Gods: The Magic of Symbols and the Practice of Theotherapy* (Element Books, 1988).

4. Ficino, Marsilio, *The Book of Life*, trans. by Charles Boer (Irving, TX: Spring Publications, 1980) 90.

5. Ibid.

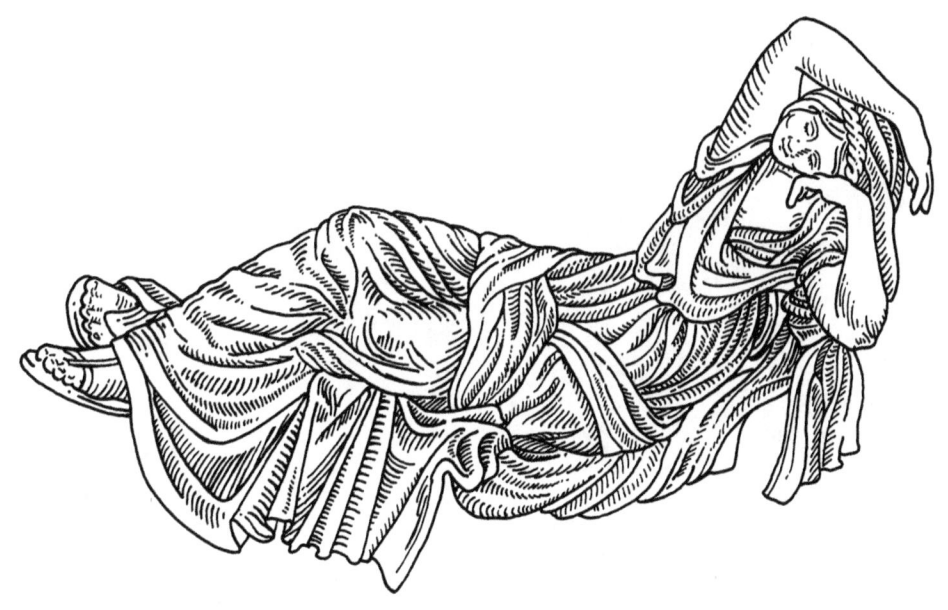

CHAPTER 4

THE HEALING POWER OF DREAMS

DREAMS AND DREAMERS

At your annual visit to your physician it may seem unlikely to hear the question posed: "What did you dream last night?" But thousands of years ago, this was routine for the ancient physicians of Egypt and Greece. Even as far back as Sumer, there are carefully detailed texts of the dreams of heroes and kings. The Bible, especially the Old Testament, is replete with references to divine or prophetic dreams, and through the ages some of the masterminds of the time have been able to come up with their best inventions, ideas, solutions to problems, and even cures for illness through dreams.

Still, no matter what we may learn from the centuries-old body of dream literature, dreams are very much a personal matter. The dreamer's personal associations to the contents of the dream are probably the best key to unlock such a mysterious realm. When you begin discussing the realm of dreams with people, the average response is either "I never dream" (which really means, "I don't remember my dreams") or "Boy, did I have a wild dream last night. Must be indigestion." Then there are the epic dreamers who dream profusely and are convinced (like tribal people) that their dreams are more important than waking life.

Adult dreamers who do dream prolifically begin dreaming in childhood. Many of those dreams become lost or forgotten because they are not encouraged, or the dreams, like myths, are deemed "fantasy" by the adults or older siblings. This is unfortunate because children's dreams are often the most numinous. Children often draw what they feel. Children who dream a lot might be encouraged to draw pictures of their dreams, rather than write them in journals, as adults do.

Prophetic dreaming is surprisingly common and frequent when we really pay attention to it, and it seems that dream lore from the ancients is full of such material. The dream process and dream state hasn't changed, but if you are working with your dreams in a clinical way in contemporary times, you will probably do so in a psychotherapist's office.

Dreams may have significance for modern medicine, too—just as it did for ancient Greek medicine. In his latest book, *Reinventing Medicine*, Dr. Larry Dossey delves deeply into our ancient past, when dream incubation was common medical practice; he argues for the resurrection of this art among physicians of today.[1]

This is good news for all of us. Why? Because dreams are another very important link to the mythic realm. Dreams are our personal myths. We cast them, direct them, costume them, and give them a setting. In dreams, we are our own film production company. What kind of story are we telling? And more importantly, is it a healthy, happy story, or is it traumatically disturbing, lingering in the shadows to haunt us throughout the day? And if what the ancients believed is true, that dreams provide exceptional keys to curing the ills that plague us? Are we solving life's problems, getting healed, and generally feeling uplifted by our dreams? And are we in contact with divine forces that will counsel us and point the way forward?

DREAM HEALING

To speak of dreams and of healing in the same context, we must first introduce the god Aesculapius (Greek: Asklepios). Like many mortals who later became divine, Aesculapius was the human child of one of the great gods. His father was Apollo, planetary god of the Sun and patron of healing; his mother was Coronis of Thessaly, a mortal woman. Coronis was killed by her lover's jealous arrow while pregnant. Remorseful, Apollo rescued the unborn child and "incubated" him elsewhere (an important word, as we shall see). Once grown, Aesculapius was sent to Chiron, the wise old centaur who trained so many mythic heroes, including the great Achilles. Though Apollo was the physical father of Aesculapius, Chiron was his spiritual godfather and teacher.

We shall have much more to say about Chiron in the proper place. But for now, let us note that there are and always will be certain mythic figures for whom no planet or major asteroid has been named. This does not mean that these figures—some of whom are important deities—are absent from the human psyche or simply absent from astrology. Instead, the archetypes tend to reach us through planets and other deities with which they have a close psychological relationship. As we shall see, Prometheus, the fire-bringer, reaches us primarily through Uranus; Dionysus, the god of ecstasy, through Neptune; and Persephone, Queen of the Dead, through Pluto, the planet named for her husband. The archetype of Aesculapius, likewise, reaches us and touches us through the planet-comet Chiron. Not only were they teacher and student, but both were wounded and both were healers. The Greek idea was that the only effective healer must be one who is himself wounded: "He who wounds also heals."[2] As in homeopathy, the cure is in the illness; the healer himself carries the disease.

So great a healer was Aesculapius that it is said he was able to raise the dead. Pluto, king of the underworld, complained to the other gods that Aesculapius was robbing the dark lord of his rightful heritage of souls. Jupiter killed Aesculapius with a thunderbolt, but on second thought brought him back to immortal life again and set him among the stars, where he is depicted with a great serpent coiled around him. This is the constellation of Ophiuchus, which literally means "the serpent-bearer." It occupies that portion of the heavenly realm that lies between late Scorpio and mid-Sagittarius.

It is interesting to note that both Aesculapius and his teacher Chiron were immortalized as constellations relating to the Sagittarian archetype, for Chiron became the constellation Centaurus, the centaur, and Sagittarius itself is of course a centaur; Ophiuchus is actually positioned within Sagittarius.

Because Aesculapius was trained by Chiron, who was famous for his herbal remedies, we might be tempted to think of him primarily in terms of "natural" healing or herbalism, but in ancient Greece he was regarded primarily as a healer through dreams.

Throughout the ancient world, there were temples dedicated to Aesculapius where people went for healing—and here we mean the healing of ills both physical and psychological. One such temple was at Epidaurus on the mainland of Greece, a site reputed to be the god's birthplace; the largest, however, was on the island of Cos. It was in the Aesculapian temple of Cos that Hippocrates, the founder of Western medicine, received his initial training, thus providing a link between the dream therapy of the gods and the origins of modern medicine. During the fifth century BCE, the cult of Aesculapius was in full flower throughout the Greek world, and dream incubation was so widely practiced that there may have been as many as 400 Aesculapions, or *dream temples*, all of which were modeled after the prototype at Epidaurus.

The origins of dream incubation, however, go back centuries before the Aesculapions of classical times. Dream healing had been practiced in Egypt at least 1,000 years earlier, and the Minoans of Crete were probably quite familiar with it as well. There is also reason to believe that the shrine of Apollo at Delphi was originally a dream oracle belonging to the ancient earth goddess Chthon. When Apollo slew the serpent and took the site for himself, Chthon retaliated. Euripides tells us:[3]

But Earth had wished to save the oracle for Themis,
Her own daughter
And so in anger bred a band of dreams
Which in the night should be oracular
To men, foretelling truth

Our modern-day psychics, astrologers, healers, and dream therapists might be envious of their predecessors. There was such an unflagging devotion and confidence that the dream temples would deliver miraculous results that the requirement for entry became stiff and some seekers waited a long time to be accepted. Whether at the Oracle of Delphi or at the Aesculapion of Epidaurus, one had to make application, wait for word of acceptance, and then offer certain sacrifices and/or perform certain rituals. Though these rituals may have varied from time to time and from place to place, there were certain universal features about them.

Some of the sacrifices may have had to do with fasting, taking cleansing baths, or offering something to the god. It was thought that bathing not only cleansed the body, but also set the soul free to commune with the healing god. Those who came to seek healing were required to isolate themselves in meditative, spiritual seclusion within the temple precincts. They undertook special diets, sometimes ingesting a certain herb or drink that would help prepare them for the healing. They received healing massages and spent a day or two in silent contemplation. Another essential ingredient to healing was music. Chiron himself was a musician and trained physicians to play. Apollo, god of healing, is almost always shown with his lyre. The patient was then ready to sleep in the inner sanctum of the shrine, but not without some sign or message from the oracle that the god or goddess had invited the patient to enter.

The shrine was called a *tholos* or *abaton,* and almost always contained a spring connected to a well deep within the earth. Running water or springs were essential elements to the healing, and many of the shrines were set up at spots where waterfalls, caves with water running through them, or the sea was nearby. Both Epidaurus and Cos are located close to the sea and additionally had a running spring nearby. In this respect, the Aesculapions resembled older holy places, shrines, and oracle sites of the most remote antiquity. The Castalian spring runs adjacent to Apollo's shrine at Delphi and the Oracle of Trophonius at Levadia contains numerous caves and waterfalls. In these two particular shrines, the dreamer shed his clothing, was wrapped in certain cloths or skins as if to be buried, and was forced to descend to a deep hole in the cave where light could not enter.

Inhabiting the womb of the earth at these ancient oracle sites might be snakes who would actually take part in the dream. Snakes were an essential element of healing in the ancient world, and they often accompany healing gods or goddesses. Mercury or Hermes, who leads souls in and out of the dream world as well as in and out of Hades, carries with him the caduceus, a staff with two snakes intertwined, originally Apollo's. Athene's shield is emblazoned with a golden serpent.

These healing serpents were especially important to the cult of Aesculapius. In Greek and Roman iconography, he is almost always shown carrying a staff (probably a tree branch) with a snake coiling around it; this symbol is similar but not identical to the caduceus of Mercury. In the Aesculapions, there was typically a statue of the god—some made of stone, others of gold or ivory—and these statues often depicted the great dream healer accompanied by his animals—the dog and the serpent. In fact, actual snakes were employed in the healing process. When the patient slept within one of the temple's special "dreaming rooms," she or he typically slept in the presence of a number of large but harmless serpents who lived in the temple and who are rather obviously linked to the "sky serpent" coiled around Aesculapius in the constellation of Ophiuchus. These serpents were true "wisdom serpents," and were believed to be a substantial element in the healing process.

The sleeper prayed to Aesculapius in hopes of receiving a healing dream; once asleep in the inner sanctum of the temple, he hoped to receive a dream from the god that would carry with it the essential elements of both the illness and the cure. The right dream equals the right cure. If the patient had in fact performed the prior meditations properly and in a spirit of integrity, such a dream usually resulted. In the early centuries of dream healing, the patient was even thought to be incurable if the right dream did not appear the first night, though the records indicate that in later times one might spend as long as three or four months in a dream sanctuary in order to effect the cure. When the right dream did appear, the dreamer was obliged to record the dream. The most significant healing occurred when the patient and physician had the same dream at the same time. Not only was this considered a healing, but a miracle. The temple priests first acted as "psychologists" in helping the patient to interpret his dream, and then as herbalists by prescribing remedies based upon the dream's message.

KINDS OF DREAMS

What sort of dreams were sought by the patients who came to these Aesculapions for healing? The ancient Greeks recognized at least two different varieties of dreams, and perhaps three.

Like almost all other pre-Christian Europeans, they believed that everyone had two souls—one was vested in the body and served as a kind of eternal life-spirit, while the other was a "free soul" or "wandering soul," typically linked to the physical body from behind. The Celts called it our *fetch*—the "double" that tags along behind us. Occultists and metaphysicians of today would call it our *astral soul* or *astral body*.

The Greeks believed that many dreams are created by the nightly journeys of the wandering soul through astral realms—in other words, many of our dreams reflect the landscapes, images, and spirits to be found in the astral world. This belief is still widely held in India today, and is part of classical Vedanta philosophy. The Greeks also seem to have believed that some dreams are comprised of fleeting images and resonances from our daily lives—what psychologists call *remnants of the day*. It is uncertain, however, as to whether remnants of the day and astral dreams were really one and the same thing—in other words, whether the pictures and images shaped in the astral realm are based largely upon emotional tones and valences left over from our daily experience. These two kinds of dreams may well have been identical in Greek thinking, and it is simply the present-day classical scholars, lacking a clear concept of metaphysics, who have confused them and assumed that they are different.

In any event, there was another kind of dream, and it was considered to be the most important kind of dream experience. Such dreams constituted direct communications with or visitations from the gods. The Homeric poems, for example, include several examples in which a goddess or god speaks directly to one of the heroes or other main characters in a dream, delivering specific and deeply important information.[4] Sprinkled liberally throughout both *The Iliad* and *The Odyssey* are examples of dreams sent by the gods. Zeus sends a dream to Agamemnon, Athene sends a dream to Penelope, and so on. But dreams in the Homeric world were slightly different than how we now view them. The dreamer did not "have" a dream, he "saw" a dream figure. The dream figure could come through a keyhole, stand at the dreamer's head, tell the dreamer he or she was asleep, and then deliver the message.[5] Homer made a distinction between true and false dreams as well: false dreams come through "the gates of ivory" to confuse or confound the dreamer, whereas true dreams come through "the gates of polished horn" and will benefit the dreamer.[6] (One can only wonder: what might a gate of polished horn look like in a dream?)

We too may experience such dreams, though we may not always recognize them for what they are. They occur whenever we dream of a powerful figure who clearly embodies an archetype—the Wise Old Man or Wise Old Woman who gives us a talisman or some words of wisdom, the Dark Lover who rides into a woman's dream when she is in crisis, or the shining Love Goddess who appears to a man to guide his way. To put it another way, in some dreams the archetypes rise up and speak to us directly, and the archetypes are, of course, none other than the Gods.

Our predecessors took such archetypal dreams seriously and literally, and their concern with archetypal dreaming goes back as far as our recorded history. The one retold here is probably the oldest one currently on record.

In about 2100 BCE, Gudea was king of the Sumerian city of Lagash. His dream experience, now kept in the Louvre Museum in Paris, was recorded on two clay cylinders, translated as follows:[7]

In the dream [I saw]
A man who was bright, shining like Heaven
—great in Heaven, great on Earth—
who by his headdress was a Dingir (god).
At his side was the divine Storm Bird;
Like a devouring storm under his feet
Two lions crouched, on the right and on the left.
He commanded me to build his temple.

Gudea, perplexed by the dream, sought the advice of the oracle goddess Nanshe in her "House of Fate-Solving." Following this came a celestial omen that Gudea did not understand: the Sun upon Kishar (Jupiter) was suddenly seen on the horizon. A female appeared, giving Gudea celestial instructions:

A woman—
Who was she? Who was she not?
The image of a temple-structure
She carried on her head—
In her hand she held a holy stylus;
The tablet of the favorable star of heaven
She bore.

As the woman consulted the star tablet, a third divine being appeared who was a male:

A second man appeared, he had the
Look of a hero, endowed with strength.
A tablet of lapis lazuli in his hand he held.
The plan of a temple he drew on it.
He placed before me a holy carrying basket;
Upon it he placed a pure brickmaking mold;
The destined brick was inside it.
A large vessel stood before me;
On it was engraved the Tibu bird which shines
Brilliantly day and night.
A freight-ass crouched to my right.

All these objects seemed to materialize during the dream. Later, Gudea commemorated the miracle in one of his statues. The oracle goddess Nanshe proceeded to tell Gudea what the dream meant. The first god to appear was Ninurta or Ningirsu, telling Gudea to build a new temple. It was to be called E-NINNU, meaning "House of Fifty." Incidentally, Ninurta was the Sumerian name for the god connected with the planet Saturn.

The sighting of the heliacal rising of Jupiter was interpreted as "the god Ningishzidda," meant to show the king the exact point in the skies to which the temple's observatories should be oriented. The female who appeared in the vision was Nisaba, who instructed Gudea "to build the temple in accordance with the Holy Planet she instructed thee." The second male, Nanshe explained, was the god Nindub, "to thee the plan of the temple he gave."

According to the tablets, not only did Gudea have a portentous dream, but, amazingly enough by our standards, certain objects were manifested to expedite his responsibility to build this most important temple. Now, modern scholars may view this part of the story as sheer fantasy or allegory, and most of us may be tempted to do the same. But the manifested objects have a bearing upon two schools of thought that were present in the ancient world (and that are still not completely resolved in the modern world), regarding the question of whether dreams were literally sent by the gods or motivated by something within the dreamer. In Gudea's example, there's an even deeper question to ponder, which also appears in Biblical accounts of dreams—that is, whether the gods themselves visit the dreamer physically and deliver to them physical objects that appear to manifest at their bedside when they arise.

In any case, it is clear that the ancients not only took dreams seriously, but also devised various ways to define them and classify them. During the second century CE, the Hellenistic world experienced a minor renaissance of thinkers and writers. Included in this group were the physician Galen, the "travel writer" Pausanias, the mystic Philostratus, and the astrologer Ptolemy, author of the *Tetrabiblos*, which became the cornerstone of medieval astrology and astronomy.[8] Another writer of the period was Artemidorus of Daldis, who resided in Ephesus, one of the leading intellectual centers of the era. He has left us with a five-volume treatise entitled *Oneirocritica (The Interpretation of Dreams)* in which almost every type of dream experience in the ancient world, gathered through his wanderings near and far, was recorded and analyzed.[9] In fact, our modern dream theorists refer to Artemidorus' work on a regular basis, because not much has really changed about the nature of dreams or dreamers since those days. Artemidorus, it seems, skirted around this thorny question of where dreams come from, though he did come up with some very interesting ideas about the categories of dreams.

Artemidorus was concerned with what time of night the dream took place. There was a difference among the hours. They too are represented by mythical persons *(horae)* with distinct personalities. Times in dreams refer to regions of the night that have distinctive qualities, such as the twelve subterranean domains traversed by the Egyptian sun-god in his ship of the night. The *Atharva Veda,* one of India's most prolific texts on dreaming, agrees, teaching that the last dream of a sequence is the most important and that the later in the night the dream occurs, the more likely it is to come true.[10] Dreams occurring before midnight were not taken as seriously, and if too much food or drink was consumed before retiring, these dreams might be complete nonsense. Dreams occurring just before dawn were considered most revealing and often most prophetic. In fact, dreams were generally considered to be the most appropriate medium for prophecy. Many Greek thinkers expressed the idea that only during sleep could the soul be liberated from the body and free from the constraints of time and space. Thus, having quieted the senses, the soul was in a position to receive messages clearly.[11]

Artemidorus also had certain classifications for dreams that are still in keeping with much modern thought about dreams. He distinguished between theorematic dreams (dreams that come true as they occur in the dream) and allegorical dreams (dreams which disclose their meaning through symbolism). In the allegorical group, there are five classes: personal, alien, common, public, and cosmic.

By the time Freud and then Jung began their work, some seventeen centuries after Artemidorus catalogued his findings, the world was once again ready to look at dreams from a therapeutic standpoint. There is no question that Jung and Freud did not originate the idea of dreams as healing tools, but rather resurrected some of the ancient material. Of course, what they both added to the field can and does fill libraries. But Jung also reminds us that most of our difficulties result from losing touch with our instincts, with the age-old unforgotten wisdom we store, the "two-million-year-old man" residing in us all. How do we communicate with him? Through our dreams.[12]

DREAMS AND ASTROLOGY

It is such "archetypal dreams" that serve as the cornerstone of Jungian psychotherapy. Oddly enough, however, very few astrologers make use of archetypal dreams in their own practice. This is unfortunate, because your dreams may give you more specific information about the planetary issues and themes present in your life than you are likely to get from a mere study of the birth chart.

Why? Because the planets are the Gods, of course, and when a Goddess, God, or archetype "visits" us in a dream, we can usually link it with a particular planet. The deities will seldom or never appear to us as they did to ancient Greeks—do not expect to dream of Mercury in winged sandals and a shining helmet. Instead, he will be likely to appear to you in a more contemporary guise—he may be that nefarious "traveling salesman" you've always heard about, or a smiling drifter with an uncanny piece of knowledge to share with you.

As we study each planet in turn, we will examine some of the ways in which they manifest themselves in our dreams, as well as what their appearance may signify for our lives.

Our purpose in delving into so much dream material in this volume is related to both our subjects: astrology and myth. Gudea's dream corresponded to a visitation by a god and also to the rising of Jupiter. Dreams are probably the best way to access myths and archetypes. Dreams for us can be both personal and archetypal. In the last few centuries, humanity has become less tribal, more individualized. While certain benefits have been gained, others have been sacrificed. One sacrifice is that we have lost our ability to stay connected to the divine world and how the Gods communicate with us through dreams. There are countless stories related by missionaries who discovered how important a dream could be to tribes as a group, how important the shared dream experience was among the tribal members, and finally, the belief that the dream world has more relevance than the waking one, with the resulting notion that this world is not as real as the dream world.[13] Jung, too, was both impressed and distressed by what he learned in his visits to primitive cultures—he was impressed by the frequency and accuracy of archetypal dreams that were a mainstay of their culture, but distressed by one tribal leader's statement that now that the white man had arrived knowing everything, there was no longer a necessity for the people to dream.

Dreams are myths—they contain the same symbolism. For instance, an astrological client dreamed of a man wearing a red hat. Now, we already have two associations with astrological Aries or its ruler, Mars. The hat is something on the head (ruled by Aries) and red is the color associated with Mars and Aries. The man was rushing across the landscape (more Aries symbolism) in a hurry, and it seemed as if he was forcing the dreamer to start running as well. When the dreamer's chart was consulted, it turned out that, indeed, she had her natal Mars being transited by Pluto at the time of the dream, and she was attempting to integrate and transform the nature of Mars in her chart. The dream was encouraging her to get on with it.

When people are embarking on therapy or having an astrological reading for the first time, they often experience something like this. They are embarking on new territory and the psyche is delighted to find a new way to communicate with them. Often, when people come to have their chart read, they will say something like, "I had the most fantastic dream last night, and I never dream."

An article appeared in the Santa Fe *New Mexican* in 1995 that is so hilarious, you would think it made up, yet it is true. At least one would believe so, having been printed in a legitimate daily newspaper. It reads:[14]

MAN SINKS INTO MOTHER'S GRAVE

A man planting mums in his mother's grave was trapped for 2 hours when the ground gave way and he sank knee-high. Kenneth McLaughlin, age 29, said repeatedly he tried to free himself, but the leg that sank into soft ground Saturday became stuck underneath the base of his mother's headstone. "Help arrived after 2 hours," said McLaughlin, a security guard. "I repeatedly shouted for help, but nobody came. I was really upset." McLaughlin was rescued by a bicyclist who called for help. A police officer used a flower pot to shovel a 2-foot hole near the grave and free McLaughlin.

This could be a dream. It could be a story. It was a *news clipping!* Did you catch the symbolism? A man planting "mums" (a flower, but sounds like *mom,* and many people say *Mum* for *mom*) on his mother's grave, sank knee-high (Capricorn/Saturn); he's age 29 (Saturn Return). It's Saturday (Saturn's day). He became stuck (Saturn again). He was a security guard (more Saturn). Nobody came but a bicyclist (Hermes/Mercury figure), who arrived after two hours, and the victim was freed by the digging of a two-foot hole.

In terms of mythic stories, Persephone's abduction to the underworld comes quickly to mind. As she goes to the underworld, she actually becomes indoctrinated into the mysteries of life and death. She is abducted while fixated on narcissus flowers. So here we have the great mother pulling the son into the underworld, into the realm of the feminine. He's having his Saturn Return, so he's probably going through some struggles about his identity in the world. He's stuck in life, and is being pulled down by "the great mother." The bicyclist is interesting because Hermes or Mercury is one of the only gods who can enter and leave the underworld without being harmed, and he is the guide of souls. In the myth, it is Hermes who intervenes for Persephone in the underworld. Two hours is the amount of time it takes one sign upon the Ascendant to rise, so it would be interesting to see which sign it was; two feet under also symbolizes the same.

Obviously, dream interpretation is very personal and quite complex. Caution is given here about trying to interpret a dream from a book. Although the better dream symbolism books might contain references that can lead you in the right direction, it's better to simply use the symbolism in such a way as to stimulate free association. It's tempting when you're first learning about a subject, like astrology, to consult a textbook to see what Pluto means—or a dream book to see what a pink pillow means. But these items that appear in your dreams are so personal that there could hardly be a universally agreed upon meaning for that symbol, though there may be a general feeling about it. The pink pillow may be the pillow from your childhood home and, as such, can have a certain meaning particular only to you. Was it something you really loved and needed in order to feel secure, or was it something your mother really liked, but you didn't and it was always a source of conflict between you and her?

So you want to look at your dreams as stories, as myths, and as something that could almost be written as a fairy tale or piece of poetry. There are, of course, personal dreams and archetypal dreams, and it's good to look for symbols that will identify which is which. So, keeping in mind what we have just said, use the ideas presented in this book—ideas that will help fertilize your own unconscious memories and attempt to relate them to the archetypes we are describing herein.

DREAM INCUBATION

So, what exactly is dream incubation and how might we use it today? Incubation (from *incubare*) means simply "to lie in wait," as a fetus would in the womb. Probably the best and most complete volume we have on this ancient practice comes to us from the Jungian psychologist C. A. Meier, who, in his *Ancient Incubation and Modern Psychotherapy*,[15] reports the essential practices and philosophies of the technique in detail. Our own contemporary rendering follows below:

- Begin with a mental exercise: empty your mind of all negative thoughts. It was inscribed thus at the famous dream temple of Epidaurus: "Let every man who enters the incense-laden temple be clean, / Yet he may be called clean who has none but holy thoughts in his mind."[16] Sit in meditation and release all the cares and worries of the day. Mentally envision your troubles as a ball of "dark" or "dirty" energy, then envision a great wave of white light dissolving the dark mass into nothingness. Do not proceed until you feel that you are in a joyous, positive, and receptive frame of mind.

- Take a bath. This was actually an integral part of the ritual at the Aesculapions and was a further way of cleansing both body and spirit. You may wish to add herbal preparations of potpourri to your bath water, for there is some evidence that herbs were used for this purpose in ancient times as well. In fact, almost anything you can do to relax and cleanse the physical body will be appropriate, for as we have seen, caves, waterfalls, nature, music, and massage were all part of the ancient technique (sounds like a modern-day spa, which is actually an excellent setting in which to practice incubation). It is also best to eat lightly before retiring.

- Those who entered the Aesculapions were required to make an offering to the god before they began their "treatment," and it is still important to approach dream incubation with a spirit of reverence. Before going to sleep, say a prayer or make some other form of thanks to whatever higher power you honor in your own spiritual practice.

- You are now in a perfect state of mind for incubation. As you lie down to sleep, be sure to keep a notebook and a pencil by your side to write down any dreams that may come. And don't be surprised if a dream that's shrouded in oracular vernacular doesn't come that same night. As we have seen, many who sought wisdom from the Aesculapions had to wait for months to achieve the right kind of dream.

- In the morning, awaken slowly and gradually, without alarm clocks or cell phones. Try to linger in bed, even beyond the time you would normally be moved to arise. It's important to stay in the aura of the dream for as long as possible, until as many details or images as you can possibly retain can get recorded. Write the dream down as if writing a factual news story that you would be reporting on the evening news. Then, if you're artistically inclined, sketch one of the scenes from it (pick your favorite, or the most colorful one, or the one that has the most interesting forms or objects in it). If you are not an artist, rewrite the dream as if you were writing a poem or a fairy tale or a fictionalized story. Read it, then leave it be. Come back to it a week later and read it again. You might remember another fragment or two that was initially forgotten.

- Share your dreams with others. In many cases, the healers of the ancient dream temples acted merely as "good listeners" rather than interpreters, for it was assumed that the patient was well equipped to understand the basic impact of his own dream. And yet there are always levels and dimensions of our own dreams that remain hidden from us, precisely because they are so close to us. Just as the wise astrologer does not attempt to read her own chart, the dreamer should not attempt to interpret her own dream completely and without assistance. Take it to an expert, or at the very least, someone well experienced with the art of dreams, and watch it unfold.

- After a dream was experienced, the seeker at the dream temple typically made an offering of thanks to the god Aesculapius. This is similar to the practice that Jungian psychologists call *honoring the dream*. The basic idea is this: if we simply write a dream down, talk about it, and then neglect it, the dream will lose its transformative spiritual power. So we must actually do something to demonstrate that we are paying attention to the voices of the Gods, the planets, or our own inner archetypes. In Kabbalistic dreaming, for example, this was taken very seriously and very literally. If you dreamed about a trip to New York, you would be advised to jump on a plane and find out what New York was waiting to show you! But even if we are able only to honor a dream symbolically, we must still make an attempt. If you dream of an old friend, give him a phone call. If you dream of an unhappy time from your childhood past, allow yourself to meditate on the incident and feel the grief, the sense of loss. And if you dream of nature, go for a hike!

ACTIVE IMAGINATION

This technique, developed in Jungian psychology, is sometimes referred to as *dreaming the dream outward*. It can help us in unlocking the meaning of dreams that remain stubbornly obscure, and it can also be used to contact the inner archetypes directly.

Dreams frequently break off at important junctures in the story. We wake up, wondering what was supposed to happen next. It is much as if we had set down a good mystery novel just when a new clue is introduced or a new suspect comes upon the scene—we are left wondering where the course of the story will turn.

Of course, we can always pick up the novel and read the next chapter when we have more leisure to do so. But how shall we accomplish this in the case of a dream?

Active imagination answers that question for us.

Let us suppose that you dream you are at a party. You constantly encounter a strange man, a "mysterious stranger" who seems to be watching you and studying you. In the course of the dream, he invites you into the garden, away from the other party guests. His eyes shine as he says: "I have something to tell you." He pours you a glass of wine. The two of you raise your glasses and touch them together. You hear the musical clink of glass on glass —and then you wake up.

As we have seen, magical personalities with powerful messages are the essence of archetypal dreaming and have been ever since Greek and Babylonian times. An encounter such as this one suggests that the stranger is an archetype, perhaps corresponding to one of the ancient gods or astrological planets. But what did he want to tell you?

In order to practice active imagination, begin much as you would begin the process of dream incubation. Sit quietly, empty your mind of all unpleasant or unwelcome thoughts, and establish a calm, joyous, receptive frame of mind.

Then close your eyes and try to visualize the end of your dream. In the example given above, try to see the garden, the mysterious stranger, just as they were in the dream. (For some people, especially those who are not particularly "visual" in their orientation, this may take a little work, but if you have kept a detailed dream journal, it will be much easier.) Mentally raise your glass and touch it to the stranger's glass, and then listen to what he has to say.

This sounds almost ridiculously simple, but it isn't. For one thing, it may require some practice at visualization or mental imagery, as we have noted. Also, it may be just as difficult to remember the stranger's words in an active imagination setting as it would be in a dream. (You may wish to have a friend present, then speak the words out loud so that your companion can write them down, or you may wish to tape-record the active imagination session.)

Beyond that, there is much in active imagination that is left to your own conscious control, quite differently than in a dream. You are free to dialogue with the archetypes you encounter. This can be quite stimulating, but it may also be disconcerting. As we noted in chapter 2, the archetypes are most likely to visit us and speak directly when they feel disturbed—when something in our psyche is out of balance. Very often, the first thing that happens in an active imagination is a kind of confrontation with our own deepest problems and issues. When we first meet the Gods, it seems as if they're crazy.

So it takes a certain amount of courage and commitment to undertake the path of active imagination. It is not a game. But it may well lead you to the astrological and archetypal source of your present issues in a way that a simple astrological reading seldom can.

Active imagination is a versatile technique, and can be used even when there is no particular dream requiring clarification. In fact, it can be used by itself to induce a kind of "waking dream" and thus contact the Gods, planets, or archetypes directly.

The technique is almost the same—empty the mind, close the eyes, and travel within. But in this case you will not be reconstructing the scenery of a dream: rather, you will simply be allowing images to present themselves to your mind.

In most cases, you will not immediately encounter a figure or personality. You are more likely to see a simple image—for example, a bird in flight. The important thing is this: do not allow your mind to wander. If given its own way, your mind is likely to float from one image to another—from the bird to a tree to a lake to an old friend. This kind of meandering will serve no useful purpose. Do not "let go" of the bird until you understand why it has appeared to you and what it means.

If practiced often enough, this form of active imagination will eventually deepen and become more complex, more vivid. You will encounter the same archetypal figures who appear in dreams, and you will be able to dialogue with them. And once again, the Gods are likely to seem "crazy" and to confront you with your deepest issues.

In the chapters that follow, we provide some symbolic figures and meanings of the planets and the deities with which they are associated. The symbolic mode of dreams and active imagination is precisely the same—the figures that might represent Venus in a dream are the same that might represent her in active imagination. This part of the book is meant simply to help you figure out *who* is speaking to you and what they may be trying to tell you.

---

1. Dossey, Larry, *Reinventing Medicine* (San Francisco, CA: Harper Collins, 1999).
2. Meier, C. A., *Ancient Incubation and Modern Psychotherapy,* trans. by Monica Curtis (Evanston, IL: Northwestern University Press, 1967).
3. Euripides, *Iphigenia at Aulis,* quoted in Patricia Cox Miller's *Dreams in Late Antiquity* (Princeton, NJ: Princeton University Press, 1994).
4. Dodds, E. R., *The Greeks and the Irrational* (Boston: Beacon Press, 1957).
5. Parman, Susan, *Dreams and Culture* (New York: Praeger, 1991).
6. Homer, *The Odyssey of Homer,* trans. by Richmond Lattimore, (New York: Harper Collins, 1975) Book 19.
7. Sitchin, Zecharia, *Divine Encounters* (New York: Avon Books, 1995).
8. Ptolemy, *Tetrabiblos,* edited and translated into English by F. E. Robbins (Cambridge, MA: Harvard University Press, 1940).
9. Artemidorus, *The Interpretation of Dreams: Oneirocritica,* trans. by Robert J. White (Park Ridge, NJ: Noyes Press, 1975).
10. Stevens, Anthony, *Private Myths: Dreams and Dreaming* (London: Penguin Books, 1996).
11. Parman, op. cit.
12. Stevens, Anthony, *The Two Million Year Old Self* (Texas A & M University Press, 1993).
13. Dodds, op cit.
14. "Man Sinks into Mother's Grave," *The Santa Fe New Mexican,* May 21, 1995, Sunday edition.
15. Meier, op. cit.
16. Meier, op. cit.

Part II

THE INNER PLANETS

CHAPTER 5

THE SUN
GOD OF LIGHT AND LIFE

ASTROLOGY AND MYTH

The Sun of our solar system, though composed of fiery gaseous materials, has been portrayed as an animate living deity in the myths of almost every human culture. As we have seen, almost any object in the sky could be deified—not just planets, but fixed stars and even the Milky Way itself have all enjoyed god- or goddess-like status in one culture or another. We can then only imagine the importance assumed by the bright and shining one, our Sun.

In Egypt, the sun god, Ra, enjoyed an exalted status that even went far beyond other cultures. The Babylonian sun god, Shamash, was said to be exalted each day as it reached its zenith. The Sun at zenith was believed to be a symbol for the king of the land, for the king was at the apex of society just as the zenith Sun is at the apex of the sky. We can see why eclipses of the Sun were such a source of worry and concern for ancient people, and why they seemed to bode ill for the society at large. Such events surely predisposed the fall or impending death of the king.

Mithras, the Persian god of rebirth and regeneration whose worship challenged early Christianity for supremacy, was in certain senses of the word a sun god. And it has been said that the Christians overcame him by transforming their own spiritual teacher, Jesus of Nazareth, into something of a sun god himself!

Religious fascination with the Sun is indeed universal. Several Celtic romances, particularly *Gawain and the Green Knight,* tell how Gawain's strength waxed until midday and waned thereafter, presumably linking him with the Sun. His father's name was Loth, which is linguistically related to the Welsh Llew and Irish Lugh—who may well have been a solar deity at one time.

In Japan, the Shinto religion likewise makes a bow to the Sun, but there the solar orb is a goddess. Her name is Amaterasu O Mikami. Never an organized religion with written texts of instruction or prescribed ritual, Shintoism was a worship centered around natural beauty—earth and nature—particularly waterfalls, trees, flowers, etc. Here we observe a theme that we will see repeated—the sun and earth as a complementary mix woven together for best results. The rising sun is the defining symbol or logo for this religion and can still be seen on Japan's flag. Like the Goddess of old, it is a religion that honors nature, particularly the beauty in all things; and it is easy to see how this belief has permeated Japanese culture, even today. And, again like the old Goddess cults, it is nonexclusive. Its members may practice other religions simultaneously.

In fact, solar goddesses are more common than one might imagine. While the Hindu deity of the Sun, Surya, is often described as a god, the same figure is sometimes called a goddess as well. And while some have groaned that the Hindu lunar deity is a god rather than a goddess, it is interesting to note that the moon god's favorite bride, Rohini, seems in many ways to be a solar deity, and the story of their love affair is in fact a parable of the Moon's emergence from the heart of the Sun each month, followed by his progress from son to consort until he returns once again into the body of the goddess.

In Greece there were several solar figures; and, as Apollo, the Sun eventually came to represent highly exalted principles in ancient Greek philosophy. Helios, Hercules, and Apollo are three figures linked with the Sun in Greek myth. Helios drove the fiery chariot that pulled the Sun across the sky each day, and his name is still a root word for all things solar. The hero Hercules (to use the more common Latin name for the Greek Herakles), first a mortal and eventually a god, performed his twelve labors, a metaphor for the Sun passing through the twelve signs of the zodiac each year. But it was probably Apollo, the exalted son of Zeus, who was most deeply associated with the Sun's archetype of leadership, kingship, or royalty.

While certain cultures still retain lunar calendars as their basis for tracking time (for example, the Hindu, Muslim, and Hebrew calendars), the Western world is most familiar with the solar-based calendar.[1] Our months and seasons make it virtually impossible (unless you're locked in your own virtual reality) for us to ignore that the Sun is the prevailing factor that establishes the predictable order and sequence of our seasons here on earth. When Earth is tilted closest to the hemisphere in question, it is summer, and when tipped away from the Sun, it is winter. Spring and fall represent a more moderate time when the earth is experiencing equal day, equal night (thus *equinox*, which in Latin literally means "equal night"). The Sun, which follows the path of the ecliptic, traces its footsteps in a serpentine pattern around Earth's equator, rising to the north in the summer and falling to the south in the winter. The moment when it is precisely on the equator, getting ready to fall southward, is the autumnal equinox. The Sun is falling to the south—we in the north are losing more and more of our light each day until the winter solstice

(*solstice* is also from Latin and means "sun standing still"). At this time the Sun literally does stand still for a few days, and then begins to head north again. There is no shortage of ancient and modern celebratory feasts in many religions honoring this moment, and it may in fact be one of the most important times in the year because of the simple fact that the Sun is returning. No wonder the birth of Christ is celebrated this time of year. Although the earliest Christian writers imply that the historical Jesus of Nazareth was actually born in April, the winter solstice birth tradition is powerfully symbolic, for the Sun is returning in the Northern Hemisphere where these religions originated, and Christ, exalted as the Son of God, has also returned.

But what's curious about all of this is the fact that even though we speak of the Sun as doing all this work, it is in fact the earth. We also speak of sunrise and sunset in our diurnal cycle, but once again it is really the earth that is responsible for this movement. Sun and Earth are integrally related, and we, as "earthlings," should not think of the Sun without thinking of its ongoing relationship with and to the earth and its effect upon all Earth's inhabitants. In the astrological chart, we say that Earth is in the center. But it is not incorrect to think of the earth as being the opposite point to the Sun—thus forming a polarity relationship.

Apollo, the Greek sun god, had his sacred place at the Oracle of Delphi. But his tenancy there was not a matter of mere chance. It is said that Zeus released two eagles and sent them flying in opposite directions. Where they met was Delphi, which was thus considered the center of the earth. But the origins of Delphi go much further back into prehistory. For centuries and possibly even millennia, it was a goddess worship shrine dedicated to Gaia and other female deities of the earth. A sacred stone called the Omphalos was placed there. The word *omphalos* means both "navel" and "center," referring both to the place in the human body where the umbilical cord is attached as well as the center of the world or the cosmos. If Gaia, our Earth, and particularly Delphi, its center, had a symbolic umbilical cord there, we might say that all of Gaia's children, no matter how far scattered around the globe, still have an ancient connection with that mystical center. And it is fitting that the earth itself should be worshipped at "the center," for the Sun, of course, is the center of our solar system.

A myth tells us how Apollo came to be the patron deity of Delphi. He slew a giant serpent or dragon called the Python, which guarded the sacred gorge.

Some feminist writers have seen the serpent as emblematic of the ancient "serpent wisdom" of the Goddess, and consequently they see Apollo in the same light as other so-called heroes, kings, leaders, or warriors bent on conquering primitive peoples and claiming the enchantingly beautiful and sacred land as their own. (Modern developers still act in their spirit.) The Oracle of Delphi itself was in the hands of a priestess called the Pythoness, who inhaled the fumes rising out of a crevice in the earth, and thus gave forth prophecies. Apollo, after taking control of Delphi, preserved the oracle—though perhaps altering the ancient rituals somewhat. Delphi remained the principal prophetic center of the Graeco-Roman world up until the end of Paganism.

Astrologically, the Sun rules Leo, a summer sign that runs its course while the Sun shines at its brightest. This is when the Sun acts most strongly as a creative ruling force. And who can argue with the force of the Sun? Of course, it's the same in an astrological chart. According to the ancient doctrine of planetary sect, those born during the day naturally have a solar orientation towards life, while those born at night are more lunar in temperament. But you can add more points if it's also a summer birth (especially Leo). A birth at noon, when the Sun is at its daily zenith, is even more powerfully solar—and in astrology, the zenith or "noon point" of the chart signifies such solar matters as power, fame, and success. Add even more "solar" points if the birth occurs while the Moon is at its dark or new moon phase, and hence at its weakest.

In such cases, the Sun's influence can be irradiating rather than just warming. The Sun's role in the chart is to focalize it, giving a point of reference to the other planets. The Sun imposes light and time and order and the seasons upon the planetary bodies that revolve around it, allowing life in all its forms to exist under its law. When the Sun is too strong in a horoscope, the individual may be so focused that all those in her or his sphere are likewise required to exist only under his "law." Such people may embody a "my way or the highway" attitude towards life. Is it any wonder that politicians and other world leaders are symbolized by the Sun? In India, this negative view of the Sun is prominent in the astrology of Hindu culture.

In India, the Sun may beat down with such force that the crops are blighted, the earth withered and scorched. Even so, political leaders and other solar types are inherently untrustworthy, because their powerful egos care but little for the happiness of others, and an overly intense politician may leave the ordinary mortal feeling as "scorched" as the summer earth. Hindu astrology regards the Moon as a much more likeable, much more friendly force.

Apollo evidently did have a shadow. For three months each year, he abandoned the land of Delphi, where social customs, law, and order prevailed. It is written that he headed north to the land of the Hyperboreans. We may wonder, why north? Doesn't the Sun itself "head south" for the winter (at least in terms of its visible position on the horizon)? But the idea of the sun god's journey north to the polar regions would seem to embody the ancient doctrine of polarities. For in a certain metaphorical sense, what this solar fireball really needs is ice. In any case, it is written that the god Dionysus came to Delphi during those months to rule in his place. Now Dionysus could not be any further from Apollo in nature and character (see our chapter on the planet Neptune as an archetypal carrier for Dionysian energy). In fact, the German philosopher Friedrich Nietzsche used these two deities as symbols for what he perceived to be the two polarities of Western culture—the Apollonian and the Dionysian.

There are a few similarities between Apollo and Dionysus, one being the fact that they are both associated with musical instruments. Perhaps this is why so many inspired and gifted musicians have important connections between the Sun and Neptune in their birth charts. Apollo, as a son of Zeus the law-giver, often functioned as the intermediary between the gods and humans, handing down the laws of Olympus and seeing that they were enacted upon the earth. He represents balance: "Nothing in excess, everything in balance"—reason, order, and politics on the one hand, but the recreational practices of civilized music, archery, and theater on the other hand.

Dionysus, also a son of Zeus, is a god of "the vine," including everything having to do with the making and consumption of wine. He represents the idea of completely cutting loose and going wild. Dionysian energy is the opposite of law and order; when one is under his enchanting spell there is no law and there are no boundaries. Dionysian energy is drunken, frenzied, and chaotic. If Apollo's law is founded upon "nothing in excess," then Dionysian behavior would seem to be the exact opposite—a celebration of total excess. Again, one might look to Sun-Neptune contacts in the chart to observe someone with both sides of this dilemma inherently present in his or her make-up.

But perhaps the most important "polarity" in which the Sun is involved is the polarity between the Sun and the Moon. This dichotomy underlies much of Western esotericism; it is part of the realm of alchemy as well as of astrology.

It is easy enough to say that the Sun is masculine while the Moon is feminine, but what do we really mean by that?

The alchemists perceived the Sun as an archetype of Spirit, and the Moon as an archetype of Soul. Too often, contemporary New Agers may use these words interchangeably, but as psychologist James Hillman has pointed out, they are really quite different.[2] Spirit strives for perfection. It wants to climb the mountain top to reach the "peak" of enlightenment—or with a more materially oriented Sun, the peak of financial or political power, pure and simple. Spirit is content to sit at the top of the mountain, in the snow-covered Himalayas of the mind, and watch the doings of mere mortals with a kind of cool detachment. At its worst, Spirit can isolate us, remove us from the world, lock us into intellectual realms—or realms of power and control—that separate us from those around us and make us insensitive to others.

Soul, on the other hand, loves nothing more than to connect with others and unite with them in bonds of love. If Spirit rejects the world and longs for the heights, Soul embraces the world and rests in her moist river valleys. Soul cares about certain foods, certain people, certain memories and experiences that bring warmth and a sense of oneness with the world all around. Spirit can too often disdain these matters as unworthy, mere "attachment." Soul also has its drawbacks—it can easily become clingy and maudlin, completely drowning in that beautifully flowing river that, at its best, makes the valley so peaceful and inviting.

If we begin to understand the difference between Spirit and Soul, we can also understand the difference between Sun and Moon, and we can understand what astrologers mean when they talk about solar and lunar types of individuals. As we noted above, these categories are not simply a matter of contemporary psychological astrology. In ancient times, anyone born during the day was a solar type, while anyone born at night was a lunar type. This had important repercussions for every aspect of interpreting the birth chart, for the ancient astrologers judged the strength of all the other planets largely by whether they were in the portion of the horoscope—day or night—that was appropriate to them.

In much the same way, the ancient "planetary cycles" recognized by our astrological ancestors (and which still survive in a somewhat different form in the *dashas* of Hindu astrology) also took their origin from the archetypes of Sun and Moon, Spirit and Soul—those born during the day counted their planetary cycles beginning with the Sun, while those born at night began with the Moon.

DREAMWORK AND ACTIVE IMAGINATION

Kings, leaders, heroes, and one's father are all symbols of the Sun. Among all of these, the father is perhaps the most important solar symbol, for most people dream about their father hundreds of times more often than they will ever dream about a head of state!

Still, we have personally heard of many people dreaming about the president, especially as presidents seem to be reaching out and trying to get closer to the people, rather than keeping a distance like the leaders did in ancient times. That might include royalty as well. Around the time of Princess Diana's death, countless women reported dreaming of her. Such dreams may fall into the category of *collective dreaming*, whereby all dreamers' psyches are interconnected and thus able to receive the same vision or dream. If in the dream, an object appears luminous or contains a bright and shining golden light around it, think of the Sun. One dreamer reported dreaming of a pile of objects lying in a field, but there was light around one of the objects. It was this object that needed to be isolated and worked with in her psyche.

Our Sun is composed of a fiery center. Though dreams of domesticated fire, as in a fireplace or hearth, would be related to the goddess (and asteroid) Vesta, the principle of fire itself, as in a drought blighting the landscape or a wildfire spreading rapidly, or in intense burns from fire, could be related to an overly active solar principle. People who have visions as a way of life have "seen" the Sun in dreams. Sometimes they will see it exploding. At other times they will see its light intensely focused on the earth in a particular way, as if to energize and heal it. In this context, healers working with light are often channeling solar energy. Apollo was, among other things, a god of healing, and the use of light in healing is quite effective, as is color, which is the spectrum of light diffused into different wavelengths.

Artemidorus, who wrote an important guide to dreams in late classical times, went into great detail about the Sun—and with good reason, for the celestial orb often appears in dreams. To dream of a sunrise, for example, is auspicious for all things, especially for business. Since each sunrise is a "birth," it may also signify the birth of children, but if the Sun appears in a dream as blood red or somehow unpleasant (as in some post-apocalyptic science fiction fantasy), it carries the opposite meanings. If the Sun actually crashes to the earth, it bodes a disastrous event or (in more modern terms) a psychological crisis of some magnitude. Artemidorus believed it to be very auspicious for a ray of sun to enter one's house in a dream, for the house is made brighter thereby; by extension, it symbolizes that our lives, which are centered in our home space, will be "made brighter." A woman reported dreaming of a friend of hers who had recently passed on. Around the woman was a very bright light, which the dreamer described as luminescent. She was assured by this dream that her friend had made a successful transition. But if the Sun itself should actually roll into your house, beware! That is a fairly destructive proposition.

More psychologically, the Sun represents a person's sense of self, especially self-esteem or confidence, and dreams that either inflate oneself or deflate oneself are inherently connected to the Sun. Entertainers, politicians, and other notable celebrities are people in the limelight—any dreams of such people relate to the Sun.

Gold is also solar. And need we mention that the creation of gold—whether material or symbolic—was the goal of the alchemists?

PLANETARY REMEDIES

While Artemidorus was fascinated by dreams of the Sun, solar remedies equally fascinated the Renaissance magus Marsilio Ficino. Ficino (who was more than half Pagan in spirit) regarded the Sun as an entirely positive planet astrologically, and seems not to have taken its "darker" side into consideration. In Ficino's view, one could never get too much solar energy!

As we have noted above, there can be different opinions about this, for too much Sun in a horoscope can lead to a massive ego. If one is already a corporate raider or a military leader, it might be best to avoid some of the more powerful traditional solar remedies.

For most people, it is generally a good idea to enhance the solar force in one's chart. Traditional gemstones connected with the Sun are rubies and garnets, which have a bright red color and hence symbolize vitality and powerful energy. Ficino drew attention to gold as a solar metal—set those rubies and garnets in a gold setting to increase the solar energetics even more strongly, or wear a gold chain. Ficino, who was a physician, even came up with ways to ingest the solar force with your food. He recommends a blend of cinnamon and honey, since in his view both are solar in nature. Beyond that, it sounds fairly tasty. He also recommends listening to powerful, stirring music.

However, Ficino's favorite planetary remedy for increasing the power of the Sun was also the most obvious: get outdoors and enjoy the sunlight! Ficino recommends walking through a meadow filled with flowers. The warm sun fills the walker with solar vitality, while the green color of the meadow as well as the flowers enhance the energy of Venus. In Ficino's view, such a practice was one of the best possible ways to fill yourself with the energies of two extremely benevolent planets. It's also very good for you. (Even the corporate raiders could benefit from a little touch of the Sun's milder side, mellowed by Venus and her floral beauty.)

INVOCATION AND AWARENESS

As will be clear from the information above, perhaps the best times to invoke or call upon the solar force within us are when we seek to achieve something of importance, whether in the spiritual or material realm. We should call upon the solar power within us whenever we need some vital energy to bring us through the hard stretches, to inspire us to something beyond ourselves. The solar energy helps us to climb the mountain, whether of mere worldly power or of spiritual achievement. If you wish to undertake powerful spiritual work, follow the Sun!

We can be aware of solar archetypes at almost any time—just look around you. In how many advertising themes (aside from Coppertone™ and other obvious matters) does the Sun play a role? And is its role not usually to symbolize life, health, and vitality? The archetype of the Sun and its power permeates our entire culture.

If we maintain awareness of the way in which the archetype is always around us, we can walk with Ficino in the sunshine almost any time!

---

1. This begs the question as to what kinds of internal timing mechanisms might differ between groups of people observing lunar rather than solar time. It takes 365.25 days for one full

revolution of the earth around the Sun, but there are only 360 degrees in a circle. Because of that, there is a cumbersome and confusing situation that puzzles school children immediately—we have an uneven number of days each month and then we have to stick in an extra day every four years to make it all work!

2. Hillman, James, *A Blue Fire* (New York: Perennial, 1991).

CHAPTER 6

THE MOON
RULER OF THE NIGHT

ASTROLOGY AND MYTH

The Moon is inescapable. Its monthly journey and its phases are part of our most fundamental observation of reality. The Moon is the most brilliant object in the night sky one week and completely invisible two weeks later.

Because of this, it is a basic tenet of archaeology and anthropology that lunar calendars are older than solar ones. The great megalithic stone circles of Europe, such as Stonehenge and Avebury, may well be markers of lunar time, lunar phases, and eclipse cycles. Some have argued that incised reindeer bones from the Ice Age (circa 30,000 BCE) are in fact lunar time markers as well, and some would go so far as to argue for records of lunar time even among the Neanderthals (circa 300,000 years ago).[1] One ancient lunar calendar is still alive and well to this very day: the twenty-seven Mansions of the Moon, which play such a fundamental role in Hindu astrology, can be traced back to at least 1200 BCE, and they may well date back to the period of the Indus Valley civilization (c. 2500 BCE).

Moon gods and goddesses have been worshipped in practically every culture. As children, many of us were shown how to look for "the man in the moon." This figure, outlined in the sky, is a folkloric reflex of the original astrological Moon: the god Sin, who, to the Babylonians, was the Father of Time. The word *sin* has nothing to do with our own English word for wrongdoing; it is simply a contraction of the Sumerian word Su-En, which denoted the crescent moon. The full moon was Nanna, yet another name for this important deity. Sin was more powerful than Shamash, the Sun, and in fact he was regarded as the father of the sun god. He was also the father of Ishtar, goddess of the planet Venus and one of the most powerful of all the Mesopotamian deities.[2]

Be that as it may, in Western astrology the Moon has always been perceived as feminine. No one is quite sure how the old Babylonian moon god was transformed into the symbol of feminine consciousness and soul. However, it should be remembered that the Moon seems to have been worshipped as the Great Mother Goddess far back into the European Neolithic period. When the Greeks adopted Babylonian astrology to their own culture, they may have been unwilling to change their outlook on the Moon's essential nature. And they didn't.

The connection between the Moon and womankind is deeply evident, and rooted in observational astronomy. The Moon's monthly cycle takes twenty-eight days to complete, and the connection between the lunar cycle and a woman's own twenty-eight-day cycle has been acknowledged since the most ancient times.[3] In fact, it is not just the female human that is linked to the cyclical twenty-eight-day lunar period, but all biological life on earth, including animals, plants, and ocean tides.

The Moon as the Mother Goddess is strikingly similar (at least in ancient Europe) to the Earth Goddess, also a Great Mother (see our chapter in this volume on Gaia). The primary difference between the Earth Goddess and the Moon Goddess is that the Earth Goddess is often depicted alone, pregnant, and about to give birth. The Moon Goddess, on the other hand, usually shows a pairing motif of mother and infant. This makes sense when we observe the Moon as a satellite or even offspring of the earth, forever destined to orbit around Earth for the whole of its existence. This concept also reveals something of the nature of the Moon's needs for nourishment, partnership, and dependence upon others in order to sustain oneself, and sure enough, that's how the Moon is treated in astrology.

If we examine the relationship of the Moon to the Sun/Earth axis in the birth chart, we will learn much about the astrological Moon. In Hellenistic and medieval astrology, the concept of planetary sect was a fundamental teaching, one that distinguished between day and night births in assessing the power and importance of the various planets. For those born at night, the Moon single-handedly has dominion over the chart, no matter what sign the native is. Second, whether born during the day or the night, note should be made of how shapely or full the Moon is (how much light it contains), as here too it would determine much about the character and destiny of the person. This last idea is still deeply important in Hindu astrology, where the Moon is usually of much more importance than the Sun. A bright full moon is said to promise a much happier and more contented life than a dark new moon. And the Moon is said to be unhappy and "lonely" when it is isolated in the chart without other planets surrounding it. The Moon, like the feminine field of consciousness for which it is a symbol, longs to connect with others, soul to soul.

This concern for brightness is important in the sense that it relates to the Moon's cycle—or more accurately, to the solar-lunar cycle. When the Moon is new, a slender crescent, she is the Goddess as nymph or maiden, still young and without a partner. When she is full, she is the mother, her belly big and round. And when she wanes again into another slender crescent, she is the Crone, the old wise woman.

Some of the most famous goddesses associated with the moon were Selene, Diana, Artemis, Cybele, and Isis. But it is Artemis, more than any other, who exemplifies the moon as maiden. The Ephesian Artemis was worshipped as a many-breasted mother, as much of an earth goddess as a lunar one. But in Hellenistic times, Artemis (Latin: Diana) had a youthful, girlish attribute, a maiden rather than a mother. Artemis was the child of Zeus and the Titaness Leto. When it was apparent that Leto would soon give birth to twin children of Zeus, Hera (Zeus' jealous wife) placed a curse on her that she should not find a suitable place to deliver the divine offspring. Wandering in search of a safe place, Leto finally came to the Aegean island of Ortygia, where Artemis was born. As soon as she emerged, the first act she performed was to help her mother to the nearby island of Delos, where, under a sacred palm tree guarded by lions, she acted as midwife to her brother Apollo's birth. This was an instinctual act upon the part of Artemis, who was regarded as the patroness of childbirth and children, and especially of orphans.

Like other, older goddesses, the Greek Artemis was said to be *virgin,* which simply meant "free," not mated for life. This is just one of the many aspects of her independent nature. By choosing to remain unattached, she chose freedom. Unlike her sibling Athene, who preferred to preside over the city or *polis,* Artemis chose to reside in the woods, with running mountain streams and wild animals. In this regard, she was the patroness of wild beasts as well. In this respect, her spiritual ancestry is ancient indeed, for Our Lady of Wild Beasts is one of the most ancient deities known to us. Artemis is often portrayed clothed in her hunting tunic with bow and arrow, and her hunting dogs beside her. We can thus see that Artemis, by remaining in nature, by remaining a virgin, and by living among the wild beasts, resonated strongly with the instinctual forces of nature, not at all unlike our astrological Moon.

Artemis was frequently paired with her brother, Apollo, who was sometimes thought of as a sun god. The sibling relationship here is profoundly important, as are the connections in one's chart between the Sun and Moon. Manilius gives Artemis rulership of the ninth sign, Sagittarius (the wild huntress), and Apollo rulership of the third sign, Gemini.[4] Vettius Valens reverses these attributes, at least in terms of the houses, and gives the Ninth

House to the Sun God and to prevailing (solar) religion, while the Third House is given to the Moon Goddess and to folk (lunar) religions.[5]

As mother, the Moon Goddess is typically associated with fertility, fecundity, and all life-giving properties. Isis is often depicted as such a mother goddess, holding her young son Horus on her lap. This imagery is almost identical to the artistic renderings of Mary holding the infant Jesus. In both cases, the mother gives birth to a magical, special child, and in both cases the child becomes a god. (Interestingly enough, the Egyptians of Hellenistic times regarded the constellation Virgo as Isis and the bright star Spica as the child Horus. When Christianity overcame Egypt in the late Hellenistic era, Virgo became identified with Mary and Spica with Jesus.)

Reflecting on how lunar archetypes so often portray a mother/child motif in art, we can't help but notice that in astrology the Moon is almost always associated with the mother—if not the mother personally, then certainly the biological inheritance from the family, most often the maternal side. In the birth chart, we look at the Moon as indicative of the way in which the child feels connected to the mother, the indications of the child's early family patterning, and the way the child is imprinted emotionally from its infancy and childhood years. These things ultimately tell of the person's capacity to be nurturing or mothering in his or her own right. When there are comfortable and flowing lunar aspects with other planets, the mother/child experience is fulfilling. When there is stress placed on the Moon from certain other planets, the individual finds personal relationships challenging and uncomfortable. The degree of sensitivity a person has, and is able or unable to express, is shown by the Moon.

The darker aspect of the Moon, its waning crescent, is associated with Hecate, the Greek goddess of witchcraft. (See our chapter on Lilith for more on this aspect of the moon.) In Hellenistic works such as *The Golden Ass* by Lucius Apuleius, she rules over some very disturbing aspects of magic indeed, much like the Hindu goddess Kali, whom she somewhat resembles.[6] Yet even the darker aspects of our personality may serve as vehicles for personal transformation, or as windows to the deepest canyons of the soul.

Like Hermes or Mercury, Hecate is a deity associated with the crossroads—the place where many paths meet and converge at the center. Such deities tend to be associated with the "spaces in between," which in turn signifies the boundaries between waking and sleeping, the upper world and the netherworld, between consciousness and the great unconscious. And the "space between" is always magical, charged with spiritual energy—in much the same way that shamans insist that sunrise and sunset are the most magical times, for they are the "spaces between" night and day. In this sense, Hecate is the Wise Old Crone, the old woman who has seen life come and go, and who understands its inner meanings—even if those meanings are not always cozy and comfortable for the rest of us.

Through these myths, we can see how the Moon symbolizes the three stages of a woman's life, and in fact the "Lady of the Night" has sometimes been worshipped in her triple form as maiden, mother, and crone. We've seen how the Moon's twenty-eight-day cycle reflects a woman's menstrual cycle. In a woman's life there are also three phases: premenstrual (maiden), menstrual (mother), and menopausal (crone). The cyclical nature of the Moon can also be broken down into three distinct periods of life in astrological progressions. In the progressed chart, the Moon returns to its original place every twenty-seven years, just as it returns to its original place every twenty-seven days by transit (hence the twenty-seven Mansions of the Moon still used in Hindu astrology). From birth to age twenty-seven is the first cycle, and corresponds to the maiden phase. By twenty-seven years of age, when the first progressed lunar return occurs, most women (and men) are biologically and emotionally ready to be parents, some often craving it. If they haven't given birth yet, they are usually at that time beginning to consider it.

(An aside here: The first and most frequently asked question of Western women visiting non-industrialized [i.e., lunar] cultures is usually: "How many children do you have?" Note that the question is not: "Do you have children?" but "How many?" And if the answer is "I don't have any," there is an empathetic look of sorrowful compassion cast one's way, as if the Gods have cursed you by leaving you barren. In more technologically developed [i.e., solar] cultures, the most frequent question is: "What do you do?")

The second phase, from twenty-seven to fifty-four, constitutes the "mothering" phase. Whether one is mothering one's children, one's career, or one's mate, there is usually great attention paid to the process. By fifty-four, when the second lunar return occurs, most parents are releasing their children to the outer world, and they are free to turn their attention inward, sometimes to spiritual matters, sometimes to hobbies or retirement. At this time grandchildren may begin to appear on the scene, and the relationship with grandchildren is often nurtured and developed in much different ways than it was with children. As a grandparent, the individual truly becomes the elder or crone—the wise man or woman who carefully and tenderly guards the young ones, protecting them, like Artemis/Diana, from the wilder elements of life.

The Moon rules Cancer and is exalted in Taurus, and these are said to be her favorite signs. But if we examine feminine archetypes from a wider perspective, we will see lunar correspondences between all six feminine signs of the zodiac and their polarity signs. The interlacing of these earth/water signs forms two perfectly equal triangles, creating a Star of David or a star tetrahedron. Consider the following:

> *The Taurus/Scorpio polarity = Moon as Lover—Mars/Venus*
> *The Cancer/Capricorn polarity = Moon as Mother—Demeter/Persephone*
> *The Virgo/Pisces polarity = Moon as Savior/Redeemer/Birth of Holy Child—Mary/Jesus; Isis/Horus*

From the many Moon markers that have dotted the ancient monuments and landscapes of the world, one may begin to understand the reverence for the number nineteen. Nineteen is the number of years it takes a greater Moon cycle and eclipse pattern to repeat itself. Eclipses of the Sun by the Moon and of the Moon by Earth's shadow were revered and feared more than anything else in the sky. All the way back to zero, the Moon has been a boundary marker or measurer of time, correlated to specific laws of karma, reward, punishment, service, or whatever. Here, we're reminded of the Greeks' personification of the Three Fates as measurers of time, represented by (what else?) three women. How many folks do you know that will tell you a story that took nineteen years of their life to conclude? What had the Fates cooked up for them during that time? And try as they might to end it earlier, when it was over, it was abruptly over.

DREAMWORK AND ACTIVE IMAGINATION

Of course, the Moon may appear in dreams or imaginal work in many different aspects, and Artemidorus devotes quite a bit of attention to her. First of all, it is entirely possible (even common) to dream of the physical Moon itself. In this respect, Artemidorus informs us that lunar symbolism is much the same as solar symbolism: a bright, healthy full moon is a symbol of wholeness, completeness, and general good fortune, while a waning Moon, eclipsed

Moon, or a Moon that appears in an unpleasant or "creepy" setting may indicate trouble—and psychologically, we may guess that it symbolizes emotional dismay in the dreamer's subconscious.

There are, of course, a number of moon goddesses, all of whom have somewhat different meanings. Artemis generally signifies the Moon as maiden—she will appear as a youthful, energetic, or even athletic woman, but never as a lover (this is Venus/Aphrodite, not Artemis!). Artemidorus (who was clearly named for this particular goddess) tells us that she helps the dreamer to obtain courage. In particular, she brings courage and strength to women who are about to give birth—if she appears to you in a dream while you are pregnant, it means that your unconscious is favorably disposed and ready for motherhood. As a goddess of nature, she may also indicate the need for a more positive connection with the wilderness in our lives. Because she is powerful and active, she bodes well for business ventures.

Some may remember the story of the hunter Actaeon, who accidentally happened upon the goddess while she was bathing in the nude. Virginal creature that she is, she became angry and sent Actaeon's own hunting dogs to tear him apart. Thus Artemidorus tells us that it is *never* auspicious to see her naked in a dream!

As Selene, the Moon is symbolically more related to the Mother. More often than not, she is the dreamer's actual biological "Mom," appearing as an actress in a dream. "Lunar types" will have more dreams about Mom than the average person, but even among people who rarely remember their dreams, Mom often shows up in the dreams they do remember. Pay attention to what she is wearing and what setting she occupies. Does she relate more to the past, present, or future (our Three Fates again)? Pay attention to how she communicates with the dreamer as well. Where, if at all, is the umbilical cord still attached?

If she does not appear as the dreamer's mother, she may appear—at least in the dreams of men—as his wife, daughter, or sister. When a nurse appears in a dream or active imagination, this is almost always a lunar figure. Again, context is everything. Generally speaking, the appearance of lunar women in a dream is positive for issues regarding travel and one's public image.

Finally, the Moon may appear as the crone—Hecate, the Dark Goddess of the Crossroads. A spooky old woman in a dream may be challenging the dreamer to face her or his fears.

PLANETARY REMEDIES

One of the most noticeable things about the Moon in the sky is that it is white in color. Whiteness increases lunar energy, and this includes the wearing of white garments. The traditional gemstone for the Moon is a pearl; not only is it white, but it originates in the ocean, which is the Moon's special realm, due to its influence upon the tides and its association with water in general. If pearls prove too expensive, one may of course use a moonstone.

The Moon is white, but it is also—in both poetry and popular songwriting—referred to as silver or "silvery." This is another lunar color, and the metal silver is associated with the Moon just as strongly as gold is associated with the Sun. In Vedic astrology, pearl rings or pendants are generally set in silver, so that the lunar symbolism remains constant. Ficino informs us that lunar talismans were always made of silver during medieval and Renaissance times.

As we have noted, the Moon is strongly linked with water—not just the ocean, but water in general. Vedic astrologers often recommend that a client with a weak or afflicted Moon try to live near water. In the best-case scenario, one can move to the seaside and take daily walks by the ocean—this is an absolutely guaranteed way to increase lunar energy in your life! If you can't manage an ocean, at least try to take a slow, meditative walk around a local lake. (The Moon is slow and meditative—if you jog around the lake, you're mixing Mars with the Moon.) If all else fails, install a pond or fountain in your yard.

In astrology generally, the Moon is associated with the food we eat. Specifically, it is associated with milk, cheese, and other dairy products. Eating these foods will increase lunar energy in your life, but this is not for everyone, since some people do not do well with these particular sources of nourishment—no doubt, types who already have too much lunar energy to begin with! Talk to your health practitioner first.

No matter what your diet is like, the simple process of cooking is a lunar thing in and of itself. The more you cook, the more lunar you will become. Gardening is also a quintessentially lunar activity. If you grow your own food, then cook it yourself; you will be immersed in the Moon's gentle vibration! How satisfied and nourished do we feel when we are treated to home-grown, then home-cooked specialties in native villages when traveling around the globe? In fact, in the Japanese macrobiotic philosophy of healing, two things about eating are apparent for maximum health and well-being: eating what's fresh and in season, and eating only those foods that are grown locally.

Finally, the Moon is associated with tranquility, compassion, and even enlightenment. And even though gazing at the Moon won't *really* make you a "luna-tic," it's probably a better idea to visualize a quiet, peaceful full moon during your meditations—especially a full moon reflected in a calm, tranquil lake.

INVOCATION AND AWARENESS

The Moon is the "planet" (technically, it's a "light" or "luminary" like the Sun) that probably touches us most often in our daily lives, and of which we have countless opportunities to gain awareness. Many of these opportunities are suggested above, if you read between the lines:

Every time you talk to your mother, you talk to the Moon. Every time you act as a mother (even if you are a male), you act as the Moon. Whether you are cooking your own food or eating in a restaurant, you participate in the lunar archetype every time you eat. And you certainly touch the lunar vibration when you're in the garden.

Just to digress here, the garden is a complex archetype. The earth in which you plant is related to Gaia, the Earth Goddess. The actual growing and nurturing of plants is connected to the Moon, for you are "mothering" the products of the earth. And while the water you bestow upon the plants is likewise lunar, you need the Sun to assist you in giving them life and energy. The boundary markers and garden stones you lay out are Saturn, and the lawn mowers, clippers, and other tools that you use in the garden are Mars. By the time you finish this book, you will hopefully be able to see everything in life this way, not just the garden!

Because we are so aware of the Moon all around us, we may find it easy to call upon or invoke her. Shakespeare's Juliet would not have liked the idea: she urged Romeo not to swear upon "th' inconstant moon / That monthly changes in her circled orb…" But with all due respect to Juliet, generations of witches and Goddess worshippers would disagree with her. The Moon has always played a powerful and important role in all the arts of magic. Spells of increase are performed while the Moon is waxing; and according to folklore, spells of black magic or malicious purpose are performed while the Moon is waning. Of course, we are not recommending that anyone should perform "spells of malicious intent!" (Nor are we suggesting that contemporary witches do any such thing.) The general rule is this: when you want to "mother" or "nurture" something, to make it increase or grow, then set your magical intent, your affirmations and visualizations to that purpose while the Moon is waxing. If you want to surrender something—like a bad habit, an addiction, an inappropriate emotion—into Hecate's underworld realm and, in short, make it go away, then put your intention to that purpose while the Moon is waning.

---

1. Hancock, Graham, and Santha Faiia, *Heaven's Mirror* (New York: Three Rivers Press, 1998).

2. Mount Sinai may in fact mean "the mountain of Sin," and there is evidence suggesting that there was an ancient moon cult in that locale. When Moses came down from the mountain with the new laws in hand, the people were dancing around a golden calf, a symbol of the moon.

3. As remarked earlier, some scholars have pointed to incised reindeer bones from the Ice Age as possible lunar markers. Skeptics have responded that these carved bones may just as easily be attributed to some long-dead Stone Age woman keeping track of her menstrual cycle. From the point of view of astrological symbolism, it doesn't really make any difference.

4. Manilius, Marcus, *The Five Books of Manilius* (1697; reprint, Washington, D.C.: American Federation of Astrologers, 1953).

5. Valens, Vettius, *The Anthology*, trans. by R. Schmidt, 3 vols. (Berkeley Springs, WV: Golden Hind Press, 1994).

6. Apuleius, Lucius, *The Golden Ass*, trans. by Robert Graves (Harmondsworth, England: Penguin Books, 1972).

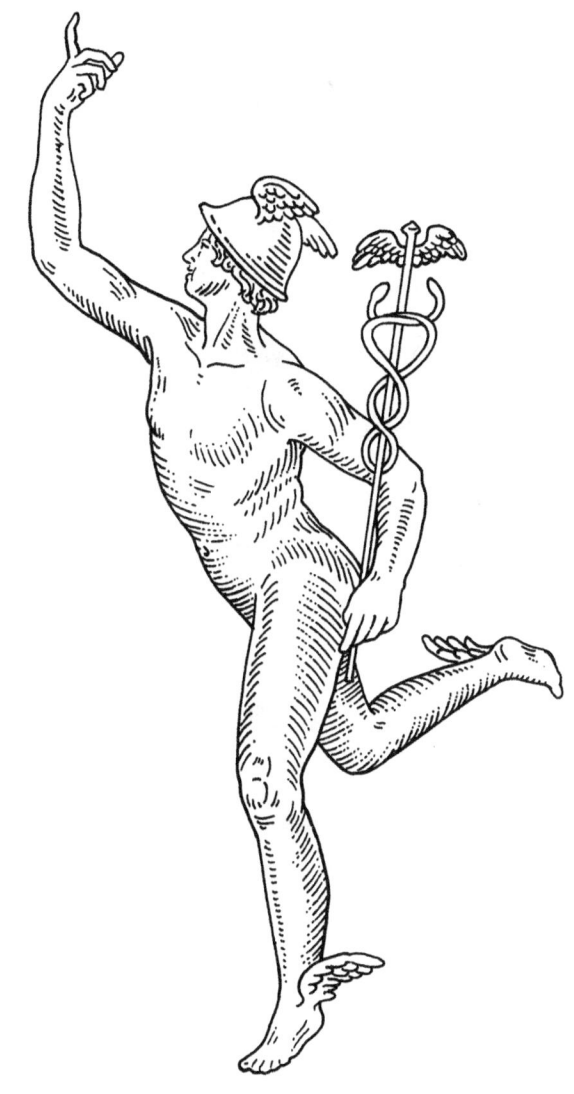

CHAPTER 7

MERCURY
MESSENGER OF THE GODS

ASTROLOGY AND MYTH

It will probably come as no surprise to those familiar with Mercury from astrological studies that Hermes, the god who forms the original of the planetary archetype, is a study in contradictions. In the most ancient times, Hermes was symbolized by a fixed standing stone embedded in the earth, called a *herm*. These herms were markers for property boundaries, and often stood at the doorways of individual homes as well. Even here, in the earliest period of history, Hermes rules the boundaries between one state of consciousness and another, the threshold between home and world, between the inner and outer realms. He is a god of liminal space, the space between; he is a god of crossroads and ambiguities.

It is no wonder that he later became identified with the arts of magic. The erect shape and size of these herms often led to their equation with the phallus. This may sound strange to astrologers—who, after all, are accustomed to thinking of Mercury as an "asexual" or neutral planet, uninvolved in passion. Yet perhaps this point of view is a bit limiting. After all, Hermes was called the "captain of the nymphs," and he was a lover of Aphrodite herself. But then again, men who seek an endless succession of "nymphs" may remind us of that notorious "traveling salesman" of folklore—and this, as we shall see, is yet another Mercury figure. His sensuality is all in the mind (his realm), not in the heart. But Aphrodite, the Venus archetype, doesn't really mind, since she is of similar disposition. They make a good match.

In later mythology, Mercury was depicted as the fleet-footed, never still, winged god that delivered the messages of Zeus and the other Olympians. In his messenger capacity, he soared to the heights of heaven on Olympus, mingling with the immortals, and then at once descended to the fiery netherworld of Hades, keeping company with the souls of the dead. On herms he was depicted as a bearded, mature man, while in his messenger-god guise he was youthful, sprightly, and the most androgynous looking of the gods (the FTD floral guy).

Mercury's most fundamental astrological significance, however, is as the planet of the mind or intellect. This link between Mercury and the mind is very old indeed, for behind the Greek planetary names lie older, Babylonian names, and in Babylon the planet Mercury was the visible form of Nabu, the god of writing—and when we remember that it was the art of writing that set

Sumer and Babylon on the fast track to civilization, we may understand the importance of this attribution.

We can see also why Mercury has been chosen to symbolize the functions of the mind. There is, after all, no apparent limit to how far the human mind can either soar or descend. Let's look at the descent first. He's a clever one, this Hermes, portrayed by the Greeks as the precocious younger brother of Apollo, a trickster figure who was, one way or another, going to rock Apollo's orderly and neat perfectionist world. Mercury's trickster nature is so well developed that one cannot but stop and marvel at the cool execution of his tricks. You may have just been sold the Brooklyn Bridge, or been subject to a con artist, sleight-of-hand trick perpetrated right before your eyes—rather like the shenanigans of Robert Redford and Paul Newman in the movie *The Sting*. Game masters and con men have Mercury down to a cool science. They are his children. And so are the traveling salesmen of the world.

This is the god who leads us to chance and teaches us to choose wisely with the lots assembled before us. His own "chance" encounters usually proved to be lucky ones. He "happened on a turtle and got himself an endless source of wealth." Now how many people can see endless sources of wealth in a tortoise? But young Hermes turned it over, slapped a few strings upon it, and created the musical instrument called the lyre. Here we see Mercurial inventiveness and entrepreneurship at work. Such chance meetings and circumstances that are seized and recognized as golden moments or opportunities quickly bear fruit for the individual. So clever may he seem that you are likely to ask: what does this have to do with his dark side? And the answer is: thieves have the same sort of intellect. Mercury is mind without a conscience. He needs other planets to endow him with a sense of responsibility. Considered entirely on his own, he can be somewhat immature.

Let's remember the precocious nature of this young god. Mercury is generally portrayed in a youthful manner, as are all the second-generation Olympians. He is the son of Zeus. There is a hierarchical, if not generational, structure existent in Olympian thought. Zeus and his siblings are portrayed in a mature and stately manner. The children of Zeus, half of whom also became elevated to the high status of the "Twelve Olympians," are portrayed in a much more youthful manner. Now, gods and goddesses are immortal and as such would not actually age in human terms. They do, however, partake of a certain archetypal imagery that may include "age." It would be hard to visualize Mercury or Hermes as a wise old man—though as we shall see, in his typically contradictory fashion, he may sometimes wear even that disguise. In general, Mercury is the very essence of youthfulness. In fact, in the old horary astrological tradition of the Middle Ages and the Renaissance, Mercury often symbolized youthful people or even children.

In a certain way, we may think of Mercury wisdom as "the wisdom of youth"—the shining intellectual wisdom of the young student who goes through college on scholarships and endowments; or the young clerk who is hired on at the bottom of the line in a large corporation and quickly rises to the ranks of top management through his or her skill and efficiency; or the young apprentice who quickly learns the art and mastery of the craft for which he is training and soon becomes the master craftsman.

Yet there is an "old" Mercury as well, and this bearded Mercurial sage is deeply intertwined with the archetype of the Wise Old Man (the Wise Old Woman is more often lunar than Mercurial). When intellectual knowledge reaches such an exalted level that it dances on the boundaries of the infinite, it is no longer merely knowledge, but magic—and Mercury is the god of magic. In Hellenistic Egypt, this god of magic was known as Thrice-Greatest Hermes, and the "Hermetic" sciences such as alchemy (and even astrology) are named for him.

This aspect of the Mercurial archetype is depicted in the caduceus, Mercury's gift from his brother Apollo. This magical healing rod with the double serpents intertwined has been handed down to us in modern times as the primary medical symbol adorning every clinic and hospital. The intertwined serpents may be suggestive of the double helix and the essential role DNA plays in human life. Others have also seen it as a diagram of the "serpent power," called *kundalini* in India. The kundalini is the source of magical energy within the human body; during the practice of yoga or magic, it travels up the spinal column (the rod) in two intertwined channels (the two serpents) until it reaches the third eye and awakens the inner vision (the wings at the top of the rod).

In the Renaissance, the magical sage Hermes was typically depicted as an old man with a long white beard, a Merlin figure indeed. But there are other mythic correspondences as well. For example, Wednesday is Mercury's planetary day (*mercredi* in French, *miercoles* in Spanish), and our word *Wednesday* signifies "Woden's Day," after the Norse god Woden or Odin. Now Odin was a wise old man with a long white beard, and a powerful magician. He was a wanderer, like Mercury—the Norse sagas often tell us of how he appears seemingly from nowhere in a long gray cloak, works his magic, then disappears as mysteriously as he arrived. In Slavic countries, similar tales are told of St. Nicholas, who, far from being a benevolent Santa Claus, shows echoes of an older Pagan god resembling Odin.

Another important thing to note, when considering Odin's travels, is that he can travel up and down the great tree at the center of the world, the axis of the world. Traveling up the tree leads him to the land of the gods; traveling down the tree leads him to the land of the dead. Like Greek Hermes, he mediates between the worlds. He is the energy that travels between realities, and he is the borderless reality in between.

Mercury is what some cultures might refer to as a shape-shifter, one who has access to all worlds simultaneously just as he belongs to none. James Hillman writes: "For Hermetic consciousness, there is no upperworld versus underworld problem. Hermes inhabits the borderlines; his herms are erected there, and he makes possible an easy commerce between the familiar and the alien."[1]

The image of the journey up and down the World Tree is a universal one, but in tribal societies it is always the same individual who does the traveling. And this individual is the shaman. As a traveler between the worlds and a god of magic, Mercury is the shaman of the planetary hierarchy.

Let us look at some of the psychological ramifications of this shamanic journeying. As Hermes led souls to the land of the dead, so may he lead our conscious minds into temporary suspension. For shamans, this is a state of hypnotic or mystical trance; but for most of us, it is the journey into deep sleep. Homer tells us that Hermes is the "bringer of dreams." He possesses a magic wand with which he puts men asleep and awakens them. It is there where REM occurs and the dream-ego takes over. The dream state is how we enter the underworld in living form.

When the dream is over, it is Hermes again who leads us back into Apollo's realm, the light of day. For some, this constitutes an instant death to the dream experience—as liquid and runny as quicksilver (Mercury's alchemical substance), the dream disappears forever back into the night. It is a narrow opening, that tunnel through which dreams may come and go, and if we are not entirely vigilant at the departing gate we may be completely and immediately severed from that realm. Like Orpheus (another shaman traveling the worlds), who lost Eurydice at the very last second in his journey up from the underworld, the dream image is lost forever.

In this process, Mercury acts as a guide or messenger, carrying the messages from our dream self to our waking self. This again calls the dualistic sign of Gemini to mind. Perhaps the duality of our nature lies in the waking-self and dreaming-self ego consciousness. The better the connection between these two selves, the better off we are at solving everyday problems, not to mention the larger issues of life. So when you do cross paths with Mercury, whether as the messenger in your dreams or the messenger you meet at the crossroads of life, sit up and take notice.

Mercury's symbolism from myth—invisibility at will, spryness, fleetness of foot; his interchange with his elder brother Apollo, whose stolen cattle are forced to walk backwards by the young god of thieves; and his dual nature—all have implications to Mercury's role in astronomy. The planet Mercury is the speediest of the bunch. It circles the Sun in a mere eighty-eight days, traveling up to two or three times as fast as the next nearest planets, Venus and Earth. Sticking so close to the Sun (Apollo), there is a frequent interchange between the two. Like the Hermes of myth, Mercury of the sky slips by like a thief in the night, invisible to us for most of the year. And when it is visible, just after sunset or just before sunrise, it is so faint that you must truly know it's there to see it.

There are inferior conjunctions of Mercury to the Sun as well as superior conjunctions. In between these events, we have what is known as a Mercury retrograde period three times a year, a phenomenon in which the planet, as seen from the earth, appears to be moving backwards. In fact, the retrograde motion of Mercury seems to emulate the backward motion of Apollo's stolen cattle—while shepherding the cattle away from Apollo's domain, Hermes had them walk backwards so that their tracks would confuse any would-be investigator of the crime.

During Mercury retrograde periods, the planet is "walking backwards," and it is the trickster element that is most alive and well at such times. Mercury-ruled functions of transportation and commerce frequently are challenged then. We can't always be sure that what we just saw, heard, or did actually happened; we can't be sure that it won't all seem like a total figment of our imagination when the planet turns direct again! It is a time when many feel they are backpedaling, or going back over things previously done.

However, when Mercury is direct and moving quickly forward through the constellations, he is said to collect great knowledge and information as he goes. He has been attributed with mastery over alphabets, names and numbers, language, science, and even the starry heavens…"he who knows the names of things." Manilius writes: "You, god of Cyllene, are the first founder of this great and holy science; through you man has gained a deeper knowledge of the sky—the constellations, the names and courses of the signs, their importance and influences . . ."[2]

Astrology has chosen the signs Gemini and Virgo for Mercury's rulership. Gemini is considered the "day" sign while Virgo is considered the "night" sign. One of the most important features to come out of the ancient material being resurrected by modern astrologers is the idea of planetary sect. Of the seven classical planets, three belong to the day sect and three belong to the night, while Mercury, true to its mythology, can go either way, depending upon its relationship to Apollo (the Sun). When Mercury is the morning star (rising before the Sun) it is considered diurnal in a chart. When it is the evening star (setting after the Sun), it carries a nocturnal status.[3]

DREAMWORK AND ACTIVE IMAGINATION

Though Mercury may lead us to the dream world and usher us back into waking consciousness, he often appears to us in the dream world as well. Because Mercury is a shamanic figure, he often appears as a "mystery man," a personage created out of dream-stuff rather than someone we know in real life. The mysterious figure may be a youngster, as Mercury symbolizes youth. In fact, it could even be an infant or toddler who sits up and talks to you in intelligible form, for we should not forget that Mercury was a babe scarcely out of his cradle when he performed his first feats. His youthful vigor relates to athletics as well, and Artemidorus regards Mercury as a figure of good omen in the dreams of athletes.

Remembering that Mercury was a god of knowledge and learning, we may look for teachers and students gathered in a classroom setting. According to the classical astrological attributions, we should expect a learning environment that covers early learning through high school years; although, as we have seen, Mercury rules over certain forms of esoteric knowledge as well (more of this below). In dreams or active imaginations where Mercury plays the role of the teacher, pay close attention to what he is teaching you.

The trickster aspect of Hermes was symbolized by his cunning and thievery, and thieves often show up in dreams. Be careful not to confuse Mercury with Pluto in such cases—the Mercurial thief is quiet and clever, sometimes charming, while the Plutonian bad guy can be brutal and overwhelming, often shadowy or dark. A Mercury thief in a dream or active imagination may represent part of our own "dark" side, an amoral or unintegrated part of ourselves that nevertheless has something to teach us. This knowledge may not always be easy for us to deal with, and hence Artemidorus tells us that the appearance of Mercury in a dream may portend "unrest and disturbances." But even if the wisdom of the depths may occasionally shake up the calm surface of our ordinary lives, we shall be much the better for it.

Merchants and merchandising are also a strong part of the Mercury realm. If a dream takes you to a marketplace where you are engaging in commerce, buying and selling or bartering, no doubt Mercury is present. According to Artemidorus, it is auspicious for those engaged in business or commerce to dream of Mercury, for he is their totem deity.

Mercury is the "totem" of writers, public speakers, and intellectuals as well as businesspeople. Artemidorus goes on to say that this god is especially favorable when he appears in the dreams of such individuals.

The Mercurial figure may be in motion, or driving a car, since the archetype is associated with movement and travel. Many of the film and societal archetypes of the 1950s were mercurial in essence, involving mysterious young men in cars. Remember, for example, the characters created by Marlon Brando or James Dean, or the fast-talking, intellectual wild men of Kerouac's *On the Road*. Actually, any vehicle may suggest Mercury, including a motorcycle, bicycle, roller skates, or some other unusual means of transportation fashioned out of dream-stuff. Hang-gliders, balloonists, helicopter and small craft pilots are especially included here, as Mercury, an air god, prefers flight.

First and foremost, Mercury is the messenger, so look for anybody attempting to deliver you a message, such as a postman. He may even appear simply as the message rather than the messenger, manifesting himself through a fax machine or e-mail message on your computer. (Don't forget the guy delivering flowers! Mercury has become the icon of many flower shops across the land.) This same concern with information is true of all the Mercurial archetypes listed above—pay attention to the teacher, the child, the clever thief. Mercury is not just any common messenger; he brings messages from the world of the gods or from the world of the dead. Therefore the information he gives us comes from the deepest level of the unconscious and represents valuable knowledge that is generally hidden from our conscious minds.

Mercury is the god of the alchemists, the master of magic and transmutation. Any time you receive information from a "higher" source, Mercury is present in some form. Though he is most often youthful, we have also seen that some mythic figures, such as the Norse Odin, represent a "wise old man" Mercury. All the same, one should not assume that a wise old woman or man who appears in a dream or active imagination is primarily or even necessarily Mercurial, for there are other planetary archetypes, notably Saturn, and perhaps even Chiron or Jupiter, that also play a role in the wise old man or woman figure.

Above all, Mercury is the mystery person you meet at the crossroads. Let us remember that a crossroads represents the four elements of Earth, Water, Fire, and Air, and thus symbolizes wholeness, completeness. It is here, at the center of all being, that the most important messages or directional changes in our lives can occur.

Although we are more likely to meet Mercury in contemporary rather than classical garb, let us not forget to look for winged sandals or sandals in general that look well-worn. Don't forget his magical cap, which also possesses wings.

PLANETARY REMEDIES

As we have already mentioned, Mercury's primary symbol is the caduceus wand, which, as a diagram of the DNA or the kundalini energy, corresponds to his more magical or shamanic functions. It can serve as a handy talisman unto itself, and one that stimulates the workings of the higher mind.

Although the colors and gemstones associated with Mercury have changed over time (at least in the Western world), his original gemstone was an emerald, and his correspondent color was green. Medieval Sufis marked the changes in their consciousness through the internal perception of color vibration; in many of their magical systems, green was the most exalted color, corresponding to the mythic Khidr, the "Green One," who is yet another archetype of Mercury as the magical wanderer. One of the most important texts of

Western alchemy—which probably originated among the Sabaeans of Harran, who preserved the old Gnostic and Hellenistic lore throughout early medieval times—is called *The Emerald Tablet of Hermes*.

In terms of lifestyle, Mercury can be stimulated by mental activity of all kinds. If you want to strengthen a good Mercury—or harmonize a bad one—you may wish to read more books, go back to night school, or learn a new language. However, it is best to study something that really feels good to you, rather than something heavy or ponderous. Remember that Mercury is youthful and charming, highly sociable, and even somewhat frivolous. Although he does indeed symbolize knowledge, his knowledge is the kind that delights the soul rather than burdens it. If your studies are too serious and practical and arcane, you are actually strengthening Saturn rather than Mercury! So keep it light.

INVOCATION AND AWARENESS

Versatile and clever, Mercury was one of the gods most often invoked and worshiped in ancient times.

Because Mercury is a god of travelers, you would want to invoke him at the start of any journey to ensure safe passage. This is especially true on a journey into foreign lands or cultures, for Mercury the shape-shifter, the adaptable master of mutability and language, will help you blend in with the crowd rather than stand out as the outsider. When you are attempting communication with someone from another culture or language and it is clear that you are not making progress, the presence of Mercury may be helpful.

Though memory is a function of another archetype (Mnemosyne), Mercury can clearly help in this regard, especially with remembering the names of people and things. At the beginning of your exams, invoke Mercury for help in recalling data of any kind. Visualize his winged airiness flying to the realm where the vault of knowledge of all time is stored. See him extracting the information you need at the moment and then rushing it back to you promptly. In point of fact, one of the present authors has noted that many people in Russia pray to St. Nicholas before an exam, whether for academics or some bureaucratic job. St. Nicholas is merely the Christianized version of the Old Wandering Sage of Pagan times, who, as we have seen, is an aspect of the higher Mercury.

Mercury was considered a god of tradesmen and merchants in ancient times, and business contracts were seldom signed unless the god had first been properly invoked. Therefore, use Mercury in the marketplace to bargain fairly when appropriate.

Mercury is such a predominant archetype in our fast-paced culture of the "information highway" that we may easily find ourselves invoking him for several different reasons at once. When you're late for that very important meeting, caught in traffic without your cell phone, or stranded on a lonely desert highway where communication modes don't exist, call upon Mercury immediately!

Mercury is an extremely versatile deity, and though we may not think of him as having connection with home and hearth, the ancients certainly did so. Herms were ancient boundary markers for property, and one can even see youthful rooftop figureheads guarding the homes in Greek villages today as protection for the home.

Nevertheless, one should be careful about invoking Mercury. Remember that he was, among other things, a god of thieves, and though his skill is unparalleled, his morality is sometimes questionable. The principle of "Be careful what you ask for, you just might get it" should always be kept in mind when dealing with Mercury.

---

1. Hillman, James, *The Dream and the Underworld* (New York: Harper & Row, 1979).
2. Manilius, Marcus, *The Five Books of Manilius,* (1697; reprint, Washington, D.C.: American Federation of Astrologers, 1953) book 1.
3. Hand, Robert, *Night & Day: Planetary Sect in Astrology* (Reston, VA: ARHAT, 1995).

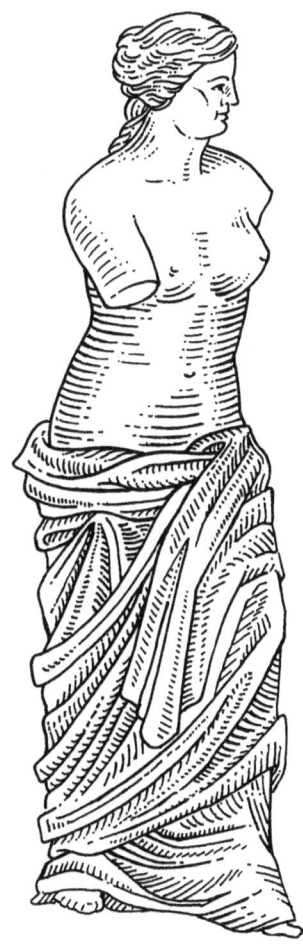

CHAPTER 8

VENUS
GODDESS OF LOVE

ASTROLOGY AND MYTH

Venus has always been the Goddess of Love.

Is there any question that the night is ruled by the feminine forces of nature? Not when we look to the sky and observe that the two brightest objects are the Moon and Venus. The Moon's brightness is, of course, obvious. But how many have awakened in the wee hours before dawn or observed the sky just after sunset and seen a planet so bright and luminescent that we are simply awed by its presence? That's Venus in the sky during the times of year she is visible. She appears as both the Morning Star and the Evening Star, and is equally beautiful in both her aspects. There is no astrological tradition in the world—whether Western, Vedic, Mayan, or Chinese—that does not accord a great importance to the planet Venus.

In terms of Western astrology, the goddess of the planet Venus has a long ancestry that stretches all the way back to ancient Sumer, where she was known as Inanna. To the Babylonians and their successors, she was Ishtar, and that was the name by which the planet was originally known.

Although astrologers have linked Venus with marriage ever since medieval times, that was not her original significance. Ishtar was the goddess of "free love"—by which the Babylonians meant precisely the same thing we mean today. The ancients regarded married love and passionate love as two distinctly different things. When young women were married in ancient Greece, they offered up some of their cosmetics and pretty clothes upon the altar of Aphrodite to symbolize that they had left her world behind them and entered the world of Hera, goddess of married love.[1] In most traditional societies the world over, erotic love and married love are not only regarded as different, but as incompatible. Until just a few hundred years ago, the Western world lived by the same paradigm. No medieval troubadour ever wrote a ballad to his own wife, and Guinevere's dilemma—her equal but different love for Arthur and Lancelot—may serve as a prototype of the problem. When she was with Arthur, she was acting in the role of Juno or Hera. When she was with Lancelot, she was Venus or Aphrodite.

If the ancients regarded marriage and passion as incompatible, they certainly regarded passion as important. Ishtar was one of the principal deities of ancient Babylon. She was a primal force of nature; she stormed the gates of hell in search of her lost lover and confronted the very Queen of the Dead to demand his return. She was unrepentant in her sensuality—she chose her lovers with little regard for propriety or caution.

And yet the Babylonians regarded her as the essence of the feminine soul. The word *ishtar* could be used as a term for the indwelling feminine spirit within all women, and even within all goddesses.[2]

Some of this grandeur survived in the persona of the Greek Aphrodite, who was often known as "the Great Goddess." The cult of Ishtar passed to the Near East, where she was known as Astarte and Ashtaroth, and hence by way of Phoenicia to the Greeks, who renamed her Aphrodite. Her sacred place was the island of Cyprus, which lay hard by the Phoenician coast. In fact, so deeply identified was the goddess with her island and her shrine at the city of Paphos that early Greek astrologers sometimes referred to her simply as the Paphian or the Cyprian, without any other name.

If Ishtar was a goddess of the desert sands of Babylon, Aphrodite was, in many respects, a goddess of the ocean. She was born when the sperm of Ouranos the Sky Father fell into the ocean; she rose naked out of the waves upon a seashell, full grown and beautiful. She was sometimes called Aphrodite Pelagia, which simply means "Aphrodite of the Ocean," or Aphrodite Anadyomene, which means "Aphrodite Rising from the Sea." One of her prettiest epithets was Foam Born Aphrodite. Others were Shining Aphrodite, Smiling Aphrodite, or Golden Aphrodite.

Later writers on myth, as well as some of the medieval poets, tended to trivialize her—to paint her as a simpering courtesan without either integrity or intelligence. In some respects, this lack of respect has passed over into astrology, so that women who embody this particular goddess are characterized as "dependent" or "a man's woman." But this was not the way she was perceived by the ancients. To them, she was a primal force of nature. To her lover Anchises, she appeared in a blaze of light, followed by herds of wild animals. She was neither simpering nor silly, but downright terrifying in her power.

Twenty-five years ago, Carl Sagan smirked at the irony of naming the planet Venus after the ancient goddess of love. He said that Venus, without a doubt, contains the most turbulent and stormy atmosphere in our entire solar system.[3] If Sagan had ever been seized by the deeper aspects of passionate love, he wouldn't be surprised by this turbulence. The greatest poets and playwrights of the ages have waxed eloquent in praise of this goddess, as well as expressing their tormented pangs of madness (or even suicide) while in the throes of unrequited love. One might think of those churning storms on Venus as equivalent to the churning oceanic foam from whence this goddess arose, and the churning human emotions one is seized by and must bow to when one "falls" in love.

The king of the gods, Jupiter or Zeus, sought to control wild Aphrodite by marrying her to Vulcan or Hephaestus, the lame, introverted blacksmith of the gods. It was not a happy marriage. Venus was constantly unfaithful to her husband and had a particular affection for Mars, the god of war. Passion calls to passion. Women who embody the Venus archetype to a large degree often have difficulty maintaining conventional relationships and may be happier playing the Muse rather than playing house. Astrologers always look to the relative positions of Mars and Venus in the horoscopes of two potential love partners in order to measure the degree of sexual compatibility between them.

Like Athene, Aphrodite has no mother and is a child of the Sky Father pure and simple. But if Athene was born of Sky Father's brain, Aphrodite was born of his genitals, and thus symbolizes the raw sexual power of the cosmos. As Jean Shinoda Bolen pointed out, this goddess functions equally well in partnership or alone.[4] She may be a muse, inspiring artists, or she may be an artist in her own right.

In fact, Bolen calls her "the alchemical goddess," and perhaps speaks more truly than she knows.[5] If Venus, almost alone among the ancient deities, survived the end of Paganism to be reborn among the poets, she also survived in the educated tradition of alchemy or Hermetic philosophy. The spiritual unity that constitutes the final goal of the alchemist's quest is often symbolized by an androgynous being—a *hermaphrodite*. This term is a combination of *Hermes* and *Aphrodite*, and refers to a myth wherein these two deities became lovers and produced a hermaphroditic child. Hermes or Mercury is, of course, the god of the alchemists and, as we have seen, a symbol of the kundalini or serpent power.

But so is Venus. She is the feminine polarity of the same power, the same energy, the same sexual-spiritual force. She is the Western equivalent of the Hindu shakti, the animating vital energy that lies within all things and that is perceived as female. This is not the "passive" or "receptive" aspect of experience that we usually associate with "the feminine"—this is the active or creative aspect of the feminine.

Venus' spiritual journey from erotic muse to alchemical goddess may be seen in the old Babylonian myths and in the sky itself. An old poem tells us of how Ishtar journeyed into the underworld in search of her lover Tammuz, who had died. As she descends deeper and deeper, her jewelry and her garments are stripped away from her by the guardians of the gates of hell. All the same, she continues to plunge on, passionately seeking her lover. She ends up naked and cold in the darkest part of hell, confronted by Ereshkigal, the terrible queen of darkness who hangs Ishtar from a meat hook in the darkness. But the world cannot survive without love, and the gods come to her rescue. (In some versions of the story, she wins a stay on earth for her lover Tammuz or Adonis as well.) When we see Venus as the Morning Star, we may imagine her as young and beautiful, the goddess of erotic love in partnership with her lover Tammuz. When she moves closer to the Sun, she will become invisible, and this represents her journey into the underworld. When she emerges once again from her union with the solar force, she will appear as the Evening Star—the Queen of Heaven who has been through the darkness and who knows all things, the alchemical shakti.

This psychological interpretation of Venus' journey, which comes from the work of psychologist Sylvia Brinton Perera, is only one paradigm.[6] There are others. For even though Venus has been identified as the love goddess from Greek and Roman times through the Middle Ages to the Renaissance and to the present, it is worth remembering the Venus, whom the Babylonians called Ishtar, was sometimes a warrior goddess as well. When she made her appearance in the morning sky—that is rising before the Sun—she was considered a warrior and was called (by Greek astrologers) Venus Lucifer, but in the evening sky, just after sunset, she was called Venus Hesperus and portrayed the love aspect of the goddess. And while Perera's interpretation is psychologically valid, this paradigm is much closer to the original Babylonian understanding of her symbolism. You don't have to be a hopeless romantic to appreciate the beauty of this planet dazzling brightly in the western sky just after sunset.

The symbolism is clear. The feminine principle ruled the night while the masculine principle ruled the day. When Venus was a daytime planet, she was armed for battle with the (solar) forces that ruled the day. Her functions as love goddess were exalted in the night. Both the Mayans and the Babylonians were aware of Venus' synodic cycle of 584 days. Five of these cycles create an almost perfect five-pointed star in the heavens and take eight years to complete. Thus, though Venus returns to our charts every year, it is every eighth return that might be seen as having more relevance to the Venus pattern in the overall scheme of our lives.[7]

Venus became, in many ways, the last Pagan survivor. The church did not deal well with the raw sensuality of Venus, and in the first millennium her image practically disappeared from view, being replaced by the Madonna. But she survived, even though driven underground. The Norse name for the Aphrodite archetype was Freya, and in the Middle Ages, after even distant Iceland had been Christianized, the Viking writer Snorri Sturluson affirmed that Freya alone, of all the ancient deities, still lived and was still worshipped. In medieval France, she can be found concealed beneath the myth of Mary Magdalene, and it is often difficult to tell whether the many cathedrals dedicated to "notre dame" (Our Lady) were originally intended as shrines to Mary the Mother or to the Magdalene—and as Joseph Campbell and others have noted, these grand cathedrals were definitely built to house the goddess.

With the emergence of the troubadours and the concept of romantic love, with chivalry and knighthood, her essence once again flowered. But it was the Renaissance painter Botticelli who really immortalized Venus, and the image that most people carry of her today is based on his painting of her just as Homer described her: ". . . naked in her radiance, floating on a shell, rising to the shore . . ."[8] (It is significant that Botticelli was a student of our good friend Marsilio Ficino.) We may wonder whether the devotion of troubadours and Renaissance painters was actual belief or simply a mere artistic convention; it is difficult to tell. But one way or the other, she has always been with us, never absent. And she is with us still, in movies, in magazines, and in our lives.

And though Venus remains very much with us, we may wonder if her archetype is severely unbalanced in our society. Aberrant social behavior, crimes of sexual dysfunction, pedophiles running rampant, and Internet sex sites are booming. Though there is much more sexual freedom now in most Western cultures, we are still struggling to come to grips with the Venus archetype.

One must remember that when a human being is embodying an archetype, there can be grave consequences. One of Shakespeare's most well-known plays

Romeo and Juliet plays out the Aphroditic love theme in its most glorious but all too tragic reality. There have been legions of real, human embodiments of Venus as well. From Cleopatra to Marilyn Monroe, there have always been women whose Aphrodite energy was so powerful that it touched and empowered the lives of all around them. And if many of these women came to tragic ends, like the fictional Juliet, it is because it is difficult for any mere mortal to shoulder the burden of embodying an immortal Goddess.

Yet there are some who made the journey successfully—although, like most women in ancient times, they remain nameless. In Tibet, there is a category of Tantric goddesses called Dakinis who are overtly erotic and who act as sexual consorts to some of the more terrifying aspects of the Buddha. Although such goddesses have been part of Indo-Tibetan myth since pre-patriarchal times, there is also some evidence that some of the legends embody a memory of real women—the nameless teachers or "Sky Dancers" who transmitted Tantric teachings to women and men alike during the early Middle Ages but who were driven underground by the Brahminical establishment.[9] These Tantric yogis and yoginis *(dakinis)* expressed Aphrodite energy to its fullest. And they still exist.

DREAMWORK AND ACTIVE IMAGINATION

The ancients recognized many different aspects of Venus or Aphrodite, and Artemidorus goes so far as to make distinctions between them in regards to our dreams. There is, for example, Aphrodite Urania, the "celestial" Aphrodite, queen of the evening star and the eternal muse. Unlike her more sensual counterparts, this Aphrodite is a spiritual figure—what Jungian or archetypal psychologists would call the *anima mundi* or feminine soul of the world—Artemidorus tells us that she is "regarded as Nature and the Mother of the Universe."[10] When she appears in a dream or in active imagination, she will seem like a goddess indeed—glowing with light, filled with wisdom. To experience this aspect of Aphrodite is a fortunate thing indeed, and it signifies that you may be about to access your own prophetic or visionary abilities. You will have absolutely no doubt that you have been gifted with a true archetypal dream or vision, a visitation from the high gods. And unlike other, more sensual aspects of Venus, the celestial Aphrodite is favorable for marriage and for partnership, so if there are other relationship themes in your dream or active imagination, the appearance of this transcendent female archetype signifies good things.

Artemidorus also speaks of Aphrodite Pandemus, which means "all people." As the lover of all, this Aphrodite is the overtly sexual and licentious goddess associated with courtesans, or, in a more contemporary context, with sexuality that lies outside the social boundaries of marriage or conventional partnership. This Venus figure is likely to strut through the dreams of men and women alike clad in a short skirt, nylon stockings, and high heels—or perhaps in lingerie, or even in nothing at all. She is the "bad girl" that mothers warn their sons about, the girl no parent wants his or her daughter to become. She has no sexual boundaries. In the dreams of men, she awakens the erotic nature, and if she takes the form of a neighbor or friend, it may be time to face up to and deal with your attraction to that particular individual. In the dreams and imaginal work of women, this Venus "lover of all" most often symbolizes *the shadow*— that part of themselves they shove out of sight and refuse to acknowledge. And yet the shadow is as much a part of ourselves as the substance, and when it appears in dreams or active imagination, it usually constitutes a "wake-up call," a cry to be heard and accepted. Women may often dream of Venus Pandemus when they are in danger of stepping over the edge, breaking the boundaries, or having an affair. Or they may dream of her simply because their own sensual and overtly sexual side has been denied, pushed out of consciousness. Either way, it signifies the need to examine the "bad girl" who lies unrecognized and unloved within. And yet Artemidorus tells us that even this Aphrodite may be a very favorable sign for all those involved with the arts; and indeed, the male artist is just as likely to be inspired by a bad girl as a good one, and female artists have traditionally been among those women who shake off the boundaries and limitations of conventional society.

We should also remember that Aphrodite was a goddess of the ocean, and perhaps it is no accident that the planet Venus is exalted in Pisces, the sign of the great ocean itself. If a mysterious and beautiful woman, whether trashy or transcendent, appears in a "watery" context, you are probably dreaming of or imagining Aphrodite Pelagia (Oceanic Venus) or Aphrodite Anadyomene (Venus Rising from the Sea). She may be a bathing beauty on the beach, a swimmer, or whatever. Like the celestial Venus, she will most often be illuminated by light, and once again you will have no doubt that you are dreaming archetypally. She may also be every bit as sensual—and without boundaries—

as Aphrodite Pandemus, the "lover of all." According to Artemidorus, she signifies travel—whether you want it or not. But more importantly, she bridges the gap between the sexual and the spiritual. In the language of India, we could say that she is a Tantric goddess, an icon of the bedroom and of eternal starlight all at the same time.

PLANETARY REMEDIES

It is easy enough to say that the best way to harmonize the energies of the planet Venus is to focus upon the relationships in our lives—although more often than not, an individual is seeking to harmonize her or his Venus energies precisely because of an absence of relationship!

However, there are other ways to make this archetype live and breathe within us. Ficino recommends dancing, listening to or playing light, cheerful music, and walking through fields of flowers. It is hard to disagree with the old master on this one, for these are very pleasant pastimes indeed and make anyone's life more joyful.

All flowers essentially come under the domain of Venus, but especially the rose, which has always come to symbolize "I love you." A bouquet of freshly cut roses, or even a single rose, can help to bring in Venusian energy. Essence of rose oil in a bath or sprinkled lightly on the skin is another way of inducing Venus. A stroll through a garden of fragrant roses will even do the trick, inhaling their essence as you go.

In Ficino's day, Venus was associated with the color green, and those springtime fields exemplified her coloring as well as her energy. As we have seen, the color green was more probably associated with Mercury in ancient times, but be creative. Whatever works, works. Let us remember that Venus is a sensualist who loves color in general. Dress your house up with flowers, colorful prayer flags, and folk art in vibrant primary colors—your Venus will be happier with you.

Stop to enjoy what you eat instead of simply wolfing it down on the run—Venus appreciates all sensual delights. But be aware that Venus is frequently excessive and may easily become overindulgent—in food as well as in love. Though Venus can be indolent and resistant to exercise, she loves dancing, which is always a good remedy for Venusian indulgences.

If you are accustomed to dressing in gray Saturnian business suits, unisex sweat clothes, or drab clothing in general, you will be making your Venus unhappy. She likes brightness, sexual differentiation, and beauty. Women and men alike should behave accordingly if they wish to please her.

INVOCATION AND AWARENESS

Venus is probably "invoked" or at least brought into conscious awareness in our contemporary lives more often than any of the ancient deities. Men in particular are very aware of her in the sense that they "project" her archetype onto the women in their lives. When a man falls in love, the woman of his affections ceases to become an ordinary woman and instead becomes an incarnation of Venus. (No wonder she may seem, in his love-struck eyes, to actually "shine" like Aphrodite.) Such a projection feels very good—in fact, it feels wonderful! It's like a drug. But it has the same dangers. The greatest danger, of course, lies in the fact that a man in this state of Venusian intoxication will be unable to see the real person, the real woman, who lies underneath his projection. If the relationship is to become more than a simple romance, he must eventually break the projection and see the lover as a human being rather than a goddess. The astrologer would do well to study the Venus position in a man's horoscope to discover which particular aspect of the goddess is being projected. (Of course, women also project the archetypes onto the men in their lives, but in their case it is not Venus who is being projected—it is Mars, or Jupiter, and sometimes even Neptune or Pluto.)

Women invoke Venus whenever they imagine themselves as the models in *Cosmopolitan* or as the latest film star—whenever they dress for a lover rather than for the business world. In short, they become Venus whenever they function as lovers. It is no wonder, then, that the Norse writer Snorri and the medieval poets declared her the only one of the ancient deities still living. She lives still, as much today as ever, in every fashion model, movie star, and lover.

In general, we consciously invoke her or call upon her when we call upon love to come into our lives. And this actually works! Focusing upon the Venus archetype or calling upon the goddess really will bring love into your life, but as with Mercury, one must be warned to be careful what we ask for, because we will certainly obtain it. Before you ask Venus to bring you a lover, you should be extremely clear about what sort of relationship you really want.

One may also call upon Venus for all matters having to do with the arts. Though the "alchemical projection" of the goddess onto mortal women may be a bit dangerous for the man who is projecting her, poets, writers, musicians, and painters will find it a necessary risk, and one they will gladly take. For Venus is the muse, and no creativity is possible without her.

---

1. See chapter 14 on Juno for more about this distinction.
2. Bottero, Jean, *Mesopotamia: Writing, Reasoning, and the Gods* (Chicago, IL: University of Chicago, 1992) 216.
3. Sagan, Carl, *Cosmos* (New York: Random House, 1980).
4. Bolen, Jean Shinoda, *Goddesses in Everywoman* (New York: Harper & Row, 1984).
5. Ibid.
6. Perera, Sylvia Brinton, *Descent to the Goddess* (Toronto: Inner City Books, 1981).
7. Sullivan, Erin, *Retrograde Planets* (Arkana/Penguin, 1992).
8. Charles Boer, trans., *The Homeric Hymns* (Dallas, TX: Spring Publications, 1979).
9. Shaw, Miranda, *Passionate Enlightenment: Women in Tantric Buddhism* (Princeton, NJ: Princeton University Press, 1994).
10. Artemidorus, *The Interpretation of Dreams: Oneirocritica,* trans. by Robert J. White (Park Ridge, NJ: Noyes Press, 1975) 120.

CHAPTER 9

GAIA
MOTHER EARTH

ASTROLOGY AND MYTH

In their endless intellectual battle with the astrologers, scientists (primarily astronomers) have alleged that astrology regards the planets—including the Sun and Moon—as revolving around Earth. This, they tell us, reflects astrology's allegiance to an ancient and discredited view of the cosmos. Thus, in their own minds, the model of the astrological birth chart—with Earth apparently in the center—serves to discredit astrology as well.

This demonstrates a profound misunderstanding of astrology. For though it is true that an astrological horoscope shows all things as revolving around an apparent point on Earth, it should not be imagined that this is intended to represent astronomical reality. Instead, it images the way the sky seems to revolve around us, based upon our own earth-centered point of view. In other words, it is not Earth that is at the center of the solar system, it is *you*. It is *your* birth chart, and *you* are the center of your own universe. Earth appears at the center of things because *you* are standing on the earth. This is important because the earth is our frame of reference—and if we are not grounded and centered in the earth, then we will not be able to make much use of that which is in the sky!

It is in that spirit that we seek to restore Gaia, goddess of the earth, as an important factor in astrology. Some years ago, British atmospheric scientist Dr. James Lovelock, in collaboration with American biologist Dr. Lynn Margolis, put forth a ground-breaking (no pun intended) concept postulating the theory that the earth is a living, breathing organism.[1] Named the *Gaia Hypothesis* after the Earth Goddess who, in the Greek writer Hesiod's poem *The Theogony*, drew forth the living world from Chaos, it has become a common ideology among scientists, biologists, healers, and just about everyone on the planet who is intent on preserving and caring for it, rather than drilling, mining, sending missiles, doing underground nuclear testing, and in short, stripping the planet of its essence. The Gaia Hypothesis has fostered a New Age earth religion and sparked the rebirth of an ancient goddess.

Though the goddess named Gaia comes to us from the Greeks, her roots are embedded in a much earlier era. Before the Greeks, before the Egyptians, and before the Babylonians, there was the worship of the earth itself. And when the Greeks began to erect shrines, altars, and temples to their newer gods—Zeus, Apollo, and Hermes—there was very often an earlier shrine lying buried beneath the shining pillars, one which honored one of the many earth goddesses who inhabited those regions from long ago.

The first agricultural communities in the Near East and in southeastern Europe developed around 8000 or 7000 BCE. Some feminist historians have theorized that these communities were centered upon the worship of a Mother Goddess. Small clay statuettes of apparent Goddess figures have been carbon-dated to sometime around 6750 BCE, right in the heart of the precessional age of Cancer. Archaeologist Marija Gimbutas believed that these statuettes had been found in sufficiently large numbers and over a wide enough area to indicate that they represented the defining religious belief among the people of the times.[2] Archaeologists may well continue to discover remnants of this culture that will date it to an even earlier time than now imagined.

Written history doesn't begin until some 3,500 years later in the southern region of Mesopotamia, so Mother Earth, as a defining deity of prehistory, had quite a reign. In many ways, she has never entirely left us. Mary the Mother of Christ is, from a mythological or archetypal point of view, the most recent incarnation of the Neolithic Earth Mother Goddess, having been elevated to a very holy and divine status in her own right. And if Western religion has been dominated by the Christ archetype (the "Son" of God) during this last two-thousand-year Age of Pisces, we must remember that the opposite sign of Pisces is Virgo, an earth sign that symbolizes the "virgin" mother.

In Hesiod's *Theogony,* we are told: "At first Chaos came into being, but then the Earth, broad-bosomed." Earth brought Father Sky (Ouranos) into being and from their union came all else. In this context, we might see the fertilizing role of the sky (rain) that mixes with the generative power of the earth to keep life flowing. Many mythologies around the world have conceived of a mating between earth and sky. Earth is usually, but not always, depicted as feminine. And of course she would be full-bosomed and womblike. Fertility is the key concept here as Gaia bore more children than anybody else. From her body sprang all the subsequent generations, including the Titans, the Olympians, and their descendants. And let's not forget the mountains, rivers, forests, and glens of the earth—these, too, we trace back to the mother of all living things.

Gaia is a patient, watchful, timeless, and enduring force. When Ouranos the Sky Father became a tyrant, she persuaded her son Cronus to destroy his father. Earth intervenes in the generational conflict between fathers and sons, always on behalf of the sons, for it is always with an eye to the future generations that she lends her aid in conflict. And why wouldn't she? Don't we always say that it is the children, in all their innocence and hope, who will ultimately save the world? But it is not just that. It is also because Earth is the ageless wisdom that human life is cyclical and that one generation can't be immortal and rule forever. The passage of time sees us all come and go in the blink of an eye, but what remains constant? In the context of precessional cycles, it is the sky that is fickle and changing, but what stays the same? The earth.

Gaia honors all the creatures of earth and embodies all of nature. Her body *is* nature. We call her Mother Nature, Mother Earth, the Earth Goddess, or Earth Mother. We all know this woman. She is Hesiod's full-bosomed being, comforting and protecting young ones from harm's way, or feeding all the strays. Many stories from myth involve babies or children who are orphaned or sacrificed for one reason or another to appease the gods. Many of these babes are rescued by surrogates who may come from the human or animal kingdom. Earth always sends a representative to look after these young, orphaned ones and in many cases it is these "magical" children who are gifted with special powers.

We are told that upon arriving in Delphi, the center or "navel" *(omphalos)* of the world, Apollo had to slay the python who guarded the sacred shrine of Gaia in order to claim the place as his own. Once slain, the spirit of Mother Earth's python became invested in the Delphic Pythia, the sacred priestess who uttered prophecy to the thousands of pilgrims who sought guidance in the ancient world. The priestesses who spoke at Delphi climbed down into the bowels of the earth—Gaia's womb—from which they later emerged to share their divine message. It is the essential wisdom of Gaia—Earth's wisdom—that was at the root of these prophecies. Anyone who is connected to the *anima mundi,* the world soul, is connected to Gaia. When there is a discordant event happening in one corner of the world, those connected to the anima mundi feel it in every other part.

Gaia is sometimes also known as Ge, from whence comes our common prefix *geo,* used in such earth-related terms as geography, geology, geophysical, and geodetics. (Geodetic astrology is the branch of astrology that postulates a correlation between the celestial zodiac of 360 degrees and the 360 degrees of terrestrial longitude on the planet's surface.) *Geocentric* astrology is the astrology that most Western astrologers practice, placing Earth at the center and looking at the sky all around us. Earth is taken for granted in most astrological charts, and though not often shown, many astrologers understand that if it were to appear in the horoscope it would occupy a position *exactly opposite the Sun*. Those who work with the heliocentric model of astrology place Earth's position beside the Moon—if the Sun is your vantage point, Earth and Moon appear as a pair. But for the most part, Western astrology is geocentric, and therefore Earth is not included as a specific point in the birth chart.

If it is true that Earth will always be in opposition to the Sun, then we must view them as an inseparable polarity pair, continually magnetized to one another. If your Sun is in the sign of Taurus, your Earth will automatically be in Scorpio. If your Sun is in Libra, your Earth is automatically in Aries. While many of the opposite signs in astrology seem challenging to one another, it is only when they are brought into harmony (the reconciliation of opposites) that inner balance is achieved. Balance is the key principle here. When someone with a Libra Sun is bending over backwards to maintain peace and harmony with others while at the same time avoiding conflict at all costs, they will often attract an Aries type who openly engages in conflict. It is Libra's function to bring peace and harmony to Aries, while Aries brings action and catalyzes movement for Libra. The relationship can only function successfully when both sides of this polarity are expressed. When a Taurus Sun person is intent on holding on to things forever, it is the Scorpio Earth, intent on transformation as the key to enlightenment, that reminds us that stagnation ultimately results in death and decay. If the Sun in the chart represents the spirit of the individual, then the earth point acts as the body. The earth point is where we are grounded and where we may be anchored.

Since Earth is not one of the planets normally placed in a birth chart, there is no real astrological sign or rulership assigned to it. However, all the earth signs (Taurus, Virgo, and Capricorn) could be seen as having a special connection to the planet Earth in various ways. Taurus, in particular, has a great affinity with Gaia. It is the more mature aspect of Taurus that relates to Gaia and comes to embody a Gaia-like presence at about midlife.

DREAMWORK AND ACTIVE IMAGINATION

Most likely, Gaia will visit us in dreams personified as a mother figure, such as the Earth Mother already described, full-bosomed, wide-hipped, and all-encompassing. Unlike some of the more personalized mother goddesses, Gaia will often be rather impersonal. That is to say, Gaia will be more archetypal and universal, without such features as a personality or character that acts angry, happy, sad, or conditional. Gaia is an unconditional presence and often can be seen acting as an observer. You might also notice that Gaia shows up in dreams simply as an aspect of the earth itself. You might be dreaming of walking around ancient ruins, excavating something embedded in the earth, or picking up a rock, a crystal, a bone, or a stone (though these can sometimes be attributed to Saturn's realm). Dreams of rivers, forests, mountains, and landscapes will involve the earth. Dreams of rain falling and mixing with the earth, producing mud or some type of clay figure that has been extracted from the earth, all suggest a visit from Gaia. Dreaming of beings who live in or under the earth may be in this same category. While animals and plants have been related to Mars and Venus respectively, they also belong to Gaia. Anything of the natural world has a deep and immediate connection to Gaia.

Archetypally, you may literally dream of the planet Earth appearing to you precisely as it is. Many people have dreams of the earth being flooded or destroyed by nuclear fallout. Others have dreams wherein dolphins swim up to the shore and instruct them on how to better care for the planet. In cases such as this, you may be one of Earth's children who have been called forth to aid in her struggle for preservation, and to be a guardian or caretaker for the body of the earth.

More Mother Earth dream imagery may be found in the chapter on Ceres. In fact, Artemidorus tells us that dreaming of Ceres or Demeter is much the same as dreaming of Gaia.

PLANETARY REMEDIES

If you are having difficulties with the Gaia archetype, you may notice the problem in one of several different ways. As we have seen, Gaia is always opposite the Sun in any horoscope. Using the examples given above, the Libra Sun, who is unable to muster any Aries energy for action or even self-preservation, may need to reconnect with the Earth Mother, as may the Taurus Sun who is so out of touch with Scorpio polarity that she just can't "let go" to save her life. Also, just about anyone who lives in the city, who feels frayed, frazzled, and burned out, will need to reconnect with Gaia.

If your connection with the Earth Mother is tentative or frayed, the best way to remedy the situation is to get close to her. In fact, this is beneficial for almost anyone, anytime, anywhere. Nothing heals and restores our balance (the Earth/Sun polarity again) quite like a long walk in nature or a picnic under the trees.

AWARENESS AND INVOCATION

To become more aware of Gaia simply means to become more aware of nature. In the traditional healing lore of Eastern Europe, it is said that the rocks are the Earth Mother's bones, and that the leaves of the trees are her long beautiful hair. To become aware of all this—or better still, to be *constantly* aware of all this—is a quintessentially healing and grounding experience.

Hence one would certainly want to invoke the presence of Gaia when one is in need of grounding, centering, anchoring, and stability. There is nothing more solid and secure than the firm ground underneath our feet. There are many who walk the earth, but never feel it underneath them. They are oblivious to it. When changes are happening so quickly that they make your head spin and you are in danger of losing your balance, call in Gaia. This Taurean element of stability will help anchor you. There are very airy folks who reside totally in their heads or up in the sky, taking earth for granted. In these cases, the physical body of the individual is often ignored to great detriment. When there is a need to survey the body's natural rhythms and cycles (bodily fluids, elimination, digestion, organs, tissues, muscles, and glandular systems, which call to mind the earth sign Virgo), Gaia may then be invoked for guidance in properly monitoring the functions of the body. In situations where management, foresight, organization, and planning are needed, when patience and the awareness of the passage of time are worth more than finding hurried solutions to current dilemmas, Gaia may be called forth.

---

1. Lovelock, James, *Gaia: A New Look at Life on Earth* (Oxford University Press, 1982).
2. Gimbutas, Marija, *The Civilization of the Goddess* (San Francisco, CA: Harper, 1991).

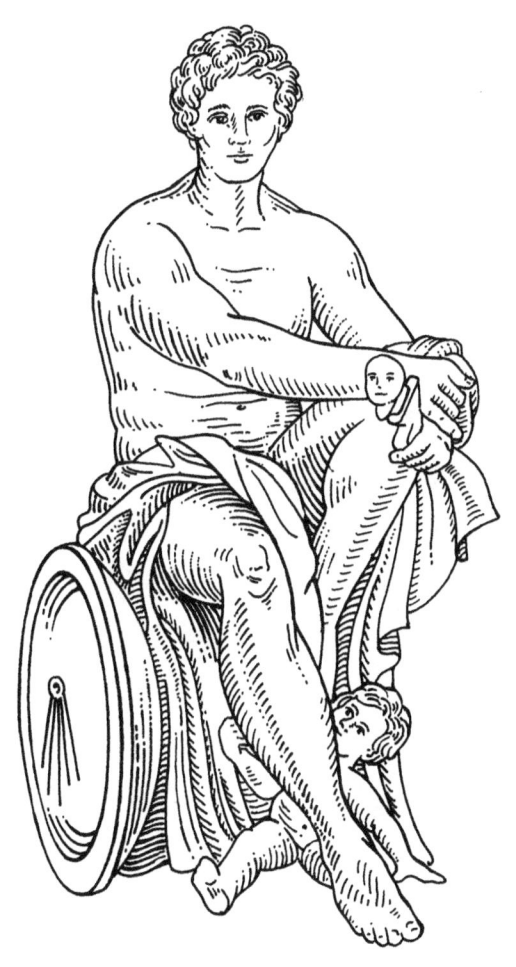

CHAPTER 10

MARS
GOD OF WAR

ASTROLOGY AND MYTH

Mars has a bad reputation in astrology. This reputation has been with him since the very beginning. In ancient Babylon, this planet was associated with the god Nergal, a deity of warfare, plague, and misfortune. Symbolically, the fiery red planet Mars has much in common with that bright and occasionally reddish ball of fire we call the Sun. But if the Sun brings life and growth to the world in some respects, it may also bring suffering through too much heat. It may blight the crops, scorch the earth, and cause us thirst. If we think of Nergal as that aspect of the Sun that scorches and blights, we shall not be far wrong.

It is said that Nergal, as a god of war, conquered everything on earth that there was to conquer. So he stormed the underworld and tried to conquer the goddess who ruled there, dark Ereshkigal (see the chapters on Venus and Pluto). He was partly successful. The two of them hammered out a compromise, dividing the Land of the Dead between them. So if Mars has affinities with the Sun, he also has affinities with Hades or Pluto. Perhaps we should think of him as the dark Sun that shines in the underworld.

The planet Mars did not fare much better when Babylonian astrology traveled to Greece. There it became associated with the god Ares (Roman name Mars), the fearsome deity of warfare. It is written in Greek mythology that there was not a single temple anywhere devoted to Ares. There didn't need to be. The battlefields were regarded as his temples, the dead as his devotees, and the vultures as his totem animals. This was a god who was feared but not loved.

While the Greeks were critical of this god of passion and war, the Romans admired him deeply, building many temples to him (as the Greeks did not). In many respects, the Romans regarded Mars as one of their principal deities, a source of power and victory. He was said to have fathered Romulus and Remus, the founders of Rome. Of course, the Romans were largely concerned with conquering the world. (Fight on, Gladiator!)

The astrological associations of the planet Mars reflect his history. In Hellenistic astrology, he was associated with danger, cruelty, disaster, and warfare. The ancient astrologers had absolutely nothing good to say about him. All the same, Mars plays an important role in the birth chart, and in reality we cannot get by without him. His archetype directly influences the quantity and quality of energy, courage, and force inherent within all of us. Without him we have no will power to achieve great things in life. Without him we have no energy and endurance to survive life's storms. Without him, we don't even have enough inner courage to stand up and talk back to a rude and nasty bank teller.

Although there were no temples erected to the god Ares in Greece, he was still regarded as one of the twelve ruling Olympian gods. An astrological scheme passed down to us by the Roman astrologer Manilius, which assigned the rulership of the zodiacal signs to the twelve Olympians, linked Mars with Scorpio; the same attribution held true in the more traditional system, where Mars was the "day ruler" of Aries and the "night ruler" of Scorpio. But Mars is more strongly placed in Scorpio, a nocturnal sign.[1] Mars is hot and dry and so is Aries. This just complicates things. In the watery, nocturnal sign of Scorpio, Mars has a chance to cool down and become feeling. In this context, we might note that his most favored and highly exalted relationship with any other planet was with Venus.

As with Venus, Mars is an active part of our daily awareness, although we are not always aware of it. While it is obvious to many that we are still worshippers of the "shining Aphrodite" within each new fashion model or screen goddess, it is perhaps less obvious that we—at least in the United States—tend to be worshippers of Mars as well.

The United States has always held Mars in high regard. From the very beginning, our heroes have been *pioneers*—adventurers who dared to explore new territory, usually at great risk to their lives. This, of course, is Mars as ruler of Aries, the sign of the pioneer and adventurer. And since the last two thousand years have been the astrological Age of Pisces, it is not surprising to find that Mars, as the soldier who performs his duties on the field of battle, has done his job with a Neptunian aura for the most part, i.e., as a crusader for God. In the United States, this crusading zeal falls under the slogan "For God and Country" or "God Bless America" (since religion is embedded in the national psyche, no matter what the Constitution might say).

As we enter the third millennium and the Age of Pisces is in its late "balsamic" phase, we may find a growing populace repelled by the smell of war, but that doesn't mean Mars isn't still alive and kicking. Not in the least. Hollywood absolutely loves Mars. The cowboy—who lives by brawn and weaponry rather than by brain—is a Mars archetype, whether in his classic "John Wayne" form, or in the more alienated and existential westerns of Clint Eastwood (in the famous Sergio Leone films, he was sometimes called "the Man With No Name," an example of Mars mixed with Pluto who wears a helmet of invisibility).

Hollywood also loves Venus (see the Venus chapter), but somehow Mars gets to run away with all the box office smashes with stars like Arnold Schwarzenegger, Sylvester Stallone, Bruce Lee, and Jackie Chan at the top of the heap. They may not win Oscars, but they sure rake in the dough, while the moviegoing public can't get enough. What does this say about the masses and their reverence to the action hero, the god of war and sport? (And of course, if you add the presence of Venus in the persona of the newest gorgeous actress, you have the potential for instant success.)

The war hero who strides across hundreds of films dressed in combat fatigues is another pure Mars archetype, and the fact that the classic soldier hero has almost vanished from our cinematic repertoire tells us something about the way our society has changed. The more contemporary movie hero with the powerful biceps who trashes rooms full of antagonists with a combination of high-tech weapons and martial arts is a Mars archetype as well—though here we find the presence of other archetypes as well. The extreme violence and disregard for human life that characterizes so many new films—beginning with *Rambo* and continuing in the *The Terminator* series and *The Matrix*—again suggests the dark shadow of Pluto at work. The increasing reliance of the hero upon technology suggests that Mars and Uranus have combined forces. All the same, the most frequent "partner" for Mars is neither Uranus nor Pluto, but Mercury. The Mars-Mercury type overpowers with Mercurial cleverness as much as Martian strength, and tends to have a youthful, boyish charm as well. ("The name is Bond—James Bond.")

Although the classic American Mars has been tempered with other archetypes, we still find him in almost all of our cultural heroes. An absolutely Mercurial hero—like Roberto Benigni's courageous little clown in *Life Is Beautiful*—may still be some years away from the American consciousness. Mars, however, is not limited simply to the cinema. Let us not forget the image of the rock-and-roll star, hugging his electric guitar with sounds that explode into the atmosphere like the crackling of fireworks. With his angry lyrics and ear-piercing sounds, he has found an outlet to express for himself and for his cheering, shouting, frenzied fans, all the pent-up emotion and angst of the teenage experience. (Like some of the examples already noted, however, the rock star is a "mixed" archetype—see our chapter on Neptune.)

There is one Martian passion that the whole world shares—the passion for sports and games and for the athletes who perform them. Professional sports, with its rules of conduct, discipline, and fair play, is one way in which society has tried to contain Martian energy. These highly paid professional athletes who have been elevated to god-like status run the risk of losing it all when they misbehave, but Mars being what it is, they still do so in increasing numbers.

Beyond that, every young woman who steals a desirous look at the bodybuilders on the local beach is worshipping Mars in secret, and in so doing, she is merely acting archetypally. Aphrodite, goddess of the planet Venus, was Mars' lover, and she must have found something admirable in the god of war. This passionate and sexy side of Mars was known to the ancient astrologers, though they tend to speak pejoratively in terms of "lust" or "licentiousness." As we have noted, they never had a good word to say about him, and yet the god Mars was strong, ardent, passionate, and full of courage. These are qualities that many women admire. If you want to know what sort of man a woman truly desires, you would do well to study the position of Mars in her birth chart.

It is interesting to note, however, that this is a cultural value. One of the authors knows numerous astrologers from India who have had difficulties interpreting horoscopes during their visits to the West because they are accustomed to regarding Jupiter as signifying the marriage partner in a woman's chart. It was with some amazement that they discovered that most American women tend to marry their Mars rather than their Jupiter!

In fact, such cultural differences go much farther than all that. Sometimes the American woman *is* Mars! It is possible to note that within the last few decades there has been a quantum shift in our gender orientation; we are now aware of the Mars force in women in a positive way that was never possible before. Female athletes are just as popular as the men (sometimes more so), and the movie "hero" who trashes the bad guys with machine guns and karate chops is likely to be a "heroine" instead.

While this is a positive shift in society that promotes the diversity inherent in our human condition, it is only fair to note that the opposite shift has yet to occur—there is still little or no respect for men who embody the Venus archetype. It may be politically correct to appreciate "feminized" men, but the world at large isn't having any. A kind of exception might be made for those who, like rock stars, embody the "Neptunian" side of Venus (see our chapter on Neptune), but for the most part a male who functions primarily as a lover is denigrated as a "womanizer," while one who takes great care about his appearance is derided as a "peacock." We may have to wait a while before the scales of Mars and Venus reach true equality in the social world! The pure Mars archetype will never stand for that kind of demasculinization. In the realm of archetypes, Mars will always "look" male and Venus will always "look" female, even though in reality it doesn't always happen that way.

DREAMWORK AND ACTIVE IMAGINATION

Mars appears often in dreams, though he manifests rather differently in the dreams of women and men. In the dreams of women, he may often be confused with other archetypes. Because Mars has such a bad reputation in contemporary astrology, there may be a tendency to attribute almost any negative male figure in a woman's dream to a "bad Mars." But with a little attention, we can learn to tell the difference between Mars and other planets. For example, the psychotic or serial killer is not bad Mars; it's bad Pluto. The womanizer or traveling salesman type is not Mars either; it's Mercury. The soldier or warrior may or may not be Mars—if he is engaged primarily in fighting, it's Mars, but if he functions primarily as a uniformed authority figure, it's Saturn. The athlete is almost always Mars. In women's dreams, Mars often appears as "the lover," especially if his attributes are primarily physical—muscular strength, courage, and so on. Women often dream of a dark, mysterious lover, cruel in some ways but an initiator in others. But this too is Pluto rather than Mars.

In fact it is very easy to confuse Mars with Pluto in the dream landscape; they rule Scorpio jointly, and do indeed share some common ground. But in dreams, where there is a tendency towards shadowy images to begin with, there's always the possibility that a shadowy male figure may be both an animus figure for women (Mars) or a shadow of the dreamer for men (Mars-Pluto). It's true that Mars can symbolize the animus figure in both a woman's chart and in women's dreams. But Mars in a woman's chart (and Venus in a man's chart) tend to portray the adolescent or undeveloped side of the anima and animus. The more developed anima and animus figures begin to appear as the individual begins to seek personal awareness and achieve self-consciousness. These may be expressed by more focused and mature figures, such as Sun and Jupiter as animus and Moon and Juno as anima. (See the chapters on the Sun, Jupiter, the Moon, and Juno.)

In the dreams or imaginal work of men, Mars is once again the athlete, hero, or warrior. The important point for men is to assess their own relationship with such figures. If the warrior fails to fight or the athlete fails to run, the man's Mars is in need of strengthening; if the hero turns cruel, the dreamer needs to transform his own Mars energy from rage into strength. If the dreamer himself plays the role of hero, then Mars is a positive guiding force for him.

When Mars has become a problem for an individual, it will often show up in dreams (for both men and women) as a figure who physically threatens or chases the dreamer. (The dreamer typically awakens scared out of her or his wits.) If there is a weakened Mars in the horoscope, these dreams will serve to "awaken" the dreamer to the fact that she or he is being bullied. Such threats do not always take the form of physical violence, either. Someone may be standing in a room continually yelling and screaming at the dreamer with no pause, so that the dreamer remains speechless, unwilling or unable to break in and make a defense; though this kind of angry, unbridled emotion might show up as a Moon-Mars problem in the chart.

Much of the animal kingdom is Mars-ruled, but especially look for dogs as symbols of Mars in dreams. Except when you have a female figure surrounded by her pack of dogs (or wolves)—which of course would be Diana/Artemis—the dog belongs to the realm of Mars. Libido is also an instinctual Martian attribute. What is the first thing most dogs do by way of introduction (once they've stopped barking at you, that is)? They stick their noses in your private parts! Most dog owners will usually admit to the serious role their dogs play in their lives and will often suspect that they serve to enhance their Mars function. But if we are prone to saying that dogs begin to resemble their owners after a time, then we might go a bit further by suggesting that the dog will also embody the psychology of its owner, especially its animus. Ownership may be somewhat difficult to decipher in, say, a family of four, where the dog owes an allegiance to all of them, but after a while it is possible to spot just which one the dog has identified with psychologically.

Another aspect of Martian libido in the modern context is one's car (perhaps in former times it was one's horse). In any case, though one might be tempted to think of a car as transportation and thus belonging to Mercury's realm, the car is a mechanical object, and for most people it has become the extension of their egos. Men, especially, will dream about their cars—how much power the engine has, what particular mechanical aspect of it they must get working correctly, how fast it can go, etc. Damaged fenders and broken windows can have obvious connotations to the dreamer's psyche. A woman may also dream about her car, but more about its color or age (its cosmetic condition!) or who is driving.

Then there are dreams where acts of physical prowess surface. One female in her mid forties began a health campaign. She lost fifty pounds and, for the first time in her life, began to work out and seriously enjoy physical fitness and strength training, particularly working with weights (pumping iron = Mars). Her dreams reflected her newly sculpted body's tone and strength: she dreamed of running marathons and winning, and running through Marine bases and outdistancing even the Marines. Much to her own surprise, she could run, skate, jog, or swim for miles (in her dreams) without ever tiring.

People who are about to compete in sporting events, or really anything— verbal competitions, piano competitions, or weaving competitions (Athene notwithstanding!)— will often have anxiety-ridden dreams of not quite making it. There may be various obstacles on the dreamer's way to the event, where they just can't quite get there.

PLANETARY REMEDIES

Violence—a distinctly negative attribute of Mars—seems to be ever on the increase in modern society. No matter where you look, there it is. The Martian presence surfaces in more ways than one can imagine—from giants sports stadiums to police forces having to break up mobs at World Cup playoff competitions, no matter whether the rioters' team won or lost! Random acts of violence are out of control and seemingly crop up everywhere. In urban areas the increase in gangs has reached shocking proportions. In many cultures terrorist activity is on the rise. But what is even more shocking today is a look at how this violent society adversely affects us all through our children. School children carry guns to school, become angry for one reason or another at a teacher or a classmate, and pretty soon a pile of bloody corpses lies on the school grounds. Such acts have fostered almost as bloody a battle in the political sector between gun control lobbyists and the NRA. No, Mars is certainly not yet on the wane.

But this is all an overstated and distinctly negative manifestation of Mars. What of his positive qualities? As we have seen, there are times when we actually need Mars energy in our lives—times when we need to be more assertive and self-empowered. During such times, we may wish to increase the Mars component within us by any number of methods. A good Mars can give you the courage to stand up to the loan officer, the IRS agent, or the intimidating lawyer who reads your lack of forcefulness and proceeds to walk all over you. In fact, when Mars is afflicted in the chart, it can cause serious consequences for the individual. Seemingly minor incidents can build up over time eventually contributing to what seems like an avalanche falling on the person who is victim to a weak Mars. It pays to strengthen your Mars, not just for self-preservation but because it's also good for your health.

A good Mars keeps a person in tip-top shape, physically and mentally. If Mars is weak, it can have serious consequences for the body's defense system. Particularly if Mars is in contact with natal Saturn or Neptune, you will want to strengthen your immune system. Red blood cells, good blood circulation, and strong adrenals are all functions of a healthy Mars. Strong chi in the body maintains good health and vitality and stimulates clear thinking and right action. Martial arts (named for Mars), especially the many forms of T'ai Chi and Chi Kung, are excellent practices to increase or strengthen Mars. And even those overly assertive souls whose Mars energy is too strong can benefit here. Perhaps the best way to balance an overly strong Mars without killing it is to take up the practice of one of these martial arts. Be careful with this, however. Choose a particular martial art that emphasizes the spiritual or meditative aspect of the discipline (*not* "killer karate"). A meditative approach to the martial arts builds focus, control, and discipline, as well as courage—all the more positive attributes of the Mars archetype. But really, any type of physical activity that strengthens or tones the body will help increase Mars, as Mars is *physical*.

Mars has always been associated with iron and the color red. Pumping iron is an obvious way to strengthen one's Mars, as well as eating iron-rich foods. Any sort of ornament made of iron increases the energy of Mars. His gemstone is red coral, and this is a fairly inexpensive, easily accessible stone that can also be used to build up the power of Mars. For best results, set a red coral in the middle of an iron cross or something of that nature. We can also increase his strength by meditating on the color red or wearing clothing that is red. This, however, is only recommended when Mars is extremely weak in the horoscope—otherwise it can tend to make a person too aggressive, since colors are very powerful forces. Those for whom Mars is simply too strong can benefit from avoiding hot spicy food, the metal iron, and the color red. Driving a bright red sports car at speeds above the legal limit is definitely *not* recommended!

INVOCATION AND AWARENESS

Mars is everywhere in our society, and all we have to do is open our eyes to see him. The real question is when do we wish to make use of him and bring his archetype into our lives? It is clear that many people have too much Mars; they need to cool down the martial fire and strengthen the energy of Venus or the Moon instead.

But this is probably not true of most of the readers of this book. Students of astrology and New Age thinkers in general tend to be peaceful or perhaps even passive types who are often unwilling or downright afraid to assert themselves, even when they need to. For such individuals, the power of Mars can be a very positive force. Whenever you feel that you failed to live up to your principles because you wanted to avoid conflict or confrontation, whenever you feel a general lack of energy and passion for life, whenever you allow others to fight your battles for you, that's when you need more Mars in your psycho-spiritual makeup. Use some of the techniques mentioned, such as taking up a sport or a martial art, to bring Mars powerfully into your life.

---

1. For more on the doctrine of planetary sect, which distinguishes between diurnal and nocturnal planets, birth times, and so on, see Robert Hand's *Night & Day: Planetary Sect in Astrology* (Reston, VA: ARHAT, 1995).

Part III

THE ASTEROIDS

CHAPTER 11

AN INTRODUCTION TO THE ASTEROIDS

ARCHETYPAL EMERGENCE

What of the asteroids in astrology? There are literally thousands of named asteroids in the asteroid belt and more are being discovered each day. What shall we make of all these floating chunks of rock in our orbital system, ranging in size from a small boulder to a large island? Are they to be considered a new archetype emerging? We think so. Consider this: it's been only about thirty years since an ephemeris was readily available for astrologers to use, citing the positions of the first four discovered asteroids.[1] As they have successfully completed their first Saturn Return, do they now constitute a serious reality, and have we as astrologers advanced our understanding of them enough to cause a paradigm shift in astrology—that is, to add them into horoscope analysis? They certainly won't all be prominent. Sometimes none of them will be that prominent. But in other cases, they will speak loud and clear, and sometimes much more clearly than the planets themselves!

Let's suppose for a moment that you have never worked with the asteroids and aren't familiar with their meanings and glyphs. Where do you begin? Let's start with the original four—Ceres, Pallas Athene, Juno, and Vesta. These first four asteroids have now come to be standard inclusion in many contemporary astrologers' charts. Why these four? It may seem that the particular names given to these four were just random. But in examining the roots more carefully, we see that these four goddesses of Greece were part of the nucleus of the Olympian family. The twelve Olympians were the principal deities said to oversee the affairs of other gods and mortals in classical Greece.

Here's where archetypal emergence also enters into the picture. Societally, culturally, and energetically, new paradigms are created. Some of these are in fact due to planetary cycle and shift. Others have to do with the evolution of the species and of the earth itself. One such dramatic shift has occurred in the last 200 years, in as much as the feminine-centered values of a society began to be taken seriously once again. And coinciding with that was the citing and naming of the first four asteroids in the early 1800s, named for female deities who coincidentally represented the same type of energies that were being honored in our culture once again.

ATHENE—THE VOICE OF THE DAUGHTER

Bolen, Woolger, and Downing, among others, gave us psychological and contemporary information on how several of the goddesses of classical Greece play out in people's lives.[2] We can't ignore the fact that this explosion of literature geared toward a feminine frame of reference was also coinciding with a cultural shift as well as a celestial point of reference. Of the seven goddesses named by Bolen, four of them are our four original asteroids, and the other three are planetary archetypes.

Bolen has recently written about "The Age of the Daughter."[3] Who is the daughter and what does she represent? An immediate mythic association to the daughter figure is probably Athene, Zeus' daughter. An oracle prophesied that the offspring of Zeus and the Titaness Metis (whose name means "counsel") would result in the birth of a son who would eventually take over. Zeus reacted swiftly and impulsively, and attempted to trick fate by swallowing the unborn child. But even Zeus is subject to the laws of fate, and soon this powerful energy could no longer be contained. He gave birth through his forehead to a dynamic emergence—Athene—who was not a man at all, but a woman! (Though Hesiod describes her as "a woman, but as if she were a man.")

The act of Zeus, the father, giving birth to this child was a very important step and symbolized more than just the act itself. The father had now given birth, allowing for a deeply committed paternal instinct that was to bond the two together in spirit forever. It also allowed Zeus to relate to this young female prodigy of his in what was probably the best relationship he has ever had with a female. Athene, as the daughter of her father, became the voice of the next generation and represented the second generation of Olympians to inherit high positions from their elders, but as every next generation does, it is now carried out in their own unique way.

By the time the Greek goddesses had achieved Olympian stature, Greek society had a very narrowly defined concept of women. The only possible way a woman could then have a strong voice was to echo the voice of the father, the husband, or some aspect of the patriarchal society in which she found herself. Thus, Athene as an archetype became identified as her father Zeus' daughter, and the goddess in contemporary times as well as the asteroid Pallas Athene has come to represent the daughter's relationship to her father. And this is certainly borne out in chart work. A strong position of Athene for a woman announces immediately the number one point of discussion: let's talk about you and your dad.

In classical Greece the father-daughter relationship may have necessitated a strict enforcement of patriarchal rule as set forth by Zeus or Apollo. In modern times, however, Athene can be seen as the daughter who is emotionally and/or psychologically bonded to her father, who has in many cases given her a firm foundation of courage and self-leadership abilities so that she may act on behalf of her own voice, whatever that voice may be. Many of our modern examples of Athene women tend to be women who have a strong commitment to voicing the needs of women collectively in our society. (The horoscopes of Jane Fonda, Candice Bergen, and Oprah Winfrey immediately come to mind, but for a glittering example of this we offer the chart of Hillary Rodham Clinton, who powerfully embodies this theme.)

Feminist historians have theorized that many of the goddesses of Greece came from previous cultures. Athene may be the daughter who sprang from Zeus' head, but she may well have more distant roots in the Near East. She has been variously linked with the snake goddess Neith, Medusa, a black Madonna, and an Amazon warrior goddess.[4] Images of those previous incarnations may have come with her to Greece by way of her helmet, sword, and serpent shield. Similarly, the oracular priestess or pythia who uttered Apollo's prophecies at Delphi may once have been a worshipper of the python goddess inhabiting the gorge, a vital energy that was honored long before Apollo's discovery of that ancient earth shrine to Gaia. Ariadne may be portrayed in literature as the maiden who steadfastly anchored the thread that eventually freed Theseus from the labyrinth in Crete, but many believe her to be an ancient goddess of the island.

Returning to the daughter theme, women have been slowly slipping into areas of the job market that were at one time solely reserved for men. Since the women's movement of the late 1960s and early 1970s, women are found in aspects of society that they were once forbidden to enter. We don't have to look too far back to see that women had very few individual rights even a century ago, before they gained the right to vote. Before that, there were no property or ownership rights. No one, not even Zeus, could have suspected that his daughter had quietly slipped in and begun to remold and reshape aspects of society as if she were kneading dough. It may have taken 3,000 years, but women are now poised and ready to assume a leadership position in most segments of society—and not by the sword of battle but by the sword of intellect, Athene's primary tool. Athene's trick was to become like one of the men, slipping in unnoticed, filling roles that were needed—women looking like men, acting like men, talking like men, and even dressing like men—until *voilà*, they are there in enough numbers to make a difference.

THE TWELVE OLYMPIANS

We have seen that there were twelve principal gods and goddesses who made up the council of the Olympians. Six of them are male and six are female, and they work in tandem, complementing one another. (That may be the only time in Greek myth that male and female rulership and power were divided equally). The first four asteroids that were discovered and charted in the early 1800s were named for four of the goddesses who sat on the Olympian council. Ceres, Juno, Pallas, and Vesta are not just additional bodies floating out there in space, but are connected to archetypal energies that define important aspects of a culture.

Each of these four goddesses is a part of Zeus' family, intimately connected to and strongly defined by the laws, culture, and myths that shaped ancient Greece. Three of these four goddesses were sisters of Zeus and the fourth, Athene, was his daughter. The three sisters served different functions. If we wish, we can link the functions of these four goddesses with the classical four elements of astrology. Ceres (Demeter) is connected to the principle of earth and was considered the Earth Mother or harvest goddess. Juno (Hera) is connected to the principle of water whose expression was through feeling; she was the mate of Zeus and came to embody the institution of marriage. Vesta (Hestia, a virgin goddess) is connected to the hearth and is hence linked with fire; her role as a priestess represents the link between the physical and spiritual realm. And finally, there is the daughter, Athene, a virgin goddess who represents the principle of air and guides heroes and heroines to make wise choices. In chart work, they play their roles accordingly. The virgin goddesses, the mother goddesses, the love goddesses—these are three main themes by which women are likely to be driven in life.

There is another reason to consider this quadruplet of goddesses as embodying a structural whole. While their archetypal energies represent the four elements, they also represent Mother, Daughter, Wife, Sister. What could be more basic to the relational aspects of human beings than this? The keyword here is *relational*. There is no better way to differentiate female from male nor any inherently greater strength that the female possesses than her ability to form relationships. These four goddesses, then, and perhaps the entire asteroid belt, can be seen as the segment of the sky that separates individual needs (personal planets) from social and collective needs (trans-Jupiterian planets). This asteroid belt can, in fact, be symbolized as the relationship segment of life.

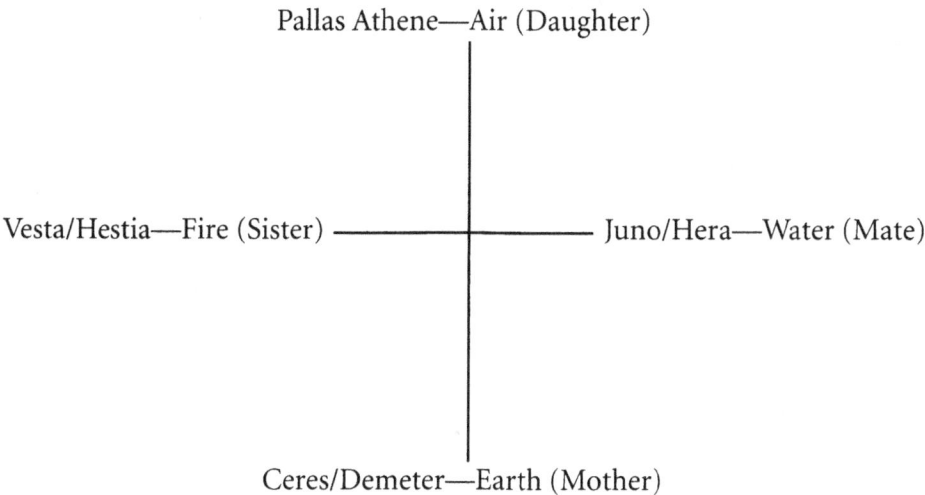

Some charts may show one of the four asteroids speaking loud and clear, while others may show all four in chorus, leaving it to the individual to decide how to play them. For the person who does have all three main themes speaking loud and clear, it can be a challenging, if not downright neurotic, set of circumstances.[5] In such a case we have four goddesses competing with one another for the individual's allegiance, such as in the mythological contest between Aphrodite, Athene, and Hera that touched off the Trojan War. Case in point: Hillary Rodham Clinton.[6]

Hillary's chart is a good example of all three goddess types at work, especially Athene. Her chart is characterized by a very strong aspect pattern called a T-square between her Ascendant, Uranus, the Moon, and Juno. Additionally, Athene is the most elevated planet and is tightly aspected to the T-square. Great, the goddesses are alive and well in this chart, but they each represent a different domain. Athene is a virgin goddess and career motivated, the Moon is a mother goddess, and Juno is a mating goddess. Juno is the wife, loyal to her mate "till death do us part."

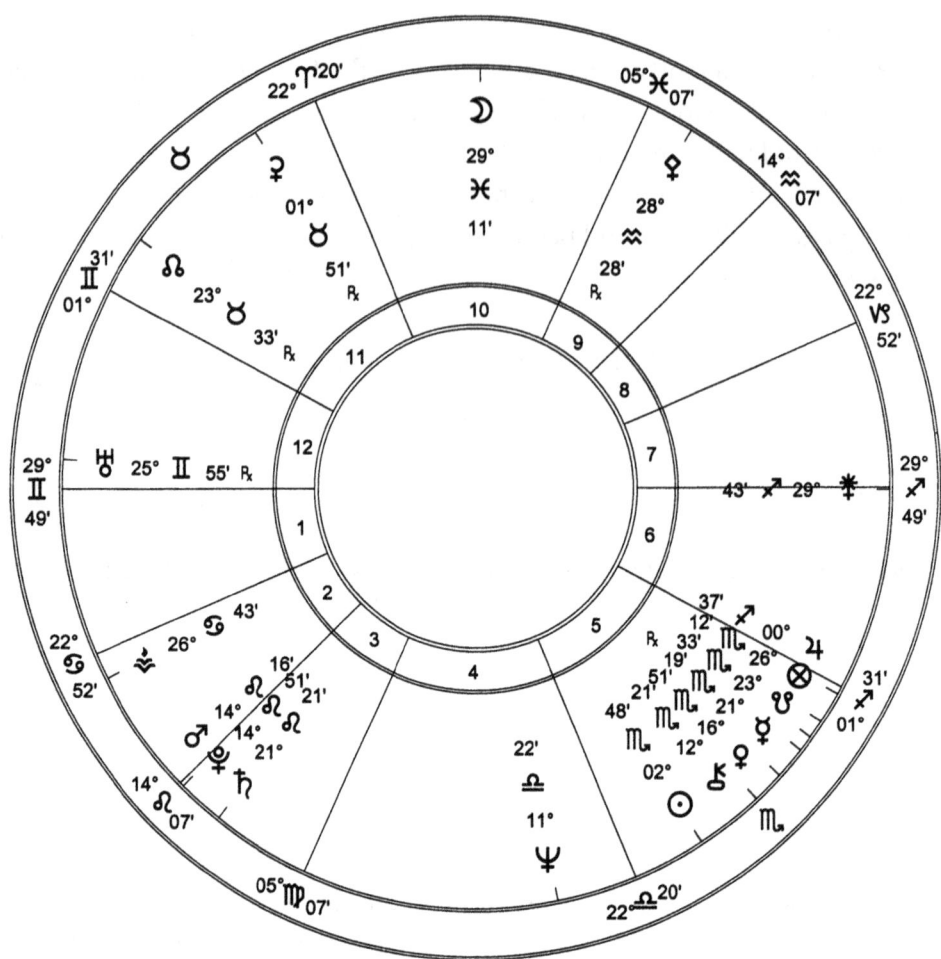

HILLARY RODHAM CLINTON
October 26, 1947 / 8:00:00 PM CST / Chicago, IL
Koch Houses

Stories about Zeus and Hera may be found in the chapter on Juno in this book. These two deities may in truth have actually enjoyed a much deeper and more all-encompassing relationship than what the ancient storytellers suggest (much of what they reported focused on marital infidelity and strife). It seems the press was no kinder then than it is now. Aside from what Hillary reveals in her autobiography, we cannot really know how Hillary reacted to the knowledge of her husband's numerous infidelities without delving too much into something that's clearly quite personal for the couple concerned. What we do know from the press reports of the day is that a myth was clearly being played out. All a first lady can really do is keep a stiff upper lip and keep smiling for the camera. (Jacqueline Onassis had to do the same even while holding the bloodstained corpse of her husband in her lap, amid rumors flying about his associations with the sex goddess of the time—Marilyn Monroe. Still, Jacqueline continued to remain composed for the cameras, and it is interesting to note that her chart also features a prominent Juno—conjunct the Ascendant and South Node—another "First Lady" aspect.)

Athene was Zeus' daughter, and Hillary may have been her father's daughter, sworn to upholding the laws of the land (she was and is a lawyer and U.S. Senator). Public support of her husband, even through the most humiliating moments of the scandal, may have made her look like a co-dependent Hera, betrayed once again. What was going on in her private thoughts with so many planets in Scorpio and a strongly placed Juno? You can be sure that if she's not expressing her rage and anger outwardly, there is an enormous amount of subterranean emotion bubbling just beneath the surface. In this case, the strong Athene in her chart helps her to keep going, giving her the courage, strength, and stamina to be strong and self-controlled, if not also whispering to her in the background: "Forget this dude, you have your own political strength and vision." Meanwhile, Hera is whispering: "Stand by him and support him; he is a good partner for you in many other respects." These are the voices that countless women face in their sometimes harrowing decision of whether to remain in an otherwise strong marriage or to leave.

Hillary's Sabian signatures are the twenty-seventh degree of Leo, which portrays "luminescence of dawn in the eastern sky," an image that welcomes the dawn of a new day after a dark night of the soul. The corresponding opposite is "a house-raising party" portraying community service.[7]

THE ASTEROIDS AS THE EMBODIMENT OF FEMININE WHOLENESS

There may be more than just a mythological correlation to all of this. The Sumerians had some very strongly shaped ideas about our solar system. Writer Zecharia Sitchin purports to have found evidence that the Sumerians believed the asteroid belt had once been a whole planet.[8] This planet had broken off into chunks of orbiting rock due to a turbulent, prehistorical celestial collision that sent all the planets and even the Sun into a new orbit. These planetary fragments were not just any planet, but were once a part of Earth. The collision had actually cleaved off an entire piece of Earth and sent it orbiting into space. The celestial turbulence continued until this chunk of our planet eventually broke off into the thousands of fragments of floating rock that now make up the asteroid belt. The Sumerians had a name for this segment of the sky.

They called it the *hammered bracelet.* If this story is wholly or even partially true, we can view the asteroids not just as separate entities, but as one body that is expressing itself in an orbital and symbolic way as many different parts of a whole being. Hence there is a very definite link between our planet Earth (Gaia) and the asteroid belt, which makes sense on a lot of levels.

Jungian psychologist Toni Wolff gives us four women who constitute two sets of polarities in life.[9]

Mother:—————————————:Hetaira
Amazon:—————————————:Medium

The four asteroids slide easily into this model: Mother = Ceres, Hetaira = Juno, Amazon = Pallas, Medium = Vesta. There is also a quadruplet of holidays celebrated by people all over the earth and symbolized by the two equinoxes and the two solstices. Because these have to do with nature (Gaia, our earth), they could be seen as honoring the earth or the feminine in some way. Additionally we have the cross-quarter days of the ancient Celtic calendar, the midpoints between the solstices and equinoxes. These are *Candlemas,* celebrated on February 1; *Beltane,* celebrated on May 1; *Lammas,* celebrated on August 1; and finally *Samhain,* celebrated on November 1, and corresponding to Halloween as well as to the Day of the Dead or *Dia de los Muertos* in Latin American culture.

While we are primarily concerned with the four asteroids mentioned above, let's not forget that the hundreds and even thousands of named asteroids have strong associations with the mythic and archetypal realm, and the laws of synchronicity being what they are, they act out the natures of these archetypes superbly. But where do we draw the line on the inclusion of extra energies into the horoscope? Well, if you think mythically and archetypally and resonate to what we're putting forth in this volume, then you certainly will want to check out some of the asteroids that are named for figures with whom you have a particular affinity. Is it Isis? Is it Guinevere? Is it Icarus? Is it Pan? Is it Lilith? Is it Marduk? Is it Atlantis? Casting their echos back to Egyptian, Celtic, Greek, Hebrew, Babylonian, or even pre-flood civilizations, these asteroids have come to announce themselves as if particle emissaries from worlds long forgotten (and they embed in your psyche by way of your horoscope in a particular way).

If you feel strongly related to any of these myths, symbols, or characters through dreams and visions, through active imagination, through meditation or through visual recognition and resonance with artists' renderings, chances are there is an asteroid or some other body in space that applies. Jacob Schwartz has given us an *Encyclopedia of Asteroid Names* published in 1996; the author also provides customized ephemerides of any asteroid name you desire.[10] Check it out and see how it fits into the framework of your chart and life. The voices speak to us in many ways, and this is one that gives a good strong physical connection.

---

1. Bach, Eleanor, and George Climlas, *Ephemerides of the Asteroids: Ceres, Pallas, Juno, Vesta, 1900–2000* (New York: Celestial Communications, 1973).

2. Bolen, Jean Shinoda, *Goddesses in Everywoman* (New York: Harper & Row, 1984); Christine Downing, *The Goddess: Mythological Images of the Feminine* (New York: Crossroad Press, 1981); Roger and Jennifer Woolger, *The Goddess Within* (New York: Fawcett, 1989).

3. Bolen, Jean Shinoda, *The Millionth Circle* (Berkeley, CA: Conari, 2000).

4. George, Demetra, *Asteroid Goddesses* (San Diego, CA: ACS Publications, 1986).

5. The three main themes are (1) the virgin goddess, embodied by Athene, Vesta, and Artemis, (2) the mother goddess, embodied by Gaia, the Moon, and Demeter, and (3) the love goddess, embodied by Venus, Psyche, Persephone, and Juno.

6. Chart data from Lois Rodden's website, www.astrodatabank.com. There is some dispute as to the correct birth time of Hillary Clinton. Besides this 8:00 PM time, there is an 8:00 AM time being used. This chart is the preferable choice of co-author Ariel Guttman. The latest report as this book goes to press (from Lois Rodden's AstroDatabank website) is: Celeste Longacre quotes her (for the 8:00 PM time). However, Eileen Applegate quotes an article from the *Chicago Sun Times* stating, "Her mother went into Edgewater Hospital after midnight and Hillary was born early on the morning of October 26." For purposes of this discussion, it makes little difference which time is used because the prominence of these goddesses still holds sway over the charts.

7. The Sabian Signature is based on Ariel's usage of material in Dane Rudhyar's book *An Astrological Mandala: The Cycle of Transformations and Its 360 Phases* (New York: Vintage Books, 1974). The signature is found in the angular separation of the lunar phase degree (Fortune) at which one was born, and its corresponding opposite (Spirit) degree.

8. Sitchin, Zecharia, *The Twelfth Planet* (Santa Fe, NM: Bear & Co., 1991).

9. Wolff, Toni, *Structural Forms of the Feminine Psyche,* trans. by Paul Wazlawik (Zurich: Carl Jung Institute, 1956).

10. Schwartz, Jacob, Ph.D., *Asteroid Name Encyclopedia* (St. Paul, MN: Llewellyn Publications, 1995).

CHAPTER 12

CERES
GODDESS OF THE HARVEST

ASTROLOGY AND MYTH

On the first day of the nineteenth century, the first asteroid was discovered. It was named Ceres, after the Roman mother goddess associated with the harvest and agriculture. Not only was Ceres the first one discovered (around 5,000 asteroids have now been identified), it was also the largest, and thus would become the mother of all asteroids. It is significant that Ceres was discovered on this date because the nineteenth century heralded a precedent-setting era for women: women's rights started to make their presence felt in an extremely vocal and political way collectively in the West.

Ceres is the Roman name for the Greek harvest goddess Demeter, whose loud cries of despair over the loss of her daughter Persephone sent shock waves through the world of the gods. Similarly, the introduction of Ceres into the heavenly pantheon of the nineteenth century may indicate to us that the Great Mother has returned to restore herself and her daughter(s) to the world. (Yes, the first asteroid, Ceres, celebrated her 200th anniversary in 2001. Pallas, the daughter, turned 200 in 2002. These could be historic times for women.) And the choice being offered—to wear one's *burka* or not to wear one's *burka*, that is the question—may be one of many dynamics at play.

There are several goddesses that may be regarded as "earth goddesses," particularly Gaia (see separate chapter). But Demeter is an offspring of Gaia—a granddaughter actually. Gaia is the quintessential "Earth Mother"; she is *the earth itself.* Ceres/Demeter, two generations removed, represents the fruits of Mother Earth—the flowers, the fields, and the food. Ceres/Demeter is primarily concerned with the growing of things and how things are nourished to provide that growth. In ancient Rome, the Greek Demeter became fused with an ancient Latin agricultural goddess called Ceres, one of the most revered goddesses of the Roman pantheon, probably due to her association with and appreciation of cultivation and harvest.

Though various mates are assigned to Demeter (Zeus, Poseidon, Iasion, Dionysus), they tend to be of minor importance to her myth. It is not the mating principle that Demeter/Ceres lives for. Rather, it is the mother/child relationship—most especially the mother/daughter relationship—that is primary in her life, and women who have a strongly placed Ceres in their horoscopes often find themselves inexplicably bound to this principle for much of their lives.

According to the myth, Demeter's young daughter Persephone was abducted by Hades, god of the underworld, and carried away to his dark realm. Her experiences there are covered more fully in our chapter on Pluto. Here we are concerned with the response of Demeter, the mother. Demeter was so distraught over the loss of her daughter that she wandered through the world in search of her—sad, weeping, obsessed. She neglected her ordinary care of the earth around her, and hence the world became cold and barren, robbed of the loving warmth of the Earth Mother. This was the first winter. The gods became so distressed over this "dying" of the earth that they intervened in the affairs of Hades, negotiating Persephone's return to the upper world. But because Persephone had already tasted of the "fruit of the underworld," she was bound to remain there for at least half of the year. Whenever Persephone is with us on the earth, Demeter rejoices. The earth blossoms into spring and warms into summer. But when Persephone returns to the dark lord's kingdom, Demeter mourns her loss all over again. Leaves fall from the trees and die; the world goes into its winter sleep. Then Persephone emerges into the upper world again, and Demeter blesses us with yet another spring.

Demeter's quest for her missing daughter was the subject of one of the great religious cults of the ancient world—the Mysteries of Eleusis.[1] In the myth, it is said that Demeter paused at Eleusis during her search for Persephone. There she acted as a nurse for the children of the king. Her adventures there work and rework the theme of mystical rebirth in ways much too complex to examine here. Perhaps the most important point is that it was Triptolemus, the son of the king, who was finally able to give Demeter the information she needed—he and his brothers had been herding livestock in the fields when Hades bore Persephone away, and they had witnessed the whole thing. In reward for helping her find her daughter, Demeter taught the Mysteries to Triptolemus, who thereafter taught them to others. He also was given a chariot drawn by serpents and taught the arts of agriculture to the world. The Eleusinian Mysteries were celebrated each year, and many renowned figures from the ancient world were initiates. It was forbidden to speak of the exact nature of the Mysteries, however, and to this day we do not know exactly what went on in the shrine of Eleusis. It is fairly certain, however, that it was a mystical passage of death and rebirth, which involved Demeter and/or Persephone giving birth to a divine child in the heart of the underworld.

Though the tale of Demeter and her daughter constitutes an important myth of the seasons, its main point for mythic astrologers is the interplay between mother and daughter—the early bonding and identification, the eventual loss and separation, and the final reuniting. And if this myth has come to represent the cyclical rhythm of the seasons, we may also observe in it the seasons of a woman's life. During virgin years, mother and daughter are one. During menstruating years when biological processes focus on the mating instinct, the daughter becomes mated to the masculine element. And finally, in menopausal years, mother and daughter once again become (hopefully) bonded.

Ceres' daughter Persephone is abducted by Pluto when she is just a young maiden. We aren't told exactly how old she is, but we may presume she is somewhere in the early throes of puberty. How many young women begin to psychologically and emotionally separate from their mothers somewhere between twelve and fourteen, wanting little if any influence or supervision? The mother, like Ceres, is all too aware of this and mourns the separation, even when it is not physical. (In many cases the separation is indeed a physical one, as the current statistical data on divorce and separation, custody disputes, and even kidnapping amply demonstrate).

Many of the earliest asteroid researchers associated the asteroids as a whole, and Ceres in particular, with the sign Virgo. In the case of Ceres, this doesn't require much of an imaginative leap since the pictorial image of Virgo has always been a goddess holding freshly harvested wheat—a symbolic image that may be linked with either Demeter, Persephone, or both. And in fact the Roman astrological writer Manilius, in an unusual system of astrological "rulerships" that assigns the zodiacal signs to deities rather than planets, gives Ceres rulership over Virgo. In the Northern Hemisphere, the Sun's annual passage through the sign Virgo comes at the peak of the harvest season (August 22 to September 21). Adding Mercury and Venus' yearly passage through Virgo just before, during, or after the Sun's time there extends the harvest time to an average of about sixty days per year. Toward the end of this cycle, once the fields and orchards are plucked, the leaves begin to drop and plant life begins its dormant phase, getting ready to go underground for the winter, the time of Persephone's descent to the underworld.

Besides Virgo, another obvious zodiacal association to Ceres is Cancer, the sign of food, family, and mothering. With the Moon and Ceres emphasized in a chart, or the signs Virgo and Cancer, these themes may gain great importance. One of the authors is closely acquainted with three really excellent cooks (who could be doing it professionally) whose horoscopes contain (1) Sun conjunct Ceres with the Moon in the Fourth House, (2) Sun conjunct Ceres with Moon and the Ascendant both in Virgo, and (3) Sun and Moon in Taurus with Ceres on the Ascendant.

In individual horoscopes, a strong and well-aspected Ceres points to fertility and abundance. People with Ceres strongly placed in their charts prefer to reside in non-industrialized areas, places where the landscape of Mother Earth and her richness may be found. A young man with a healthy Ceres may feel a bit like Triptolemus, the young lad whom Demeter instructed in the arts of plant cultivation and food production. These young men find themselves quite at home in the garden as well as the kitchen, and among feminine energy in general. Men with strong Moon-Ceres or Sun-Ceres aspects tend to deify their moms as well as emulate them in some way.

It is curious that Saturn's glyph (♄) and Ceres' glyph (⚳) are so similar, both shaped like sickles. In the ancient world, these deities were known as a harvest god and goddess respectively, and it is a unique kind of energy that they share. Similarly, the blend of energies between them in a chart may produce an emphasis on this theme. Difficult aspects between them might indicate a lack of harvest or nurturing, not enough to go around, or a profound sense of learning about frugality in this area. Aspects between Jupiter and Ceres may indicate an abundance of harvest, and similarly, very healthy appetites (sometimes prone to overindulgence in this area). Ceres and Mars may produce a combination of someone who burns their food or likes it spicy and saucy (or has a spicy hot mama and partner!).

Ceres and Pluto are a truly archetypal pair, symbolizing a sort of "forced release" that the person must experience, resulting in life-changing transformational events. A person with Ceres-Pluto might also relate more to the part of the myth that involves the separation of mother/daughter or to the death-and-rebirth theme of the Eleusinian Mysteries. Yet another pair that suggests Eleusis is Ceres and Neptune. As we shall see, the planet Neptune in many ways suggests the archetype of the god Dionysus, and in the Eleusinian Mysteries Demeter and Persephone become one, and her (or "their") child is sometimes identified with Dionysus. This also suggests the astrological polarity of Virgo (Demeter/Persephone, the Divine Mother) and Pisces (Dionysus as the archetypal Divine Child).

DREAMWORK AND ACTIVE IMAGINATION

Dream images involving the archetype of Demeter or Ceres may have all sorts of associations of earth, food, or harvest. The abundance of the harvest and also the scarcity of crop production in any given season (due to things like soils and plants being blighted by draught, flood, fire, or pesticides) can show up on the dream landscape.

The part of the body said to be associated with the sign Cancer is the stomach; Virgo rules the digestion. When these areas of the body are persistently problematic, there is often a connection to a lack of proper nurturing or nourishment in one's life. People experiencing these themes, whether in life or in dreams, will need to be more careful with their diets. People who are experiencing family or relationship difficulties will typically have dreams in which the food they are being served is insufficient, distasteful, or sometimes even rotten. Look to other images in these dreams to whence or from whom the distastefulness or indigestion springs.

This tendency towards nervous anxiety in regards to the Demeter archetype is noted by Artemidorus, who says that she may often signify "fear and danger"—though he goes on to say that the outcome of the problem will be positive, and that anxiety will give way to delight. He also asserts that this archetype is good for marriage, which is to say that a dream or imaginative session that awakens a positive image of the Earth Mother is favorable for all kinds of connectedness.

One woman dreams repeatedly of being at a restaurant and ordering her meal. When the meal arrives, it is not at all what she asked for. What does the restaurant or the server remind her of? And how does she respond to the food that is being served? Another heavily Ceres type had repeated anxiety dreams over not having enough food to serve when guests arrive. Another woman dreamed that she and her husband were gathered around a formal dining table where his entire family was present. As the food was carefully being served to each individual, it passed her up not once, but twice! She was forcefully being excluded from the meal, mirroring her feelings of how she felt her husband's family regarded her—ignoring her if not downright excluding her from the family group.

Another woman, a westerner, had been traveling in the tropics for several weeks when she began having the runs for days on end. Dehydrated and unable to eat or drink a thing without losing it immediately, she went to sleep and dreamed of an elderly man leading her up a dark winding staircase to a large, stainless steel vat where he motioned for her to come and fill her glass. In the vat were hundreds of pineapples being juiced. She awakened craving pineapple juice, which was readily and freshly available in her locale. She started drinking it and became rejuvenated almost immediately. Another woman dreamed of a more archetypal-looking Ceres presenting the harvest in a cornucopia on the dreamer's kitchen table. This dream foretold of good fortune ahead for the dreamer, which indeed was happening in her life. And of course, any dream involving mother and daughter, especially in the kitchen in a context surrounding the preparation or eating of a meal, is a sure sign of Ceres energy manifesting in one's life.

PLANETARY REMEDIES

Because Ceres was not one of the "seven ancient planets," there are no traditional remedies such as gemstones or planetary talismans that relate to her archetype. There are, however, many behaviors that allow us to enhance or harmonize her energy in our lives.

First, let us remember that she is an earth goddess, and in many ways related to the archetype of Gaia. Just as it is helpful for us to spend time in nature in order to reconnect with Gaia, a walk in the woods is equally helpful for enhancing the energy of Ceres in our lives. And yet for the most part, Ceres is a goddess of the cultivated (as opposed to the wild) earth. Any time we plant and grow things, we touch her very soul, for this is her function. Plants that can be used for food—a patch of tomatoes or carrots, or even an herb garden—are more linked with the Ceres archetype than flowers or other purely ornamental plants.

But roses and other flowers of beauty may have their uses; for no matter how much love and attention we give them, they fade in time. Having nurtured and mothered them, we must then surrender them back to the earth. But in time they shall return again, as Persephone returns each spring. Connecting with nature in her growth cycles is a very healing experience for those who may have difficulty in psychologically relinquishing their own children in life.

INVOCATION AND AWARENESS

Obviously, if one is in the business of food production or service, as are growers, organic farmers, grocers, restaurateurs, caterers, and even deliverers of such items to the market place, one might want to invoke the ancient goddess of the harvest. If one is having a problem in life with illnesses relating to the intake of food (too much or not enough, such as bulimia or anorexia), one might invoke Ceres to restore balance. Most girls suffering from such conditions have a rather low self-esteem, often resulting from the lack of a nourishing relationship between parent and child, especially the mother. When one is struggling to maintain a continuity of life after the sudden loss or separation of a loved one, Ceres would be an appropriate remedy.

---

1. Kerenyi, C., *Eleusis: Archetypal Image of Mother and Daughter*, trans. by Ralph Manheim (New York: Shocken Books, 1977).

CHAPTER 13

PALLAS ATHENE
WISDOM'S WARRIOR

ASTROLOGY AND MYTH

As an archetype of the warrior and of wisdom, one might be tempted to confuse Pallas Athene with other planetary deities such as Mercury/Hermes, the youthful god of intellect; or Mars/Ares, the war god; or Saturn/Cronus, the elder statesman of wisdom; or even Jupiter/Zeus, the kingly father figure of benevolent guidance. While she shares attributes with all of these figures, Athene belongs distinctly to her own realm.

Temples to Athene exist throughout Greece, but her most famous shrines or sacred sites are the tholos of Delphi and, most especially, the Parthenon of Athens. The city was named for her, and she was its patron deity.

The Iliad and *The Odyssey* are replete with instances of Athene's abrupt materialization to many heroes when they are faced with a difficult decision or thwarted by the other gods. Athene's appearance, soothing voice, and wise counsel give the hero clarity, confidence, and an ability to take immediate action.

Mentioned elsewhere in this volume is Hesiod's description of this goddess: "a woman, but as if she were a man." This suggests that Pallas Athene was endowed with qualities and traits that society most often identifies as masculine (such as a glittering intellect). But she is a woman, and thus her own brand of "warrior wisdom" expresses itself very differently than that of Mars—a kind of philosophical clarity inherited from her father Zeus as well as feminine intuition from her mother Metis. Most importantly, Athene's wisdom is "useful." As a woman, she refuses to lose herself in philosophical speculation; everything must have a purpose. For example, she is the patron deity of the art of spinning and weaving, a "useful" art indeed, and her identification with the city of Athens goes beyond the mere name. She was the "goddess of the city," which is to say that she was the deity of civilized life generally.

Gender is not really an issue with Athene because she is in many ways androgynous. All the same, most mythologists maintain that she certainly had a bias toward masculinity and the identification with her father. This has to do largely with her birth story and with the fact that she was Zeus' favorite daughter. And even though she is born from her father's forehead and hence has the reputation of being engendered by the father alone, she did have a mother, Metis.

Metis was one of the Titans, the "former gods" who ruled the world before the Olympians. Her special realm was that of wisdom. Zeus made love to her and impregnated her with twins, a boy and a girl; then an oracle told him that the boy child would someday overthrow him. Hence Zeus, acting like his father Cronus (see Saturn), devoured Metis. But as he was walking by the shores of Lake Tritonis in Libya, he was seized with a raging headache. He called upon Hephaestus, the young god of the forge, to relieve his pain. The smith god complied, splitting open the head of Zeus with his golden mallet, and out popped Athene, daughter of Metis, fully grown, shielded, and helmeted. When Zeus laid eyes on his newly born daughter, it was instant and mutual love at first sight.

The archetype of Pallas Athene and the story of her miraculous birth have figured prominently in the ongoing debate regarding the origins of Greek myth. The poet Robert Graves popularized the idea that the deities of the Greek world were a synthesis of genuinely Greek gods and goddesses with those of earlier, pre-Hellenic times (which, for reasons of his own, he called *Pelasgian*).[1] He theorized that pre-Hellenic Greece had been matriarchal in character, and that the Olympian goddesses had been "married" to (or, in Athene's case, born from) the sky gods of invading Indo-European tribes and thus demoted in status. In the case of Pallas Athene particularly, he took the Libyan locale of her birth story to mean that she had originally been the titular deity of a powerful female warrior cult in North Africa whose strategies, tactics, and mechanics would be stored in her memory.

The concept of a matriarchal Europe was enunciated by Graves and, earlier, by scholars like Bachofen and Briffault who found its fullest expression in the work of archaeologist Marija Gimbutas—though it is worth noting that in her final days Gimbutas abandoned her idea of "patriarchal" Indo-European invasions because it was unsupported in the archaeological record. The real origins of Pallas Athene may remain forever obscure. Although it is true that she has no clear parallels in other Indo-European mythologies, some recent scholars have purported to find her in Minoan Crete (rather than Libya) where she was known simply as "the Goddess of the City" (which of course is how she functioned in Athens).

Born from her father's mind, she is distinctly his daughter. She conveys his judgments and decrees to the world at large, and as such, she was widely worshipped throughout the ancient Greek world and deeply respected. Considering that women's roles in the politics and philosophy of Greece were almost nonexistent, Athene's elevation to the status of Zeus and Apollo says a lot about the mantel of power she possessed.

Though Pallas survived among the Romans as Minerva, goddess of wisdom, there was very little place for her in Christian Europe or in the Middle Ages. If anyone in that thousand-year span of history even remotely resembled Athene, it would be Joan of Arc, who embodied the Amazon or warrior side of Pallas. There are a few others, primarily female rulers such as Eleanor of Aquitaine or Queen Elizabeth I and, more recently, Queen Victoria. But it is really only in the last century or two, since the discovery of the asteroid Pallas in 1802, that we have begun to see the Pallas Athene archetype emerge once again and steadily but slowly infiltrate the political and business world. Because she is a "daughter" rather than a mother, it is archetypally appropriate that she should be reborn in a "new world"—in this case America, which has something of a national specialty in Athene-type women. America's natal chart contains a Moon-Pallas conjunction in Aquarius, suggesting America's highly supportive environment for the independent and free-thinking entrepreneurship that springs from so many of its citizen's heads.[2] And there is probably no symbol more American nor more Athene-like than the Statue of Liberty in New York Harbor, the first American image that greeted most immigrants of the nineteenth and early twentieth centuries upon their arrival.

In the last twenty-five years of the twentieth century, thousands of women clothed themselves with three-piece business suits and accessorized with briefcases or donned their hardhats or went through boot camp; these contemporary Athenes are now finding their ranks statistically significant and growing more so in the work force. We may ultimately have women like Margaret Sanger and Susan B. Anthony to thank for getting the ball rolling on the current resurgence of Athene in the world. And now? Athene is everywhere you look. The popular TV show *Xena: Warrior Princess,* a huge hit among young girls, attests to this.

The major asteroids—and even most of the minor ones—orbit between Mars and Jupiter. Athene, the second asteroid, was discovered in 1802 and just recently celebrated her 200th birthday—a time when her voice rings loud on the world stage. As a daughter of Zeus and part of the Olympian council of the twelve, she ranks as one of the "big four" asteroids along with Ceres, Juno, and Vesta. (For more on these four, see the previous chapter, "An Introduction to the Asteroids.") Though she was one of the twelve principal Olympian deities in Greek myth, and is part of the quadruplet of the four main asteroids, she is the *only* one of the four who was a second-generation Olympian. The others are all first-generation—the children of Saturn rather than Jupiter. Thus, she is distinctly the *daughter*.

The asteroid Pallas Athene takes approximately five years to complete its orbit around the Sun. And like its mythological counterpart, the asteroid Pallas rises to great heights. There are few if any bodies that rise and fall as far off the ecliptic as does Pallas. When Pallas is in strong relationship and favorable aspect with Jupiter or the Sun, there is typically an archetypal relationship between father and daughter such as Zeus and Athene enjoyed. Difficult relationships between that pair may produce what Jungians term the *animus possessed woman,* which refers to a woman more strongly oriented towards traditionally male preserves such as politics or career—or even the academic world of the "higher intellect"—rather than towards mothering, relationships, etc. Strong aspects between Pallas and the Moon give people strong intuition, but with oppositions and squares, they may question or doubt their own instinctual feelings and have a barrier or "shield" between themselves and their mother.

Strong aspects between Mars and Athene can indicate an enjoyment of sport and game between siblings or partners, and the difficult aspects may suggest a more intense kind of sibling rivalry, gender disputes, and competitiveness. Aspects between asteroids like Juno the marriage goddess and Pallas the virgin goddess, or Venus the love goddess and Pallas, may often emerge as dilemmas for the individual between choosing to mate or remaining single, and, if taking a mate, cautions heavily towards making the right choice. An angular Pallas or a highly aspected Pallas indicates an individual with strength, courage, wit, and wisdom, and a cutting-edge sharpness—like the goddess herself. Pallas possessed many skills. The individual with a strong Pallas should typically have no problem finding ways to market those skills.

Strong connections between Pallas and the dark gods and goddesses such as Pluto, Neptune, Lilith, or sometimes Venus, Juno, and even the Moon (depending on the condition of those planets) may involve the *shadow* or repressed part of Athene represented by Medusa, whose image appears on Athene's famous shield. Medusa, the dark snake-haired goddess, calls forth this image of the dark goddess as part of her heritage. (For more on the

Medusa image, see the chapter on Pluto.) In fact, many women whose charts contain a difficult aspect between Pallas and these other goddesses may actually find themselves playing out lifetime struggles between themselves and their sister(s) (whether blood or not). For women who feel that they are the black sheep of the family, rejecting family values but also being rejected by the family in turn, the Athene/Medusa struggle is present; those who accept this projection will typically gravitate toward the Medusa energy.

DREAMWORK AND ACTIVE IMAGINATION

Athene's dress reveals a great deal of her inner nature. She is both regal and sportily attired—in battle dress, but wearing a ceremonious, flowing frock vested with armor, a jeweled helmet upon her head, and a shiny jewel-encrusted sword in her hand. Upon her shield is the image of Medusa, the daimonic female figure with snakes in her hair and a symbol of the dark wisdom of the underworld. The owl, another symbol of wisdom, is always at her side. These are all images that might appear in dreams, but they also represent Athene's power totems. She is as beautiful as any of the goddesses in her long flowing robes and jewels, but she also carries a powerful set of tools, such as armor and sword that convey the message loudly and clearly that she is not to be messed with or violated in any way.

In modern times, however, Athene will rarely appear the way she looks as the goddess, dressed in her battle garb. Instead, she is likely to show up in dreams dressed in a business suit, with hair closely cropped, wearing glasses to indicate an intellectual superiority, looking more like a Janet Reno, Hillary Clinton, or Margaret Thatcher. This brings us back to Hesiod's "woman, but as if she were a man." The dreamer would then have to determine what role this masculine woman plays in his or her life, but more important than how she looks is what message she is communicating to the dreamer. This is Athene's wise counsel speaking to the dreamer, at least at an unconscious, if not fully conscious, level.

Other symbols for Athene in mythology that might surface in the dream landscape might be the olive tree or the loom. The weaving process or the acquisition of finely woven fabric is another symbol of Athene. One female client has dreamed repeatedly of beautiful hand-woven vestments being presented to her, and these might well carry the strength and protection of Athene. Many ships' bows had carved female figureheads upon them to guide them on their oceanic voyages. This is reminiscent of Athene's frequent appearance and presence on the ship of Odysseus, always guiding him on his journey. Particularly important in dreams might be Athene's appearance as a warrior woman, similar to Xena or an Amazon archetype. Like Xena, Athene is not a woman who goes out inciting war and strife. Instead, she is the defender and protector of innocent and weak victims who have fallen prey to hostile or savage warriors. In such cases, she then easily defeats the competition, not just through her brute strength and force, but also with her ability to cunningly size up the competition, predict their moves, and outsmart them. Recently we have seen these women excel in *Crouching Tiger, Hidden Dragon*.

Medusa (see also the chapter on Pluto) symbolizes the darker, repressed or split-off side of Athene; it is necessary for Pallas to gain dominion over this side of herself, and this is why the image of Medusa is placed upon her shield. If sibling rivalry exists, especially between sisters, there may be an Athene/Medusa conflict going on in a dream setting. Especially look for "good sister/bad sister" scenarios in family dynamics—this is the Athene/Medusa drama in action.

In the dreams or imaginal work of men, Pallas Athene most often plays an entirely different role. In Homer's *Odyssey*, young Telemachus, the son of Odysseus, is guided and advised by an older counselor named *Mentor*—from whence our common English word for a "life coach" or "life teacher." But the elderly man named Mentor is in fact Pallas Athene in disguise! When a man dreams of a woman who gives sage advice and counsel, one who "mentors" the dreamer and who is devoid of the sensual affect associated with the Venus type—one who might just as well be a man like old Mentor—then the dreamer has encountered Pallas Athene.

Artemidorus draws a clear distinction between Athene's presence in the dreams of women and men. For example, he asserts that for a woman who is involved in any kind of an erotic relationship (especially one that is a bit socially daring), Athene's appearance in a dream is somewhat unfavorable. He reminds us that the goddess avoided relationships with men—thus she may be said to be warning the relationship-oriented woman to back off from too deep an involvement. On the other hand, Artemidorus goes on to say that Athene's appearance in the dreams of men who seek to marry or become involved in relationships is favorable! Apparently, the idea is that wisdom, dignity, and a "philosophical" concept of woman that goes beyond the merely erotic are on this fellow's side. The old Hellenistic dream master assures us that Athene is, of course, favorable for philosophers. And well she should be. For those who think and ponder deeply about life, the Athene archetype in a dream signifies that wisdom itself is by one's side as a mentor.

PLANETARY REMEDIES

Since Pallas, as an asteroid, was only discovered in comparatively modern times, there are obviously no "traditional" remedies in the form of gemstones, talismans, and so on. However, there are ways to introduce the archetype of Pallas Athene into one's life through the activities we perform.

As "goddess of the city," Pallas had an interest in politics, and, as we have seen, her wisdom is of the practical kind; it needs to be applied to something definite. Those who wish to increase her power within themselves would do well to take a more active interest in local politics and to become more involved with civic affairs and projects. Beyond that, she is, of course, to some degree a goddess of battle. As with Mars, becoming proficient in the martial arts can do a great deal to expand the influence of Pallas in our lives—especially for women.

But to speak more in the realm of "magical correspondences," there is another—and seemingly somewhat unlikely—activity that is associated with Pallas, and that is weaving. Some of her principal myths deal with her status as the patron goddess of this art. Although sitting contemplatively in front of a loom may seem light years removed from the powerful and politically active stance we have come to associate with Pallas, mythologically and archetypally it works—weaving is one of her primary signifiers.

INVOCATION AND AWARENESS

We may see Athene everywhere these days; she is, in a sense, the "totem" goddess of contemporary feminism, especially in the United States. It should be remembered that many Western territories such as Wyoming and Montana gained their statehood by endowing their independent-minded pioneer women with the right to vote. Pallas Athene has been alive and well in the U.S. for well over a century! And as we have noted, she still lives among us, not only as a television Amazon, but increasingly more often in business conference rooms and executive offices.

It is relatively easy to keep Athene in our awareness. We don't have far to look, and it is useful to have her close by us, whether as a friend, role model, or "mentor." Athene is a desirable archetype to have on hand as a transmitter of higher wisdom. When there is lack of clarity and direction in one's life, when there is lethargy, when there is immobilization due to fear to act, Athene's strength and courage are welcome. When trying to market oneself in the workplace, call on the skill and sharpness of Athene to help.

---

1. Graves, Robert, *Greek Myths* (New York: Penguin, 1984).
2. There are many charts in circulation for the U.S. (see Nick Campion's *Book of World Horoscopes,* England: Aquarian Press, 1988). A generally agreed upon date for the U.S. horoscope is July 4, 1776, and on this date the Moon was transiting through Aquarius, conjunct the yet-to-be-discovered asteroid Pallas Athene.

CHAPTER 14

JUNO
GODDESS OF SACRED UNION

ASTROLOGY AND MYTH

In many cases where the gods and goddesses of Greece were assimilated by Rome, they lost much of their earlier glory, power, and prominence, sometimes taking second place to imported Oriental deities. In Juno's case it may be the reverse.

As Hera in Greece, she was the Queen of the Gods as legal and rightful spouse to Zeus, the supreme. And as Juno in Rome, she was also Queen of the Gods, married to Jupiter. But she was rather more than that. We have already mentioned that in Babylon a woman's "indwelling spirit" was referred to as her *ishtar*. In other words, the Babylonians perceived the essential nature of woman as lover, pure and simple, bold and free. In Rome, a woman's indwelling spirit was her *juno,* and our common word *genius* is derived from that term. (One's genius was originally one's inner essence; the word had nothing to do with scientific or intellectual prodigies.)

Since, as we shall see, Juno was quintessentially the goddess of marriage, her status as "indwelling spirit" could mean one of two things. It could mean that the Romans acknowledged feminine nature as based essentially upon relationship, connectedness, or union—in distinction to the Babylonians, who saw her as a "free agent." Or it could also mean that the Romans were simply incapable of imagining feminine nature as being anything other than married and shackled to the kitchen. We shall leave it to our readers to decide for themselves.

To the ancients, marriage was primarily a social contract. It was not an erotic union. This concept of marriage still prevails today in traditional societies like China and India, and it is only in the last 200 years that Western civilization has recognized romantic passion as an acceptable cause for marriage. To the ancients, the ideas of marriage and eroticism were incompatible, and even in the Middle Ages, it was deemed inappropriate for a troubadour to write poetry to his own wife—on the grounds that marriage could never inspire *eros*. When a woman of ancient Greece married, she first went to the temple of Aphrodite and sacrificed her "pretty things." She made an offering of cosmetics or sexy clothes to the Goddess of Love to demonstrate that she was leaving her world behind and going to Hera's world instead. Hera and Aphrodite occupied two opposite polarities of the sphere of feminine consciousness, and there was very little connection between them. The myths suggest that the two goddesses were not exactly friendly with each other. Hera had a venomous hatred of Aphrodite's promiscuity and punished her by making her give birth to a monstrosity—Priapus, her child by Pan. On the other hand, it is said that Hera sometimes borrowed Aphrodite's magic girdle and thus revenged herself on Zeus by driving him helpless with lust.

In Rome, Juno was also the goddess of marriage and childbirth, and became supremely honored as such. She was also protectress of women from birth to death. She was especially devoted to and revered by newlyweds, not only helping to bless the sacred union and offer whatever assistance she could in the process of childbirth, but also assuring the longevity and stability of the family unit. The month of June was named for her, and it is still is the month most favored for marriage. Women gathered at her sanctuaries for healing and therapy when their marriages were troubled.

Because Hera was married to Zeus, the supreme ruler of the gods, all of Olympus celebrated the occasion in a glorious and elaborate marriage ceremony and feast that lasted for days—a tradition still carried on today with great pomp and ceremony, not only by royalty and people of high social standing, but also among members of traditional or tribal cultures. In many villages around the world, the marriage ceremony is the focal point for the entire village; the music, dancing, and feasting last for days. In contemporary society, a marriage may still become the social event of the season (or even the entire life) for many young women.

The wedding of Zeus and Hera was a glorious event, and the honeymoon was said to last 300 years. But what does 300 years really mean in the lives of the immortals? But after the honeymoon—read that as the period of fidelity and monogamy when they still were very much relating to each other—the relationship quickly began to deteriorate. The goddess who had been assigned to the institution of marriage gave it questionable success as a role model, for sure, since the stories that have lived through the ages have been almost solely about her *bad* marriage. Zeus' numerous affairs, followed by Hera's explosive jealousy and subsequent acts of revenge upon his lovers, became the norm. The more she raged and nagged, the more he strayed. The more he strayed, the more she raged, creating a vicious cycle that kept endlessly repeating. However, Hera's stormy marriage did not deter people; they took up her worship and engaged in their own rites of marriage. Although she raged at home, she did serve her people with dignity and grace. Perhaps the ancients were cynical about marriage in general and regarded Hera's experiences as normal.

Still, it is difficult to look to Mount Olympus as a very good model for marriage. Of the Olympian family, it was the marriage of Zeus and Hera, troubled from the start, that became one model. The only other married pair on Olympus was Aphrodite and Hephaestus (see the chapter on Venus), which was scarcely a marriage at all. Western civilization may occasionally still follow a long tradition of arranged marriages (especially among royalty and families of status and wealth or strong religious beliefs), but nowadays people typically seem to marry for love. And yet the state of marriage is really no better off. Until very recently, divorce was not really an option. Now that it is an option, the divorce rate continues to soar. So, has marriage as an institution really progressed, really improved? Perhaps until the archetype of Hera is restored to balance, it never will be. In spite of the current bleak statistics on marriage, there is an underlying belief by many people—men and women alike—that their lives will not be complete until they mate. And in Hera/Juno types, this mating instinct is particularly strong and is what fuels their lives.

Obviously, the primary relationship here for a Juno/Hera type of individual is the idea of matrimony, monogamy, fidelity, and stability within a relationship. While other goddesses are identified primarily as mothers (Demeter, Gaia), virgins (Artemis, Athene), or lovers (Aphrodite and to some extent Persephone), it is Juno's role as a marriage goddess that sets her apart. What sets Juno off is infidelity or any action by a potential mate that might be deemed threatening to the longevity of the relationship. When we observe that this goddess had been given the domain of ensuring marital bliss and stability while enduring her own *unstable* marriage and blisslessness, one can understand her rage. She was given control of a domain that was totally beyond her control, and she reacted with emotion. In the Olympian tales, she always raged at the other woman, never at Zeus himself. In the modern-day context, it is not always the other woman who is a threat to a Juno type. Sometimes it is the job that keeps the mate distant, or even the computer!

Juno or Hera stands out in mythology as a one-woman campaign in favor of absolute monogamy. Not only does she punish Aphrodite for her numerous affairs, but she relentlessly pursues Zeus' lover Io around the world and coldly causes the death of Semele, another one of Zeus' paramours. In so doing, she nearly robbed the world of Semele's divine child Dionysus, though one suspects that Hera had but little use for the god of ecstasy and intoxication who persuaded women to cast aside their Hera-style decorum and go wild in the streets.

Hera also persecutes Heracles, simply because he was Zeus' son by another woman. His name, of course, means "Glory of Hera," and was allegedly given to the hero to help turn aside the wrath of the goddess (the trick didn't work). Lest it slip past the reader, note that the word *hero* is also derived from Hera. It is in the service of social institutions that true heroes act—all those other fascinating bad boys are "anti-heroes" instead.

Juno was the name given to the third asteroid, discovered on September 1, 1801.[1] She was at 7° Virgo conjunct the Sun at 8° Virgo. Of the four "major" asteroids (Ceres, Pallas, Juno, Vesta) who are an important part of the Olympian family, it is Juno who is generally believed (by astrological asteroid researchers) to be connected with the element of water. The element of water carries with it a constantly moving uncertainty about tomorrow—the ebb and flow of the tides, the crashing of the waves to the shore, and the constant movement of the river to reach its journey's end. Water types long for intimacy with their mates and desire emotional security above all, something that is quite temporal. In astrology, water is the element most associated with feeling. Contrast this with Juno's spouse, Jupiter, a thunder god, who originally represented a primal force of nature. A fire god and a water goddess—representatives of the two elements in astrology that can and often do create steam (fireworks!). Jupiter throws thunderbolts and Juno has strong emotional reactions.

Charts of individuals with strongly placed Junos may be faithful to the end and often withstand periods in their marriage where the spouse has strayed. Don't forget that the asteroid Juno appears in the charts of men and women. It is not always the man who strays to the strong reaction of a jealous wife; sometimes it is the other way around, especially in the modern era where women are not so tightly bound to the home. But a stronger theme for Juno is the idea of equality in the relationship. Juno does not want to be subservient to the spouse, but unlike Lilith who fled the moment she was asked to submit, Juno stays with a relationship as long as possible, trying to make it work, always hoping it will change. In this context, it is interesting to note that the goddess Hera confronted Zeus on this matter of equality and subservience, from *The Iliad* when she is attempting to convince Zeus to see her viewpoint:[2]

> *"I am likewise a god, and my race is even what yours is,*
> *And I am first of the daughters of devious-devising Kronos,*
> *Both ways, since I am eldest born and am called your consort,*
> *Yours, and you in turn are lord over all the immortals.*
> *Come then in this thing, let us both give way to each other,*
> *I to you, you to me, and so the rest of the immortal gods will follow . . ."*

Zeus heeded her words and acted swiftly on her advice.

In modern times and even down through the ages, a strong Juno/Hera archetype is embodied by aristocratic women. These women are born into or married into a class of privilege, wealth, and social standing where the feminine function takes on the role of formalizing or ritualizing the social structure. Hosting and organizing banquets, teas, state dinners, and the like are often skills that are finely honed. Dignity and elegance are necessary ingredients to ensure the smooth functioning of such occasions, and here is where the Juno archetype radiates. In fact, in modern times weddings often become the one time in a person's life where these rituals are carried out to their fullest. A marriage ceremony can be anything from a simple civil procedure in a judge's office to the elaborate social event of the year. Many weddings take a year or more to plan, wherein no expense is spared at choosing the correct adornments—from the setting, be it a church or synagogue or country club, to the flowers, to the food, to the garments of the bridal attendants, to the background music, etc. No detail is left unattended. It can also become an extremely stressful time for many young women and their families. But this kind of stress is usually underscored by the titillation and excitement of the impending marriage.

Juno, then, rules marriage as a social institution. But in our present society, where men ordinarily marry their favorite Venus and then attempt to transform her into a Juno, the two archetypes become mixed—just as the astrological functions of the asteroid Juno and the planet Venus likewise frequently become mixed—and even deeply confused. In medieval astrology, it was in fact Venus who signified "the wife," although she also signified "lovers," who, as we have seen, were regarded as something entirely different and even incompatible with the notion of marriage. So it is helpful to have Juno in contemporary horoscopes, for she helps us to see how individuals relate to the different facets of relationship—social and erotic.

Countless Hera or Juno types show up for astrological consulting. Many have given up their own promising careers or stalled completing their education in order to marry a Zeus and support him while completing his education or providing a comfortable home for him and their children. Some are doctors' wives, lawyers' wives, politicians' wives. The marriage is typically one of status for both. She is provided with a comfortable, if not elegant, existence. He, in turn, has the appropriate wife, trained in all the social graces, to host and accompany the many functions of his life. But privately he may have been having affairs for years, and suddenly comes the moment when the children are grown and the wife begins to show signs of wear and tear (age); he reaches out for the younger, more attractive woman, announcing quite coolly that he wants to divorce. Of course she rages.

Since any archetype may flow both ways, the man who marries a strong Juno type but fails to perform like Zeus may find himself bumped in favor of a more socially prominent lover. Annette Bening's Juno-driven real estate broker in *American Beauty* sought the Jupiterian glory of another successful realtor, turning her back on her husband, portrayed by Kevin Spacey—a guy who preferred to work at a hamburger stand rather than shoulder the responsibilities of an American Zeus. Strong Juno patterns in a chart may involve participation by the individual in any one of the three parts of a relationship triangle. Many times it is the "innocent" third party, in love with a married (wo)man, who is wounded by such a circumstance.

The Juno woman may sometimes be a bit lacking as a mother. It is recorded that when Juno gave birth to Vulcan (Greek: Hephaestus), she was disgusted by his ugliness and threw him out of heaven to the earth below. He later became her favorite son by fashioning nice jewelry for her. Juno mothers, concerned as they are with the maintenance of the social order, may favor the child who gets good grades, leads the football team or cheerleading squad, and generally performs like a "hero" or "heroine" on behalf of the social order. And she may unwittingly or unintentionally neglect the child who is "different," or, in extreme cases, even cast her or him out of the family structure entirely, as Hera tossed Hephaestus off of Olympus.

DREAMWORK AND ACTIVE IMAGINATION

Juno was always portrayed as a mature, sometimes even matronly goddess, though in her youth she was beautiful enough to attract the attention of and capture the hand of Zeus. She carried herself with dignity and grace, even though she was suffering much emotional turbulence internally. She was portrayed as crowned and carrying a scepter of power, her astrological symbol. She wore long flowing robes and was usually accompanied by her bird, the colorful peacock. Because the realm of marriage was her primary domain, any dream involving a wedding or marriage ceremony will feature Juno's presence. One woman, aged thirty-eight, dreamed of choosing wedding garments very carefully for herself and her bridal attendants, yet she was not engaged, never had been, nor did she have any prospects of a mate on the horizon. Within a year, however, she met her mate. An elaborate wedding was planned, and during the preparation stages she recollected the dream, as she was actually reliving many of the images of the dream.

Then there is the other side of the coin concerning marriage. After Jupiter and Juno's initial honeymoon was over came the time of strife and conflict within the marriage. When themes such as marital infidelity, jealousy, triangular relationships, and strong quarreling among couples resulting in explosiveness emerge in dreams, the function of Juno in the dreamer's life may be sending a message to the dreamer. One woman dreamed repeatedly of having strong arguments with her spouse, resulting in her own eruptions of rage, though in reality there was no communication at all. Dreams like this are often called compensatory, allowing the dreamer to act out in the dream what she could not act out in waking hours.

So closely are Jupiter and Juno linked that the dream sage Artemidorus tells us they mean more or less the same thing, but he goes on to say that Jupiter is more important for men, while Juno is more applicable to women's issues. Because Juno and Jupiter are royalty, any Juno archetype in a dream suggests health, fortune, and prosperity. But if the Juno figure in a dream is poorly dressed or connected symbolically with the sunset, it means that there is some sort of challenge to one's health or wealth.

PLANETARY REMEDIES

An unbalanced Juno archetype, whether in life or in the birth chart, most often manifests through an unhealthy focus on social propriety or an equally unhealthy propensity towards fits of jealousy. When Juno is out of balance, one may value social status above human warmth; a husband becomes merely a financial object, judged by his success, and children likewise become objects, their worth measured by their scholastic or athletic achievements rather than by their inner qualities. An unbalanced Juno also shows itself in jealous rage, whether warranted or not; every glance or handshake the partner makes towards a member of the opposite sex becomes an occasion for smoldering wrath.

The best way to overcome these negative emotions is simply to wash them away. The goddess Hera bathed regularly in a spring near Argos to renew her virginity—although the word virginity should be understood in its ancient sense of "completeness within oneself" rather than in its current medical sense. Begin with a shower, and imagine that all of Juno's negative qualities—status addiction, jealousy, vengefulness—are being washed away. Then prepare a bath. Be ritualistic about it. Use candles, aromatic herbs, or whatever is needed to evoke the right mood. While bathing, imagine that you have become a completely new person, and one who embodies the positive attributes of the archetype—loyalty, stability, and poise.

INVOCATION AND AWARENESS

Despite the fact that Juno often shows up in a chart in terms of some of the difficulties mentioned above, it is worth remembering that she was much revered in ancient times, and her presence in one's life may be helpful at times. In ancient Greece there were temples to Hera and sacred precincts where pilgrimages were made to bless and sanctify a marriage. These places also served as healing shrines where women could go alone—or where men and women could go together—to help strengthen a troubled marriage. The obvious time to invoke Juno would be in instances like this; also remember that Zeus and Hera did enjoy a time of love and bliss together (their 300-year honeymoon!) when they were courting and newlyweds. In former times, young girls would keep hope chests for their future marriage. If something like this is undertaken, Juno would be a helpful presence. When emotion is all but out of control and needs to be expressed, especially over a troubled relationship where infidelity is involved, the invocation of Juno could be helpful.

Finally, let's remember Juno's annual pilgrimage to a sacred spring to "renew her virginity." This accomplished a much needed alchemy for both her and her partner. Married couples who find they are fused together at the hip after many years and who have never considered being without the other may well wind up in the therapist's office. On the other hand, an allowance of independence, separate life experiences, and rebirthing in sacred springs or on fishing trips may be just what the doctor ordered for an ailing marriage. The visit by Juno to her sacred spring renewed not only herself, but also her partnership.

---

1. Schwartz, Jacob, Ph.D., *Asteroid Name Encyclopedia* (St. Paul, MN: Llewellyn Publications, 1995.)

2. Lattimore, Richmond, trans., *The Iliad of Homer* (Chicago: University of Chicago Press, 1951) Book IV, v. 59–62.

CHAPTER 15

VESTA
GODDESS OF HEARTH AND HOME

ASTROLOGY AND MYTH

Vesta or Hestia is the goddess of the hearth. In ancient times, each home had a central fire or hearth, as did every public building. It is this "eternal flame" that represents the goddess Vesta, and thus she dwells in every home and in every public building.

Of the twelve Olympians, Hestia was by far the most modest. As you will read in our chapter on Saturn, that grumpy old deity swallowed all of his children so that they would never dethrone him; the ruse didn't work. Hestia was the oldest child of Saturn or Cronus; some might say that her shyness comes from the fact that she was imprisoned inside of Cronus for the longest period of time. Others say it is because what she represents is not about ego but about spirit. One explanation is psychological, the other is mystical; both are probably true.

People have always gathered round fires for shelter, warmth, and cooking. It feeds, it nourishes, it calms both body and soul, and it becomes a unifying principle. Hestia/Vesta was said to be the embodiment of this flame. In fact, she was the inner "presence" symbolically connected with Gaia, Mother Earth, at Delphi, the center of the world. There she was said to be the spirit of the glowing charcoal which was the *omphalos* (navel).[1] Though it may be difficult to find references that connect Hestia to the *pythias* of Greece or the *sybils* of Rome—the oracular priestesses of Delphi and Cumae, respectively—this association to the embers at Delphi may provide a useful link to her oracular gifts, as it was a tripod with burning embers from which the pythias inhaled the hallucinogenic fume before uttering their prophecies.

Hestia may have been the deity most frequently invoked by the citizenry of the ancient world because feasts were always begun and ended with offerings to her.[2] She may even be regarded as the defining principle for seeking refuge and sanctuary. Refuge from what? Most likely from the elements—from nature's unpredictable whims and storms. The hearth or central fire was the guiding light in every ancient home and city. And the ancients likewise invoked Hestia or Vesta's presence for the safe-keeping and continuity of the family, of every enterprise, and of the city or community itself.

In Rome, Hestia was known as Vesta, and it wasn't just her name that underwent a change. There she was the patron goddess of the so-called Vestal Virgins, a spiritual sisterhood that occupied a position of great political importance even in patriarchal Rome, but that was subject to very restricted and controlled rules of "proper" conduct. As temple priestesses, they kept alive the sacred flame that was the central hearth of the vast Roman Empire itself, never letting the fire go out. They also took vows of celibacy, and this part of their lives was under particularly strict scrutiny. It is said that the punishment for breaking their vows of chastity was, first, public humiliation, and then being buried alive—whether or not the act was consensual or perpetrated upon them. Public servants, especially politicians who are supposedly setting standards for their populace, who have been caught breaking their marriage vows can attest to the public humiliation and raking over the coals by the media and subsequently their constituents that was subsequently experienced!

Thus Vesta is yet another "virgin goddess." In ancient times, the word for "virgin" didn't necessarily have the physical or medical connotations it has now; it simply meant that she chose no mate. But more importantly, Hestia or Vesta was endowed with a certain kind of immunity to the love arrows of Eros and the seductive qualities of Aphrodite, making it much easier for her to live a life of celibacy. Though in Greek and Roman incarnations she seems to have strictly adhered to the laws of celibacy, her pre-Hellenic roots may well have been different. Based upon the writings of the poet Robert Graves, some feminist thinkers have speculated that temple priestesses kept the sacred energy alive but also engaged, when necessary, in the sexual act. No marriage resulted from these acts, but occasionally a child did. When a child was born of these sacred unions, it was said to be divine.[3]

All of this brings us to the ultimate inner meaning of the goddess Vesta. In the thinking of most traditional peoples, one's own village is considered to be "the center of the universe." Beyond that, in an even more personal metaphor, one's own home is likewise the center of the universe—the *omphalos*, or navel of the family or clan. Throughout ancient Europe and the Near East, this universal center is depicted as a great tree—the Tree of Life. Although it is never said that a fire burns at the base of the Tree of Life, it is often implied that a fiery energy animates the Tree. This energy is generally perceived as feminine, like the Kabbalistic Shekinah (see the chapter on Lilith).

Ancient peoples also believed "As above, so below." The cosmos was within. If there was a Tree of Life at the center of the universe, there was a Tree of Life within the human body. That tree is, of course, the spinal column, and the fiery feminine energy that animates the Tree of Life is present within the human body as the kundalini, the feminine serpent power that yogis and mystics harness to gain their powers. Many ancient deities symbolize or embody this power in its various aspects. We have already noted the examples of Mercury (Hermes) and Venus (Aphrodite). Soon, we shall meet with Lilith, who in many ways is yet another kundalini metaphor. This energy is present within us largely as sexual energy. The yogi or magician who wishes to make use of that power may engage in periods of celibacy or asceticism in order to gain control over that vast inner energy, and this is one reason why the priestesses of Vesta—the yoginis of the ancient Western world—were celibate. They were the keepers of the kundalini energy for the entire Roman Empire. So even though Hestia is a virgin while Aphrodite and Lilith are promiscuous, they all represent aspects of the same energy.

Vesta is the fourth largest asteroid and the fourth one to be discovered and named. Her discovery took place on March 29, 1807.[4] It is fitting that she is the goddess associated with fire and light, because she is the only asteroid that can be seen without a telescope, she is so bright.

When Vesta manifests itself strongly in the astrological chart, an individual may choose an inner marriage, pursuing a life of isolation and retreat rather than choosing to mate. However, Vesta is also apparent in the charts of single mothers—as is Ceres—where the father has not really played an important part in the life of the mother or child for very long. It's sort of like the virgin birth, and the image of the Madonna and Child that has become so universal as an archetype might not be far off from this. This may be especially apparent between mother and son, whereas with Ceres it is more apparent between mother and daughter.

There are many people who decide they would like to pursue a life of spiritual service, but instead of doing so within the cloistered setting of a monastery or ashram, they choose to be pilgrims and travel in pursuit of their goals. A life of service or a strong commitment to something that vitalizes the individual is what is most important to those with a strong Vesta in the natal horoscope. The path of service may be a career, a sport, spiritual service, or the dedication to the home and family. Whatever path they choose, they do it with focus, dedication, and integrity.

Vesta is the goddess that always provides the place of sanctuary and retreat. In the astrological mapping of one's planets around the globe, it is curious to see how many people wind up settling on or near a Vesta line. It is where they feel "safe," where they may find shelter and refuge. Typically, the people who are living on their Vesta lines maintain their homes in a beautiful way, whether the home be modest or grandiose. In fact, when one enters their home, it looks like a temple. On the other hand, when Vesta is a problematic theme in the birth chart, there is a sense of wondering and wandering about where to settle, where the true home lies, and where the place of comfort is, the person having moved from place to place searching for the ideal. The place of comfort, safety, and sanctuary, obviously, is within, so if it is not first found there, it would be difficult to achieve it externally.

Because of the extremely dichotomous nature of Roman Vesta and pre-Hellenic Vesta, people who have Vesta strongly constellated in their charts may find themselves faced with conflicting views about sex. On the one hand, there is a strong sexual nature, be it on the surface or buried deeply below. But because of the severe punishments exacted upon the Vestals, an imprint may exist in the memory of the individual so that the sexual nature may actually be buried very deeply in their psyches, so afraid they are of expressing it for fear of retribution. This theme may be further reinforced in the present life through one's religious upbringing, deepening the conflict even further.

It is important for people with a strong Vesta to recognize that they may be devoted to a life of service to an individual, to a corporation, or to an institution, but there is a fine line between devotion and self-sacrifice. It is easy for Vesta types to sacrifice themselves to whatever they deeply believe in. The challenge for Vesta types is to give to the point of inner satisfaction, but not overdo it because giving too much can create a pathology of victimhood.

Many complexes can and do arise from people with an afflicted Vesta, but especially look for Vesta in a troublesome aspect to Saturn, as that was the archetypal pair (Cronus swallowed his children, and Hestia was imprisoned for the longest time). It is interesting that Hestia was the ancient ruler of Capricorn, and Saturn is considered the modern ruler of Capricorn, so it is people with a strong Capricorn that will recognize some of these themes.[5] Both of these bodies are concerned with dignity, tradition, order, and proper conduct. Both archetypes are also extremely self-disciplined, so one might also notice strong internal perfectionism-driven qualities in their natures. Because Hestia spent so much time within the confines of Cronus, there is also a deep introspection or introversion in her nature that may also be apparent in Saturn's nature.

People who have Vesta stated in a dominant way find it easy to focus. Focus is required for success in achieving a job well done in any area, but it is especially required in meditation. Many who are adept at yoga, meditation, and working with unseen energies (as in healing, psychic work, mediumship) usually have a very strongly placed Vesta in their charts. A person with a strong and healthy astrological Vesta is someone with indomitable strength, usually devoted to the care and concern of others.

DREAMWORK AND ACTIVE IMAGINATION

Very few images of Vesta exist. This is not surprising, as it is difficult to put what represents spirit or soul into form. However, it has been said that Mother Mary has a very close resemblance to the idea of the original Hestia. Mary appears to many devout seekers in visions and dreams and is called upon quite frequently (as in invocation).

No matter how we may envision her, Hestia's status as the keeper of the fire of life gives her a powerful importance in dreams and active imagination. Artemidorus says that when intensely powerful and successful individuals dream of Hestia, it confirms them in their power and status, and suggests that soon they will be elevated to even greater heights. He goes on to say that for the ordinary mortal, the appearance of Hestia in a dream suggests life itself.

Women (and men) who attended parochial school in their youth, especially Catholic school, will often dream of those days. If there were strict rules and regulations, harsh authority figures, and swift punishment for not sticking to the program, they may be haunted in later years by images of their stay there. Of course, one of the most common universal images is that of the Mother Superior or the Sister with whom a more rebellious child might have had an ongoing conflict. These images will continue to emerge later in life via the dream process. More pleasant memories of this period could also manifest in dreams—such as young school girls running and playing together or a special initiatory religious ceremony such as a holy communion or even Bar Mitzvah.

PLANETARY REMEDIES

Because Vesta is not one of the seven original planets of classical and medieval astrology, there are no traditional remedies associated with her. And yet there can be no hesitation in advising the reader how to strengthen and increase her focused, centering energy in her or his life: light that fire. Whether a simple candle or a blazing fireplace, Vesta's presence in the world is always marked by a fire in the home.

The hearth fire is symbolic of another fire—the fire within. As we have seen, Vesta is one more manifestation of the kundalini or serpent power—as are Mercury, Venus, and Lilith. But with Vesta, the association with actual spiritual practice is much stronger. One of the best ways to build up the power of Vesta in the birth chart is to "raise the inner fire" through techniques of breathing and meditation. When one is attempting to "center oneself," it is Vesta's energy that emerges. Vesta is one of the few planets so benevolent and so helpful and she can almost always be safely strengthened, no matter what her actual position in the birth chart.

INVOCATION AND AWARENESS

Because Vesta was one of the deities most frequently invoked in both Greece and Rome, a modern-day invocation to her may be appropriate in many occasions. She was most often invoked at the evening meal and offerings to her were generous because of the protection people felt she gave. If one is truly looking for sanctuary, for a place to rest, for a place to lay down their weary bones, an invocation to Vesta is in order. If one requires focus and commitment to complete a particular task, Vesta will provide assistance.

As we have noted, images of Vesta are hard to come by. This was quite obvious recently during one of our Mythic Astrology seminars in Greece. Participants who strongly identified with the Vesta/Hestia archetype or who were striving to achieve it looked in the many souvenir shops that permeate the Plaka. There were images galore of Aphrodite and Athene, of Artemis and Hera and Demeter. But none were to be found of Hestia. How would they find an image that would embody those principles? One way is to create an altar. The altar itself reflects what Vesta is about. Her energies are unseen, but her presence is strongly felt. It is really quite simple to create an altar or another area in or around your home that could be construed as "sacred" space. Take as little or as much space as you need.

Occasionally, someone will say that they have no space in their home, that it is taken up by everybody else, or that they share their room with another and truly can't find a spot for themselves. If this is the case, then an invocation to Vesta is really needed, as she is the defining principle of giving one the space to center, focus, and find themselves. If you have just a small amount of personal space in your home (or office), even a simple corner of your desk or dresser can serve as a foundation for a candle or other objects that have particular meaning for you. The objects themselves are not important; it is the meaning of those objects to the seeker that is important.

---

1. Kirksey, Barbara, "Hestia: A Background of Psychological Focusing," in *Facing the Gods*, James Hillman, ed. (Dallas: Spring Publications, 1980).

2. Charles Boer, trans., "The Homeric Hymn to Hestia," in *The Homeric Hymns* (Dallas, TX: Spring Publications, 1979).

3. George, Demetra, with Douglas Bloch, *Asteroid Goddesses* (San Diego, CA: ACS Publications, 1986).

4. Schwartz, Jacob, Ph.D., *Asteroid Name Encyclopedia* (St. Paul, MN: Llewellyn Publications, 1995).

5. Gleadow, Rupert, *The Origin of the Zodiac* (New York: Castle Books, 1968).

CHAPTER 16

LILITH
DARK GODDESS OF THE NIGHT

ASTROLOGY AND MYTH

As we have seen in chapter 11, "An Introduction to the Asteroids," archetypes tend to emerge into our consciousness whenever we need them, and they usually appear somewhere in the sky as well. The three outer planets certainly manifested themselves in world consciousness as soon as they were discovered. We have noted how Pallas Athene—more than the other major asteroids—has become a powerful contemporary icon, and soon we shall see how Chiron is at work doing the same thing.

But let's not forget Lilith. Actually, Lilith won't let you forget her. If you try, she will haunt your dreams, drive you sexually crazy, and steal your soul. After all, she's the Queen of the Demons. And hey, she's proud of it! This Wild Woman from Hell is everywhere in pop culture. And she grows more powerful and manifests herself more clearly with each passing year. And as we shall see, that's a good thing.

Lilith's story does not appear in the Old Testament, but in other sacred texts of Judaism—occasionally in the Talmud and most notably in the Kabbalah, where her myth reaches its highest level of development.[1] We are told she was the first wife of Adam—but she was not merely a reconstituted piece of his rib. In some versions of the story it is said that she was created at the same time and from the same earth—in other words, she was created equal. Other versions claim that she was actually created first!

There is also a Kabbalistic legend that says that Lilith was not really created by that patriarchal old god Yahweh at all; instead, she arose from chaos as a pure primordial energy, created by the universe alone. Either way, the story goes that she demanded equality right from the start. When Adam demanded that she be his "helpmate" (i.e., slave), Lilith responded: "Why should I lie beneath you, when I am your equal since both of us were created from dust?" (We might remember that Juno told Jupiter the same thing.) In our contemporary society, one thing that becomes quite evident in the personality structure of women embodying the Lilith archetype is that she does not do well in subordinate situations of any kind. She must always be in control, and if threatened with submission, she will most likely bolt. Though the author of the Talmudic legend in which this quote appears probably intended it to demonstrate Lilith's dark side, contemporary women—who have raised the same question—will hear it as a battle cry of freedom.

According to author Laurence Gardner, no female ever achieved such fame in terms of a career as Lilith.[2] She was said to be incarnate as Abraham's Egyptian mistress Hagar, as Moses' wife, Zipporah, and as King Solomon's lover, the Queen of Sheba. She then became the queen-consort of her grandfather, Enlil. Like Anath (Ashtoreth), Isis, Kali, and other goddess figures, Lilith was a paradox, embodying both light and dark.

From the very outset of her career, Lilith was regarded as an unusually free spirit, and because of this she was dubbed by the male-dominated Hebrews as being demonic—the original *femme fatale*. Though she was strikingly beautiful, men were warned to fear her.

Almost every culture in the world has one or more female deities that represent the "dark" feminine. In Judeo-Christian lore, the honors go to Lilith. She has, however, been seen primarily as a sort of female demon or devil. Lilith has been the repository for everything a predominantly patriarchal society fears, denies, and represses concerning women. Her cultural ancestry has nothing to do with Greece and Rome and doesn't even originate in Judaism; rather, her origins extend back into Babylon and Sumer. Some have seen her as a handmaiden to the goddess Inanna (see the chapter on Venus).[3] In part of the Gilgamesh epic, she appears as the spirit inhabiting a willow tree—a tree with a dragon coiled at its base and a mythical bird nesting in its crown.

But to return to our story . . . for "getting uppity" with Adam, Lilith was banished into the night and was said to come haunting as a demon in her guise as a screeching night owl. (It is interesting to note that the owl is also Athene's totem. Athene carries the snake-encrusted Medusa on her shield—a figure similar to Lilith. But Athene served her father and the patriarchal ruling class of Greece. Lilith, on the other hand, refused, and went her own way. Lilith could almost be thought of as the dark, banished sister of Athene.)

Lilith fled Eden entirely and took up residence around the Red Sea (associated in Hebrew myth with all things dark and demonic). It is said that Yahweh sent messengers to demand her return, but Lilith rebelled against God himself, delivering a defiant "No" as her answer. Instead, she contented herself with a promiscuity so wild and absolute that she gave birth to at least a hundred demons every day. Even this extraordinary degree of sexual activity, however, could not satisfy her, for she was also thought to seduce mortal men in their sleep.[4] She is generally depicted as extremely beautiful (even though she does have the feet of an owl), and the Kabbalah assures us that she is a redhead.

It was also sometimes said that Lilith had borne children to Adam, and that she murdered them. (In Greek myth, there is a similar tale involving Medea, the sorceress.) Society has always had a hard time with women who reject the role of dutiful wife and mother, women who express their sexuality blatantly and freely such as Lilith did, and who refuse to "belong" to anyone, be it father, mother, spouse—and most especially their children. Greek myths of Uranus, Saturn, and Jupiter all featured fathers killing (swallowing, stuffing) their children. Here we have a mother doing likewise. Like every mythic figure of stature, the stories passed down about Lilith mushroomed into something big, something dark, and something to be fearful about. The fear and loathing that certain segments of society have toward women who choose abortion is an another example of this. (A horrific example of Lilith gone awry in the contemporary landscape is the current flock of abortion-clinic killers that have cropped up, along with the religious fundamentalists and politicians who turn the other cheek to these occurrences, because in their hearts and minds they also condone such actions. This has got to be Lilith at its most afflicted.)

In addition to her beginnings as the bride of Adam, Lilith has been called the bride of the dark angel Samael, and even of God himself. Ordinarily, the Kabbalah asserts that God's "bride" is the Shekinah—who may also be regarded as the feminine aspect of God. But occasionally, it is said, Lilith seduces even God and takes the Shekinah's place.

The notion of a "whore of the gutters" as a bride of God may seem truly bizarre to some, but it was a common metaphysical paradigm in the Hellenistic Near East (from whence the Kabbalah originated). The Gnostic teacher Simon Magus was said to have taken a woman from a brothel to be his consort, and to have worshipped her as an incarnation of Sophia, "the Wisdom of God." In fact, some of the "heretical" or "forbidden" Gnostic Gospels from the Nag Hammadi Library[5] strongly imply that the prostitute Mary Magdalene was the physical consort of Jesus of Nazareth.[6] (No wonder they were "forbidden"!)

The solution to these apparent paradoxes lies way back—all the way back in Lilith's Sumerian or Babylonian origins. We may remember that she was the spirit who inhabited a willow tree, dragon coiled at her feet and a mythic bird in her branches. This suggests that she is a "Tree of Life," for the archetype of the Tree of Life generally always includes a dragon and a bird as well. The Tree of Life, of course, is a cosmogram—a picture of the universe itself. It's no wonder that one version of Lilith's story claims that she was a pure, primordial creation of cosmic energy. Lilith *is* the cosmos!

But the cosmos is within as well as without. The Tree of Life is also a symbolic portrait of the human psycho-energetic system, the kundalini (as dragon) coiled at the base of the spinal column (the tree) and culminating in the crown chakra, symbolized by an eagle or other mythic bird. As the spirit within the tree, Lilith is the kundalini itself, and the kundalini is said to have its most natural correlate within the human body as sexual energy.

In Kabbalah, the Shekinah or feminine aspect of God is said to be equivalent to the Tree of Life, and she is also said to represents God's *energy*. Lilith and the Shekinah both serve as "Brides of God" because they both represent cosmic energy as embodied in the kundalini. But Lilith is most certainly the wilder, crazier, more ungovernable aspect of that energy. (Interestingly enough, some feminists equate Lilith symbolically with the lotus flower, and link this not only with the crown chakra but with female genitalia, thus incorporating the full spectrum of the kundalini. Lilith is also the lily, like her name—a flower of chastity and purity!)

Like Chiron, whose mythology and ephemera quickly filled volumes of astrologers' libraries, Lilith is a mythic archetype whose presence has permeated the astrological landscape. Though no *planet* has been named for her, there is not one but *three* orbiting bodies named Lilith! Asteroid researcher and astrologer Demetra George explains this by saying that the Goddess in general often manifests in triplicate.[7] Be this as it may, we have asteroid #1181 called Lilith, discovered on February 11, 1927, at 7° Leo;[8] a dark moon Lilith first introduced to us by Ivy Goldstein-Jacobson;[9] and a third figure called *lune noire,* or "black moon," that is very popular among astrologers in Europe, and especially among the French.[10] Because we have so many orbiting bodies named Lilith, it has been more difficult to obtain any meaningful statistical data about how she is working in a chart, although Jacobson's early work on

Lilith delved pretty deeply, as did Delphine Jay's work on the same body, the dark moon Lilith.[11] George's book *Mysteries of the Dark Moon* gives some great historical and mythological background of this material.

Lilith is currently experiencing a major rebirth among women, especially those who have adopted one of her primary philosophies—fleeing from submissive relationships. She has come to represent female defiance and strength. While she may have little in common with the intellectual feminism of the past decade or so, which was characterized primarily by the Pallas Athene archetype, she has become the virtual archetypal ruler of a younger, wilder, more sexually explicit generation that thrives on raves, "grrl" power, and general mayhem. A good example of this archetypal difference lies in attitudes regarding the issue of pornography. The Athene feminist wants to outlaw pornography altogether and may occasionally be willing to pass a whole series of repressive "blue laws" in order to do so—and in this sense it's no wonder that Pallas Athene is the patriarch's favorite daughter. The Lilith feminist, on the other hand, says: "Laws? What laws? Laws bite!" She dreams of chasing the men out of the pornography industry, taking it over for herself, and making a fortune out of her sexual fantasies.

Pop icon Madonna, who really has made a fortune portraying this sexually explicit, in-your-face, defiant archetype, has the black moon Lilith in her Second House conjunct her South Node and in direct opposition to the asteroid Lilith in her Eighth House and conjunct her North Node—the two houses most associated with sensuality, sexuality, and money. She has performed in corsets, pointed bras, and lingerie, and filled her songs with references to a variety of alternative sexual practices, including bondage and discipline. Courtney Love, who gained notoriety by striding across the stage in high heels, torn stockings, and a way-too-short dress screaming out lyrics of wild, unfocused rage, has the same black moon opposing her turbulent Mars-Venus conjunction in Gemini. It must surely have been Lilith who inspired her infamous (and physically dangerous) leaps off the stage and into an audience comprised of drunken, drooling men.

Considering that the most highly developed mythology involving Lilith is Kabbalistic, it is interesting to note that both Madonna and Courtney Love have both professed themselves, at one time or another, to be students of the Kabbalah! (The Goddess knows her own.)

A very popular musical festival that took place every year from 1996 to 1999 was called "Lilith Fair" by organizer Sarah McLachlan, primarily because it featured an all-female line-up of performers, breaking the pattern of predominantly male performers that are the norm of most large-scale rock concerts. It proved successful, playing to sold-out audiences throughout the U.S. and Canada.

So Lilith is alive and well, and she grows more powerful every day. She is the wildest of all Wild Women. When movie heroines Thelma and Louise blew up that eighteen-wheel gas tanker, it must have been Lilith who put them up to it. And when they made their final desperate leap into infinity, it must have been Lilith who enfolded them in her loving arms.

DREAMWORK AND ACTIVE IMAGINATION

Lilith quite often appears in the dream landscape, as she was said to rule the night. In fact, she is one of the few astrological archetypes in this book whose mythology is explicitly connected with the process of dreaming.

She is generally said to haunt men's dreams at night. There are numerous accounts in Hebrew literature of how she comes to men in their dreams, fornicating with them, producing nocturnal emissions. In this context she is portrayed as seductive, wanton, demonic, and sinful. Especially prone to her seductions are men who sleep alone. Her visitations are timed usually to the late waning moon, the time when the moon's light doesn't reach the earth. The moon is absent from view, thus allowing the "dark moon" energies to manifest. This dark moon period that occurs each month in Earth's lunar cycle is Lilith's special time.

It may be said that Lilith is perhaps the original archetype of that medieval folkloric figure called the *succubus*—the female demon who produces erotic dreams and thus steals men's souls. In times past, men connected their life force symbolically with semen and had a dread of "losing" any of it. Thus Lilith and her sisterhood of succubi were perceived as dangerous. Fortunately, most contemporary men have discovered that their real life force lies within them, and rather than fearing Lilith, they probably enjoy her dreamtime visitations.

Lest the ladies feel neglected in this Lilith Fair of erotic dreaming, we may remember that medieval folklore also warns against the *incubus*—the male equivalent of a succubus, and thus an erotic "demon" who visits women at night. In the Kabbalah, there are, in fact, a group of male "Lilins" who perform this function.

Many men and women have reported Madonna appearing in their dreams. As she has become a living archetype in our culture, it is no wonder that this is so. For the dreamer this can suggest many things. In the dreams of men, the meaning is painfully obvious and needs no further interpretation. For a woman it might be an inducement to act out repressed sexual feelings—perhaps by dressing more sexually, as in the type of lingerie Madonna made popular. Lilith may be urging the dreamer of either sex to enjoy some "forbidden fruit."

PLANETARY REMEDIES

Although Lilith is not one of the seven traditional planets, she sparked a host of planetary-type remedies nonetheless. All of these, however, were remedies *against* her. There is no historical record of anyone making an amulet or talisman to increase her strength!

During the first few centuries of the Christian era, Jewish families often painted or inscribed charms against Lilith on their food bowls and other crockery. In this context, Lilith was mostly feared as a stealer of children. Jewish mothers of the third and fourth centuries CE were prone to become nervous if a baby chortled or gurgled in its sleep, for it was believed that Lilith was playing with the child invisibly, causing it to laugh happily—just before she took its soul. Many deaths that would today be attributed to SIDS (Sudden Infant Death Syndrome) were in ancient times blamed upon Lilith.

So charms were written on the family's eating bowls. If you are feeling a bit too wild and crazy and want to put Lilith to rest—if you are a man who has always had a fatal attraction to "bad girls" or a woman feeling like she's about to become a "bad girl" herself—then try attaching an affirmation or positive statement to a bowl. You can write it down and tape it to the outside base of the bowl, or, if you are creating a long-term charm and feeling artistic, you can write it out in nice calligraphy. Always make a positive statement, such as: "My passions and my rebellious anger are now entirely under my control." For those who feel that they need more passion and more righteous anger, it goes without saying that you can make the same magic *for* Lilith as against her.

AWARENESS AND INVOCATION

As with all invocations to the Gods, this is one deity where the phrase "Be careful what you ask for" comes to mind. Bringing Lilith into your life means facing your own wildness, your primal rage, and the unbridled aspects of your sexual nature. If you are a man, bringing Lilith's archetype into your life may mean dealing with women who manifest such qualities.

However, there are situations in which the archetype of a strong woman with the courage to act on her own can be helpful. For instance, in situations where domestic violence, subjugation, or child abuse is occurring, Lilith can give you the courage to get up and walk away and not waste any time doing it. (The demons that were said to follow her may be symbolic of the guilt and fear people have when confronted with situations like this. They become plagued by these thoughts and blame themselves rather than their perpetrators.)

There are other reasons to allow Lilith into your life. Some men may actually find such wild and untamable women to be extremely stimulating company. And women need only visit the nearest university campus and ask some of the radical young Liliths how they feel about life to get a sense of her value, her power, and her passion.

Lilith takes no b.s.

And she takes no prisoners.

---

1. Stevens, Anthony, *Ariadne's Clue: A Guide to the Symbols of Humankind* (Princeton, NJ: Princeton University Press, 1999).

2. Gardner, Laurence, *Genesis of the Grail Kings* (Boston, MA: Element Books, 2000).

3. Bell, Robert E., *Women of Classical Mythology, A Biographical Dictionary* (Oxford University Press, 1993).

4. Starck, Marcia, and Gynne Stern, *The Dark Goddess: Dancing with the Shadow* (Freedom, CA: Crossing Press, 1993).

5. Robinson, James M., ed., *The Nag Hammadi Library* (San Francisco, CA: Harper, 1990).

6. There is a plethora of literature supporting this theory that refuses to be silenced, and which the public eagerly consumes, starting with the book *Holy Blood, Holy Grail* by Michael Baigent, Richard Leigh, and Henry Lincoln (New York: Dell Publishing, 1982); and more recently the phenomenon of Dan Brown's best-selling book *The Da Vinci Code* (New York: Doubleday, 2003).

7. George, Demetra, *Mysteries of the Dark Moon* (San Francisco, CA: Harper, 1992).
8. Schwartz, Jacob, *Asteroid Name Encyclopedia* (St. Paul, MN: Llewellyn Publications, 1995).
9. Goldstein-Jacobson, Ivy, *Dark Moon Lilith in Astrology* (Alhambra, CA: Frank Severy).
10. de Gravelaine, Joëlle, *Lilith: Der Schwartz Monde*, translation of the original French *Le Retoil de Lilith* (Wettswil, Switzerland: Edition Astro Data, 1990).
11. Jay, Delphine, *Interpreting Lilith* (Tempe, AZ: American Federation of Astrologers, 1981).

Part IV

THE PLANETS BEYOND

CHAPTER 17

JUPITER
KING OF THE GODS

ASTROLOGY AND MYTH

The largest planet in our solar system has always been the king. To the Babylonians, the planet we now call Jupiter was known as Marduk, or sometimes as Nibiru. The god Marduk was the king of the Babylonian pantheon. When all was chaos, confusion, and disorder, it was Marduk who went to battle for the sake of the gods, defeating the primal dragon Tiamat—symbol of "chaos and void"—and shaping her bones and body into the world, placing the very stars themselves upon their allotted courses. While each city in Mesopotamia may have had its own patron goddess or god, it was Marduk who always symbolized the king or leader of a given polity. In other words, it is Marduk who maintains cosmic order and keeps things running smoothly.

When Babylonian astrology made its way to Greece, Marduk was logically equated with the Greek god-king Zeus, who performed many of his same functions. The Greek word Zeus was equated with the Latin Jupiter, hence the present name of the planet. Most of its current symbolism corresponds to the Greek god Zeus.

Zeus' home and exalted place of worship was Mount Olympus in northern Greece from whence he ruled over the world, but his humble beginnings were associated with the island of Crete. First, we are told that he was taken to Crete as a child, to be hidden from the tyranny of his father, Cronus. There, on Mount Ida, he was raised by the goat-nymph Amalthea (sister of Pan). As he grew into adolescence and young adulthood, he assumed the form of a bull, and as such abducted a Phoenician princess named Europa to Crete. Europa then bore his offspring and hence became known as the mother of the European people.

Minoan Crete reached its apex during the Age of Taurus, and in that land the image of the bull appears everywhere you look—in vases, sculpture, and frescoes. The Minoan civilization flourished a thousand years before classical Greece, and then fell—apparently to an invasion from the Greek mainland. The tale is preserved in the myth of the young Athenian lads who were regularly sent to King Minos, Crete's ruler, to be sacrificed to the bull-headed monster known as the minotaur. The Athenian hero Theseus put an end to this by slaying the minotaur, signifying a shift of political power from the island of Crete to the mainland of Greece.

As a son of Cronus, Zeus' lineage was royal and immortal. But like any young warrior prince, Zeus had to earn his status as hero and chief commander of the gods. He raised a rebellion against his father, and by defeating Cronus he carved out his own destiny, ensuring wealth, power, and position, and installing himself as the new sovereign. He and his brothers drew lots to determine the rulership of the three worlds. Zeus received the heavenly realm, while Hades and Poseidon were given the underworld and the oceanic realm, respectively. This is not unlike the three gods of Babylon—Anu, Enki, and Enlil—who divided the three regions of the sky into domains north, south, and right along the center of the ecliptic.

Like Marduk before him, Zeus had to establish order in the universe by defeating a primal dragon, symbol of chaos. Though the myth is seldom heard nowadays, it is said that Zeus fought with and ultimately destroyed a great dragon by the name of Typhon. Thus he, like his Babylonian predecessor, put the cosmos in order.

Zeus chose for his mate the goddess Hera, who was also his sister (see the chapter on Juno). Transforming himself into the form of a lovely, sweet-talking cuckoo bird, he seduced the goddess and made her his bride. They enjoyed 300 years of connubial bliss—certainly the longest honeymoon on record. Then matters of state and the rulership of both gods and men required his attention on Mount Olympus. Once engaged in his giant office in the sky, Zeus began interfering with many of the affairs of earthlings below. Many of these involved shape-shifting into one disguise or another in order to impregnate healthy, beautiful young women. There was little discrimination here—some were married, some were not; some were mortals, others were immortals. If a beautiful woman caught his eye, he was typically there in no time flat.

Though looking and acting like a much more benevolent ruler than Cronus, once in power Zeus took advantage of every opportunity that availed itself to him, carrying out acts that would sometimes wind up looking just like his father's. One such act was to swallow his own unborn child (along with her pregnant mother), just as his siblings had been swallowed by their own father. This peculiar little act of tyranny resulted in the birth of his most favored child, Athene.

There is no doubt that Zeus represents a figure of great power, size, and stature. One can sense this awesome presence at the Temple of Olympian Zeus inside the city limits of Athens. Though only a few pillars remain and though the temple is set significantly closer to the bottom of the hill while

Athene's temple is at the top, Zeus' special place still commands a mighty presence. There is no question that all looked to him as subjects would look to their king or president, to resolve matters of state, to offer protection, and to hold the moral and philosophical laws of the land intact.

Although Zeus was supreme and his word was final, there were limits to his authority. One such limit was the power vested in the Fates and in the underworld realm of Hades. Decisions about the life and death of all beings—even those favored by the gods—were governed by the Fates, who could even supercede the decrees of Zeus. Marriage to Hera also posed problems of limitation for Zeus. They were constantly involved in quarrels and disagreements, not just about his numerous amorous adventures with other women, but also about matters of state—enough so as to cause him a constant headache.

Like Zeus, who lived on the highest mountaintop (Mount Olympus), Jupiterians can often be found living in beautiful and stately hilltop homes that dot the landscape in the most picturesque areas of town. As Zeus' royal lineage would imply, Jupiterians typically belong to a class of wealth and privilege. Even those whose family fortunes have been lost, or those who have lost their title, become disinherited (usually through making the wrong marriage or career choice), or been exiled from the family or the social order, will still possess a distinctly Jupiterian carriage. Even bankrupt Jupiterians live their lives in a very high style, waiting to grasp the next opportunity for gain that waits around each corner. There is an aura around the Jupiterian that suggests to others "this person is important" or "this person can help me in some way" or "this person will protect me." The Jupiterian is attracted to the fields of law, economics, politics, speculation, development, and religion. But whatever field they're in, the instinctive motivation is to rise to the top. Jupiterians are terrible at being underlings or following directions from others—humility is practically unheard of.

Like Zeus, Jupiterians show their disapproval when things don't go their way. Zeus himself threw thunderbolts. The more contemporary Jupiterian may just throw fits or make sudden decisions that will adversely affect the lives of others, rippling out much further afield than Jupiter realizes. In creating their world just as they visualize it, Jupiter's favored folk often don't pay attention to the small details in front of them (including people, businesses, or landscapes that might get in the way). Jupiter gazes from afar, creating the perfect world. His is the broad vision; it needs Saturn to take care of the details. Jupiter has no use for details—his signs, Sagittarius and Pisces, are in fact notorious for their "spaced out" lack of attention to practicalities. But if Saturn sometimes can't see the forest for the trees, Jupiter can envision a most magnificent forest.

Some bits and pieces of this portrait of Jupiter may look a bit more ruthless than one would generally think, but we have to remember that all the archetypes can and do display shadowy sides of themselves. Jupiter's shadow is greed and arrogance. Jupiter's appetites are large. The dark side of many leaders—those who hold special positions of privilege and power, whether political or religious—often involves the greedy amassing of wealth for personal gain, no matter what the cost, be it in the human, animal, plant, or mineral kingdom. No wonder Zeus incurred the wrath of goddesses like Hera and Gaia when he committed inappropriate acts. But Hera and Zeus (as mentioned in the Juno section) are the perfect partnership to work out polarity. Zeus' outrageousness at times attracted an outrageous response that only a Hera could provide.

Sometimes the various deities of Greece were associated with particular totem animals or trees, like Aphrodite with the dove or Apollo with the laurel. Zeus' tree was the oak. This "king" of the old European woodlands was regarded as the stateliest and most powerful of trees. In fact, one of the present authors has heard traditional East European folk healers speak of the oak and its magical powers as if it were a mountain rather than a tree.

Zeus had his own oracle, based upon the oak tree. Though not quite as renowned in legend and literature as the Oracle of Delphi, the Oracle of Dodona in northern Greece was deeply reverenced among the people of ancient Greece. There was a grove of oaks there, and the oracular priests listened for the voice of Zeus in the sound of wind rustling through the oak leaves.

We should not be surprised to find such deeply religious sentiments attached to the big, blustery god king, for in ancient Greek or Hellenistic astrology, Zeus was in fact the planet of religion. Both of Jupiter's signs, Sagittarius and Pisces, have a reputation for sparking spiritual interests in those who have a nice helping of these mutable mystics in their charts. The old Hellenistic astrologers like Paul of Alexandria or Vettius Valens would have read the ups and downs of a client's spiritual life primarily from a consideration of

Jupiter's position in the horoscope.[1] But before you look to Jupiter for an interest in Eastern meditation or alternative religions, let it be remembered that Jupiter's place in the chart usually symbolized the "official" or "state" religion. Jupiter was concerned with maintaining the order of things, not with breaking it. In our own society, a strong, well-placed Jupiter is more likely to make a minister than a guru, although a stressed or challenging position of Jupiter may indeed lead an individual into a deeply personal spiritual quest—if only because her or his relationship with conventional religion is "challenged" by Jupiter.

Let us not leave the impression that such serious concerns as religious and political leadership have left Jupiter somber and grim—far from it. One of his nicknames is *Jove* (based on the Latin *Jupiter*), and words such as *joyous* and *jovial* are derived from his name. There is a bright, good-hearted, and eternally optimistic spirit to the true Jupiterian—a spirit that encourages laughter and delight in even the most serious of undertakings. And astrologically, Jupiter is thought of as the helper, the benevolent one who bestows good graces upon the masses each time it returns to a key position in the chart.

It is no wonder, then, that so many astrological clients would like to see more of Jupiter and less of Saturn or Pluto. In fact, one of the most common questions among people consulting astrologers is "When is Jupiter going to be strong in my chart?"

It may be that a Jupiter transit comes along, and you're wondering why you haven't been showered with gold quite yet. If so, take stock of current inventory. What you will typically find during a Jupiter transit is that you are enjoying Jupiter's excesses in a certain area of your life (the part of life ruled by Jupiter in your chart). Jupiter does things in a big way. Doors open, travel opportunities avail themselves, Jupiterian-type people enter your life. But the best way to enjoy a Jupiter transit is to acknowledge the blessings and gifts you already possess and share the abundance with others. This automatically opens you up to receiving more.

It's no wonder that Jupiter is our largest planet and was named for the grandest of the gods. On a smaller scale, Jupiter has its own planetary system going for it, with its enormous body of orbiting moons. Jupiter moves around the Sun in a twelve-year orbital pattern. Thus every year it will move through one complete sign of the zodiac, and at such a time it will touch whatever planets occupy that sign in a most dramatic way. Jupiter is given rulership over Sagittarius (modern), Pisces (traditional), and Leo (Olympian), and is exalted in Cancer. Two of these signs are fire signs and two are water signs. It would seem that Jupiter's power in a fire sign relates directly to the qualities of heroism, fearlessness, adventure, leadership, and taking command of situations that life presents (such as overthrowing his father's tyranny—something that no one else could do). There is a success with risk-taking and venturing into unknown avenues when Jupiter is dignified in these signs. Its powerful presence in water signs is directly related to the compassionate nature that is required in any leader who ultimately chooses first to protect family and home (exaltation in Cancer) and have compassion for others (rulership in Pisces).

In Hellenistic and medieval astrology, certain planets were said to "rejoice" in certain houses. Jupiter rejoices in the Eleventh House. It is here that he can best exercise his political and social aspirations, and also express his "jovial" nature with friends and other acquaintances. When Jupiter is pleasantly balanced in our own nature, we are in command of our lives, and thus are given opportunities to command others. It is the wise use of that position, the compassionate use of that power, that brings out the best possible Jupiter in humanity.

DREAMWORK AND ACTIVE IMAGINATION

If you dream about the president, the prime minister, the queen, or the king, you can be sure it's a Jupiterian dream. Even a dream involving your guru—whether that should happen to be the Pope, a cardinal or bishop, a rabbi, or a minister—falls under Jupiter's domain. But if the person is unrecognized and happens to be driving through your dream landscape, how will you recognize him or her? The bad-ass wardrobe might characterize Pluto riding up on his motorcycle, but Jupiter will be decked out in style, tailored and well coiffed, wearing only the chicest labels. He will probably be driving a Rolls, Mercedes, or Lexus—but let's not forget SUVs, which, because of their size, can allow the driver to gaze down from a lofty height upon the lesser world below. Garments and vestments of taste and style, like the velvety purple robes of Zeus and Hera, may appear, signifying command of their world. Zeus/Jupiter is sometimes equated with the Emperor card in the Tarot.

Where are you, the dreamer, in all of this? Are you part of this world, or are you gazing into it from outside looking in, like Alice? The answers to these questions can tell you a great deal about your attitude towards yourself—whether you feel empowered or powerless, in control or out of control.

Typically Jupiterian settings can be stately palaces, large homes on hills, banquet halls, gatherings, or the "in" party, "in" restaurant, or social event where all the celebrities and important people gather. One dreamer related that she showed up at a trendy restaurant that was totally booked, where not a table would be available all night. But just as she was leaving, the chef/owner spotted her, recognized her, and said, "I'm holding a table for two for you," and quickly ushered her in. Needless to say, the dreamer was on the verge of a major success or at the very least an upswing in her sense of well-being.

The eagle is Zeus' bird. Though huge in size, its aerodynamic design is expertly crafted, allowing for smooth and graceful flight. The eagle spots things from a distance and has such precision, focus, and timing that it can swoop down and capture whatever it desires in a flash. The eagle may be flying you through your dream landscape, encouraging expansion and exploration.

In reading one dreamer's story recently, many of the words she used stood out as markedly Jupiterian. First she wrote, "I had two *big* dreams this morning." The setting was a *giant* stadium where a World Series game was being played. In the dream that immediately followed were phrases like "large church," "giant plaza," "people wearing huge buttons," "we watched from upstairs balconies and verandas," "a large crowd of people," and "a large auditorium." Every other sentence has a "big" Jupiterian reference to it. The World Series is the biggest game of the season, with the top players displaying their talents for the largest sums of money involved and the largest audiences watching the game—here is Jupiter.

In another dream, the visionary, prophetic quality of Zeus emerges, as it did for the ancients in the Oracle of Dodona. Homer calls Zeus "cloud-gatherer," as his home in Mt. Olympus was often shrouded by clouds. He can see out, but others can't see in. A woman dreamed that she was driving through the beautiful red-rock Indian country of the American Southwest when out of the clouds appeared a woman's face. The "cloud woman" looked like a Native American elder. She spoke twice, both times instructing the dreamer to phone her old friend James. (E.T., phone home!) When the woman awoke, she wrote down as much as she could remember from the dream, but her comments were: "I haven't seen that person in over twenty years. I wonder why I dreamed that this woman told me to phone him. I don't even know how to contact him or where he lives." In a few days, the woman remembered a mutual friend who had suddenly started e-mailing her a few months earlier. She e-mailed the friend, asking for James' e-mail address or phone number, and they connected within a few days. Their connection was instant and permanent. Within two months they were happily cohabitating as a couple, a circumstance that changed both their lives dramatically. The dreamer followed up on her dream, tuning in to the woman in the clouds and recognizing her as a spirit guide.

Listen to the voices from the sky. Is there a message of something big waiting around the corner?

PLANETARY REMEDIES

Most people want more Jupiter in their lives rather than less. After all, Jupiter symbolizes prosperity and abundance, and few of us would choose to be without these things.

In order to increase the power of Jupiter in your life, try something gold. After all, it is the king who receives all the golden tribute, and gold naturally pertains to Jupiter as much as it does to Apollo. In old Hellenistic lists of places associated with each planet, Jupiter is given rulership over "treasuries" and "treasure houses"—the places where all the gold is kept. (These days, we would say that Jupiter rules banks.)

In terms of gemstones, a yellow sapphire, yellow topaz, or large citrine works very well, especially if it is set in gold. If it's a ring, wear it on your index finger. There is a correlation between planets and fingers in traditional palmistry, and Jupiter corresponds to the index finger. You can always garb yourself in saffron—especially if you want to be your own guru! (And what a very Jupiterian thing to do!) Royal purple is another good color to arouse the energy of the "jovial" planet.

Marsilio Ficino was a great proponent of the idea that each planet has its special kind of music, and that we can effectively bring that planet's energy into our lives by listening to its music. For Jupiter, Ficino recommended powerful, stately, and majestic music. A good example of Jupiterian music—in fact, any planetary style of music—may be found in Gustav Holst's orchestral suite *The Planets*. The suite's tone poem "Jupiter: The Bringer of Jollity" is by turns boisterous, jovial, celebratory, and stately. Holst was in fact using the astrological meanings of the planets for his piece, and one can gain a fundamental idea of what each piece of planetary music should sound like by listening to him.

And make sure that your next home has a big oak tree growing in the yard.

INVOCATION AND AWARENESS

It is easy to be aware of Jupiter in our lives. Since his energy is much sought after, his presence is everywhere. When the movies depict wealthy and powerful individuals living in stately mansions, they are playing upon Jupiterian themes. The banker, architect, or CEO who lives above your local golf course is a Jupiterian too. The Western world in general, and the United States in particular, has a love affair with Jupiter. Bigger is better! Of course this isn't always true. The building so tall that it obscures the local landscape and falls out of harmony with nature is an example of Jupiterian excess. If you should happen to go to a party, become overly lively and "jovial," hoisting a glass of wine as Jupiter used to raise his golden goblets, then the other partygoers might see you as a veritable Jove—but the results of your Jupiterian excesses might make you feel like Saturn the next morning.

Whether you invoke Jupiter by using some of the magical planetary remedies listed here, or whether you simply choose to maintain respectful awareness of the Jupiterian grandeur around you, loving and cherishing prosperity, abundance, and success, it is favorable to bring in Jupiterian energy for almost every purpose. There is, however, an old Greek dictum that applies here: "Everything in moderation." Even prosperity or expansion has its limits. If a balloon expands too far, it bursts. Be abundant, but learn the Saturnian wisdom of knowing how to limit Jupiter's exuberant expansiveness.

---

1. Greenbaum, Dorian, trans., *Late Classical Astrology: Paulus Alexandrinus and Olympiodorus* (Reston, VA: ARHAT, 2001); and Vettius Valens, *The Anthology*, trans. by R. Schmidt, 3 vols. (Berkeley Springs, WV: Golden Hind Press, 1994).

CHAPTER 18

SATURN
LORD OF TIME

ASTROLOGY AND MYTH

If Jupiter expands, Saturn contracts, and in almost all ways, the two constitute a necessary and natural polarity to one another. In Greek, Saturn was known as Cronus—named for the god of time. Time's slow, inexorable march is precisely what we see when we examine the night sky, for Saturn is the most distant planet visible to the naked eye, and hence the slowest in motion.

The Babylonian name for the planet was Ninib, another name for the ancient Sumerian god Ninurta. In very early times, Ninurta was regarded as a king of the gods and a powerful dragon-slayer. However, he was replaced in the hearts and minds of the Mesopotamian people by Marduk, a "younger" god and another dragon-slayer, associated with the planet Jupiter. Ninurta, or more properly Ninib, survived as a god of agriculture, a kind of celestial magistrate over fields and their boundaries—and, by extension, the boundaries and limits of consciousness that are suggested by Saturn's position as the visible limit of the solar system. He also governed the irrigation technology that helped move ancient Mesopotamia along the road to achievement, and that made the fields prosper.

When astrology made its way to Greece, Cronus or Saturn was the logical magical correspondence for old Ninib. Saturn (to use his Roman name) was an ancient king of the gods who had been replaced by his son Zeus or Jupiter (the Babylonian Marduk). And since he was said to have ruled over the archaic "Golden Age" of humankind, when the earth bore abundant fruit and everyone had enough to eat, his status as an agricultural deity matched that of Ninib as well. But Saturn had come by his exalted status through patricide. Urged on by his mother, Gaia, he had lain in wait for his father Uranus, the Primordial Sky, the earliest god-king and something of a tyrant. With a sickle, he tore apart his father's genitals and thus brought his reign to an end. Saturn succeeded him.

Let us note that Saturn killed his father at the behest of his mother. The Sun and Moon are, as we have seen, the archetypal father and mother pair in the sky. Before the discovery of the outer planets, it was Saturn who ruled the two signs (Capricorn and Aquarius) that stand opposite the signs of the Moon and Sun (Cancer and Leo). In a horoscope, any contact between Saturn and either the Sun or Moon usually shows deep-seated and difficult parental issues.

Like Uranus before him, Saturn eventually became tyrannical. Afraid that his own children might destroy him even as he had destroyed his own father, Saturn devoured each of his children as quickly as their mother Rhea could give birth to them, and the Golden Age rapidly became an age of darkness. But Rhea substituted a stone for Jupiter or Zeus, the youngest, who secretly grew to manhood, retrieved his siblings from their father's belly, and started a war for dominion over the universe. Jupiter, of course, was the winner, and Saturn was banished to Tartarus, a deep prison at the boundaries of the cosmos.

It is in his aspect as a god of boundaries and limits and in his archetypal role as "Father Time that Saturn, and the planet that bears his name, has had the greatest influence upon Western astrology. In fact, our picture of Father Time is based directly on the archetype of Saturn. He is an old man, as befits the most ancient king of the gods. He carries a sickle, and we have already seen how Saturn employed that agricultural instrument. Of course he also carries an hourglass, the symbol of time itself. Saturn's Greek name, Cronus, is linked to our word *chronology*, which refers to the passage of time. Other words stemming from this root are *chronometer* and *chronic*, as in chronic conditions of life. In medical astrology Saturn has always been associated with the teeth, the bones (especially the skeletal system), hair, skin, and nails. What happens when we age? The most visible signs of human aging show up in these Saturnian parts of the body. The hair and teeth begin to fall out, the skin and bones and nails become dry and brittle, and the skeleton begins to become hunched. Osteoporosis, a common problem for aging women, deals with bone loss, and the best remedy is calcium—Saturn's mineral. Thus, as we age, we may reach our golden years, Saturn's period, a time when we can put aside the daily responsibilities to enjoy retirement; but Saturn being what it is, we are also asked to stay fully vigilant of those bodily ailments and conditions so that we may be around to enjoy it!

Because we generally think of the planet Saturn as a symbol of delays (slowness of time), old age (passage of time), and inner difficulties (the boundaries of consciousness), many people find Saturn to be one of their most challenging planets, and its transits tend to indicate periods of difficulty. But for those who have a positive Saturn in their charts, or who simply make the effort to get friendly with Saturn, the planet may play an entirely different role. It may help us to achieve success in fields such as engineering or agriculture (reflecting Ninib's original status as a god of agriculture and irrigation technology). It may also simply help us to accept our boundaries and limitations in life, and as such it may truly become the planet of the Golden Age. Those who are able to deal gracefully with the myriad delays and annoyances of daily life often have a kind of peace and wisdom about them—they are tranquil, unruffled, and calm. This is the peace of Saturn, and it is a most valuable asset for anyone to have psychologically.

There is another important archetype that has been associated with Saturn since very early times, and this is Pan. Let us remember that Saturn rules Capricorn, and the "goat" of that constellation is Amalthea, the nanny goat who nurtured the god Pan. Many of us are not aware of it, but Pan was one of the most important deities of ancient Greece. His name means simply "all," and he is the All Father, the primordial god of earth—another symbolic link with the Saturn archetype. We tend to think of Saturn as a cold and repressive planet, so we may have some trouble associating him in our minds with Pan, who roams through the forests with penis erect, drunk and lascivious, frolicking with nymphs and piping his way through the wild. Surely this cannot be Saturn? But let us remember that the concept of Saturn as a "repressive" or "cold" planet is a fairly recent psychological concept. In medieval astrology the planet Saturn did indeed have a certain cold or detached aspect—mostly associated with the sign Aquarius, which was ruled by Saturn before the discovery of Uranus. But medieval astrologers also associated Saturn with all kinds of lechery and lasciviousness (as do contemporary Vedic astrologers). The wildest bacchanal of ancient times was the festival of the Saturnalia, where servants became masters and all moral boundaries were set aside.

But if Pan is the wild god of the earth, he may also be the god of our nightmares and phobias. Stories abound throughout Greek mythology of individuals who were frightened in the wilderness by the terrible roar that Pan often gave forth (arbitrarily and for no good reason). This induced in them a state of "panic," which is the same word. So anxiety attacks and panic attacks tend to fall under the rulership of Saturn astrologically.

Saturn's astrological transits often show our success or failure in obtaining that kind of serenity or maturity. When you reach the age of twenty-eight or twenty-nine, Saturn will return to the zodiacal position it occupied at the time of your birth; this is the dreaded Saturn Return that astrologers talk about, but it need not be dreadful. It simply means that the archetypal meanings of Saturn—maturity, boundaries, limitations, practicality—will impinge upon your life powerfully at this time. Your personal response to these themes may be turbulent and stressful, or it may be fairly easy. The events of your life at this time will give you a fair idea as to whether you are dealing with Saturn properly or not. Of course, you may also study your dreams for "inner" information about how Saturn is working in your life; watch for some of the dream images listed below while you are in the midst of your Saturn Return.

There is, of course, a second Saturn Return, which occurs when we are in our late fifties. For many people, this is a much more enjoyable Return than the first. During the first Saturn Return at age twenty-nine or thirty, the individual is very aware of the ticking clock, and he or she knows that it is time to get on with one's work. The internal timepiece (Saturn) is pressuring one to move into life. Saturn likes productivity and abhors stagnation or procrastination. For many women, this is a time when the biological clock ticks very loudly, as they have also had their first Lunar Return just previous to this. But at sixty comes a Jupiter Return (which recurs every twelve years). So the second Saturn Return is crowned by the fifth Jupiter Return of life, and a real feeling of inner satisfaction and accomplishment may be present during this time if one has truly responded to the needs of her or his personal Saturn. Because both planets symbolize fathering in some ways, it is a time when many begin to truly enjoy the parenting process, that is, by way of grandchildren.

There is another Saturn transit that is considered particularly important in India, and this is the transit of Saturn over the natal Moon. Rather than being geared to specific ages, this transit is dependent upon the angular relationship existing between Saturn and the Moon in your birth chart; a person whose Moon is in a waxing square to Saturn will experience this transit at the approximate age of twenty-one, then again at forty-nine or fifty, while someone with Saturn and the Moon in opposition will experience the same transit at the age of fourteen and then again in his or her early forties. This transit is important for several reasons. First of all, there is an inner relationship between Saturn and the Moon based on the number twenty-eight: the Moon takes twenty-eight days to circle the zodiac, while Saturn takes twenty-eight years. Astrologers who use secondary progressions will of course be aware that the progressed Moon likewise circles the chart in twenty-eight years; therefore Saturn and the Moon are always involved in interpenetrating cycles with each other, the microcosm and the macrocosm.

The Moon is symbolic of everything that nurtures us in our lives, whether it be our home space, our actual mother, or our state of mind. Saturn is at odds with the Moon in many ways (their signs, Cancer and Capricorn, oppose each other), but because of their cyclical similarity and because they rule the parental houses, the Fourth House and the Tenth House, the Moon and Saturn are alike in many ways. When there is a Moon-Saturn aspect in an individual chart, it is important to balance this natural polarity. Typically, such individuals feel a lack of nourishment, either physically or emotionally, from their early environment, creating a situation wherein they must provide this nourishment themselves, even as they are attempting to build gigantic structures around them to protect themselves from further pain. One of the best ways to reverse this pattern is for them to become parents themselves and provide for their own children the love, care, and nourishment that was lacking in their own early development.

DREAMWORK AND ACTIVE IMAGINATION

In dreams or imaginal work, Saturn typically appears as an old man. Whether or not he is a wise old man or a total pest will depend upon your relationship with Saturn at the time.

Because Saturn is a challenging or "difficult" planet, we may often experience his archetype in terms of our own Shadow. In Jungian psychology, the archetype of the Shadow is everything we would prefer not to acknowledge about ourselves. Because we cannot acknowledge it, we tend to "project" it upon others. For example, the soft-spoken liberal who absolutely cannot tolerate fundamentalists probably has a very zealous and authoritarian side to his own nature, one that he doesn't even recognize. He is likely to dream of such individuals persecuting him, and such a dream is a wake-up call for him to acknowledge that aspect of himself. In an earlier chapter (Venus), we gave the example of the faithful housewife who suddenly begins to dream of "bad girls." In this example, Venus is the planet that carries the woman's Shadow (the Shadow is almost invariably of the same sex as the dreamer). But for many or perhaps most of us, it will be Saturn who most often plays the Shadow role.

Saturn is the cranky old man who refuses to be reasonable. He may be senile, dour, limping, or lame. Even if he does not appear as an elderly person, he is still likely to be stern and authoritarian—look for him wearing some sort of uniform, like a soldier or policeman (or even a termite exterminator, since Saturn rules dirt and infestations). Look for him in old or dirty surroundings, like a ramshackle house or garbage dump. In ancient and medieval astrology, Saturn was associated with toilets and bathrooms, and he still may be, although sometimes these themes may signify Pluto rather than Saturn.

It is not uncommon for ailments related to Saturn's medical correspondences to show up in dreams. People with chronic back problems, for instance, may be individuals who have taken on too much responsibility and don't feel any reciprocal support from the others they are caring for. Many people report of dreaming of their teeth or hair falling out, or some strange growth on their skin. These dreams could well be warnings that the Saturn factor in their lives is out of balance.

A very common occurrence in people's dreams is the idea of Saturn as the Lord of Time. If one dreams of clocks, watches, or even the idea of racing against time, such as rushing to the plane, train, or boat and just missing it, one may not be managing one's time very well. If, on the other hand, a dream concerns the dreamer receiving a new watch, perhaps a beautiful gold watch or some other decorative time piece, it may suggest that one is working with time (Saturn) quite well and also perhaps quite creatively and beautifully.

Finally, Saturn really may appear to you as the Wise Old Man. In this sense, he will resemble the "old Mercury" we mentioned in that chapter—the wandering sage or magician or the village elder—an image rather like the magician Merlin (whom we have mentioned previously). This would definitely be an example of old Mercury and Saturn coming together in a most positive way. Such an appearance, however, is rare, and signifies that you have stretched your consciousness to its limits and then taken a quantum leap beyond. Artemidorus tells us that Saturn or Cronus, like the other Titans, is associated in Greek cosmology with the outer limits of the world sphere, the very boundaries of the cosmos. (This, of course, fits with Saturn's role as the most distant planet in our solar system that may be seen with the naked eye.)

Mythologically, we should remember that Saturn and his fellow Titans were imprisoned in a place called Tartarus, which was indeed perceived as a place beyond the "boundaries" of the world. Therefore, says Artemidorus, Saturn is a good deity to dream about only if you are a philosopher, for the minds of philosophers journey to the very boundaries of the cosmos. For other people, a dream of Saturn is generally a troublesome one. This is another way of saying that for most of us, Saturn represents our Shadow side and our deepest challenges, while for those who have done their inner work and achieved a measure of spiritual maturity, Saturn may well become an archetype of wisdom.

PLANETARY REMEDIES

As mentioned previously, many so-called planetary remedies are simply methods for *increasing* the energy and power of the planet involved. This is something we may wish to think about twice in regard to Saturn—as you can plainly see, his influence over our lives tends to be very strong naturally, and we should be cautious about giving him even more strength. One of the authors has a friend who spent some years in India with the Peace Corps—he was puzzled and surprised to discover that all the villagers were apprehensive and uncomfortable with his beautiful blue sapphire ring. He remained there for a couple of years without ever learning what it was that made people so nervous about his ring.

The answer, of course, is that a blue sapphire is a Saturn stone. The villagers naturally assumed that his ring would increase the power of Saturn over his life—and might thereby also shed its questionable influence over the projects he was working on for them. A Saturn stone is only recommended for those who genuinely like Saturn, and who have a very positive Saturn in the birth chart. For most of us, the best Saturn "remedy" is simply hard work. In fact, there are a number of astrologers, both in India and in the West, who would question the notion that Saturn is in any way amenable to stones, mantras, talismans, or whatever. Saturn tends to resist the "quick fix"—as the Lord of Time, he has very little tolerance for anything that is easy and quick. In general, the best way to deal with a Saturn problem is to face it head on. Roll up your shirt sleeves, put on your working gloves, and get down to business.

There are, however, a few things that we can do to make the work go more smoothly. In the European alchemical tradition, Saturn represents the *nigredo*, or "blackening"—the dark, sad, and difficult phase of alchemy that marks the beginning of the work. In many alchemical works, this phase—and, by extension, Saturn—is symbolized by a crow or raven (a black bird). During difficult Saturn transits, many people in India purposely put out food for the ravens and crows as a way of honoring Saturn.

Gardening is generally associated with the Moon because it has to do with nurturing and growing things, but Saturn was the god of agriculture, so there is also a Saturn connection here. The plants that grow, and that you tend so carefully, may be ruled by the Moon, but the earth in which they are rooted is ruled by Saturn, and the brick borders or garden stones you lay out are the province of the old Babylonian Saturn, Ninib, god of agricultural boundaries. As already noted, some of the most difficult Saturn problems are those that involve the Moon-Saturn relationship. Whether this relationship shows up in your horoscope natally, by progression, or by transit, gardening is a good way to deal with Moon-Saturn issues. Building any kind of structure comes under the domain of Saturn, so putting one's energy into architecture and construction is a great way to work with Saturn as well. Remember, Saturn likes the world of form, and it honors us most when it can see our accomplishments in terms of tangible results.

As archetypal psychologist James Hillman has pointed out, panic attacks are associated with the god Pan, and usually indicate that we are out of balance with our own "wild" side, or out of touch with nature and the earth.[1] The best remedy for panic attacks, therefore, is time spent in the wilderness, and the reclaiming of our own inner wildness.

INVOCATION AND AWARENESS

Very few of us would care to invoke Saturn into our lives—although the authors have encountered a few individuals who were so "ungrounded" that they actually *needed* Saturn's help! For most of us, however, Saturn is already an overpowering influence upon our daily affairs, and one that we would rather mitigate than enhance.

Nor do we need to practice awareness of Saturn, for we are all too aware of his presence! Every time the astrological student encounters a leaky roof that needs to be repaired, a long official document that needs to be filled out, or even a long, slow line at the bank, she or he becomes abundantly "aware" of Saturn's presence.

But we may do well to make ourselves aware of Saturn's positive influence in our lives, which is a little bit harder to do but infinitely more rewarding. Whenever you can congratulate yourself on a job well done, give a little thanks to Saturn as the taskmaster. Whenever you gaze upon carefully laid-out fields growing in abundance, remember Saturn's status as the king of the agricultural Golden Age. And whenever you meet a truly wise and wonderful elder in her or his own "golden age," remember that Saturn governs the wisdom and inner grace of maturity and aging.

---

1. Hillman, James, *Pan and the Nightmare* (New York: Spring Publications, 1972).

(Aesculapius)

CHAPTER 19

CHIRON
TEACHER AND HEALER

ASTROLOGY AND MYTH

Chiron skirts the edges of our definitions. Is it a small planet or something called a "planetoid"? Should we perhaps regard it as an asteroid? Or is it more properly the remains of a burned-out comet? Chiron, discovered in 1977, orbits midway between Saturn and Uranus. And just as Chiron straddles the boundaries of astronomical definitions, he moderates between the two opposing forces symbolized by these planets.

The Chiron of Greek mythology was an enlightened teacher and healer of the centaur race of beings. The centaurs were a crude mixture of animal (horse) and human, and because of their horse-like animal energy, they generally had a reputation for raucous, rousing behavior. Chiron, their leader and sage, rose above the others. He was a son of old Cronus, the ancient god-king, known to us as the planet Saturn. Cronus chased a nymph by the name of Philyra, and they went through many animal transformations during the chase. He was in the form of a horse when he caught her, and thus their son Chiron came into the world half human and half horse, a member of the centaurs. He stood halfway between the dark and earthy world symbolized by animal consciousness and the reasoning, logical world of human thought.

The centaurs of myth lived outdoors, on the slopes of Mt. Pelion in northern Greece. They roamed through the forests and fields there, wild and free. Chiron was both their king and their sage. Like a primitive, he dwelt in a cave. But the philosophical and mystical thoughts that poured out of him in his mountain retreat, and the teachings that he gave forth, were far from primitive.

Chiron was wise indeed, but his was a practical wisdom, one grounded in that which is useful. He tended to such serious matters of inquiry as the study of "celestial mechanics," by which the ancients meant astrology and astronomy. He was a renowned herbalist, and he was often assigned the task of tutoring or mentoring the great warrior heroes of the classical age, including Achilles.

However, Chiron was best known as one of the greatest healers of his time; he was the teacher of Aesculapius, who later became a kind of demi-god of the healing arts. But as fate would have it, Chiron's friend Hercules accidentally inflicted a terrible wound upon him—one that even he, the great healer, could not heal. Because Chiron's suffering was so great, he eventually asked to be released from the physical body. After all, he reasoned, he had lived for centuries and had experienced everything in the consciousness spectrum of humans and gods—except for death. This was a new challenge for him.

There were powerful repercussions to Chiron's death. When the great Titan Prometheus, the light-bringer, had been chained to a mountaintop for disobeying the gods (see the chapter on Uranus), it had been decreed that Prometheus might go free if one of the immortals should agree to die. This, of course, was something of a cruel joke on the part of the gods, for what immortal would ever choose to become mortal, to give up existence by preference and leave the world of the gods? But Chiron did in fact choose death. He walked into the underworld voluntarily and without fear. His soul, however, was placed in the heavens; some say that he is the constellation Centaurus, while others say that he is Sagittarius. Both, like Chiron, are half horse, half human.

Chiron's sacrifice set Prometheus free. The light-bringer returned to humanity to continue his work of advancing human evolution. It is interesting to think of Saturn as symbolic of the rule of the gods, as well as symbolizing the chains that bound Prometheus to the mountaintop. And, as we shall see in the next chapter, the planet Uranus may be archetypally identified with Prometheus. Chiron lies between the two, the mediator between these two vastly different modes of consciousness, between boundaries and limitless freedom.

Since the discovery of the astronomical Chiron in 1977, the themes and issues that relate to his archetype have come into our cultural landscape in a most profound way. For instance, the field of alternative medicine, which includes acupuncture, massage therapy, homeopathy, herbalism, chiropractic, and a host of other disciplines, has become a huge industry since the introduction of Chiron into our night sky. All of these things may logically be connected with the centaur of myth. His mastery of herbalism is specifically mentioned in the ancient Greek texts, and while he is not linked in classical myth with a Chinese system such as acupuncture, it should be remembered that in some sense he may be regarded as the master of all traditionally based healing systems, and that acupuncture is such a system. Chiron's name means "the skillful handed one," and the word *chiropractic,* meaning "practice with the hands," is derived from the same Greek root as is Chiron's name. Speaking of skillful hands, we can also see how this archetype might be linked with massage therapy as well.

But there is more. Chiron was a member of a race of beings that lived close to the earth, and his own wisdom was earth-centered and based in the practicalities of herbs, plants, and so on. Therefore Chiron has been regarded as a symbol of traditional or earth-centered wisdom in general. Shortly after his discovery, the Native American Religious Freedom Act was passed, which allowed Native American medicine men and healers and Hawaiian kahunas to begin practicing their earth-centered wisdom openly and publicly again after years of repression. Also, let us not forget that Chiron chose death as a conscious path, of his own free will. During the year of his discovery, Elisabeth Kübler-Ross opened her first hospice for conscious dying.

In many traditional or indigenous societies, a physical disability—such as a limp or a bad leg—is considered to be the mark of a potential shaman. This is why shamans are sometimes referred to as "wounded healers." Chiron's magical wound in the thigh, as well as his expertise in the healing arts, serve to link him with this important archetype. In many ways, Chiron is the wounded healer of the astrological world, the archetypal shaman among the planets (although Mercury shares some shamanic attributes as well).

Shamans are healers; aside from Chiron himself, there is one other archetypal healer linked with this peculiar little celestial body, and that is Asklepios, commonly spelled Aesculapius. This son of the god Apollo, born of a human mother, was in time elevated to the status of a god because of his healing powers, and therefore he is called the god of healing. Chiron was the teacher of Aesculapius, and in some ways Chiron "carries" the archetype of Aesculapius, by which we mean that all matters symbolized by the myth of Aesculapius have their astrological correlate with the planetary body known as Chiron. If there are Aesculapian themes in your life drama, you will probably find them emerging and growing during the transits or other astrological events of Chiron.

In some ways, the god Aesculapius stands at the forefront of modern medicine. Hippocrates, the founder of classical Greek medicine, was trained in the healing temples of Aesculapius. Nevertheless, the rituals associated with those temples strike the contemporary imagination as more akin to magic than science. As noted in chapter 4, dreamwork was a powerful tool for healing in the temples of Aesculapius, and large but harmless serpents were kept on the premises as symbols of regenerative power—and in a sense as healers in their own right. As the constellation of Ophiuchus or "the Serpent Bearer,"

Aesculapius still carries his snake through the night sky, and the symbol of medicine, a staff entwined with a serpent, commemorates the healing god. (The medical staff is in fact slightly different from the caduceus of Mercury, for which it is commonly mistaken.) Chiron and Aesculapius were both "magical healers," and it is fitting that the archetypal themes common to both of them should be shared by the same celestial body.

As noted earlier, Chiron has been variously classified as a planet, a minor planet or asteroid, a comet, and then again as a planetoid. There is an entire group of newly discovered celestial bodies called the Centaurs that partake of Chiron's properties and physical attributes and that are located out beyond the orbit of Pluto; ironically, Chiron is in a completely different neighborhood, orbiting the solar system between Saturn (his mythological father) and Uranus (his mythological grandfather). Because he is considered a bridge between the well-defined, methodical world of Saturn and the free, unconstrained world of Uranus, Chiron can be thought of as the key to uniting the two.

Chiron was named by the astronomer who discovered it—Charles Kowal. When astrologers began using Chiron in horoscopes, they developed a glyph or symbol for him that resembled a capital *K*, for Kowal. Many people thought that it actually resembled a key. This has turned out to be somewhat significant, for it inspired astrologers to develop the idea of Chiron as a "key" that opens the door to bridging Saturn and Uranus.

Though Chiron has a very uneven elliptical orbit, it does return to its own place approximately every fifty to fifty-one years. Thus, we can begin to see Chiron emerge in people who reach the age of fifty, their "golden" anniversary, a time when the beginning of wisdom or great healing opportunities may emerge. This astrological event has, in fact, proven to be a powerful and significant one for those who are "Chiron sensitive." It tends to open us to new and unique revelations that resist both the conservatism of Saturn and the wild eccentricity of Uranus. For example, we have already mentioned the fact that Elisabeth Kübler-Ross opened her first hospice for conscious dying during the year of Chiron's discovery. We did not mention that she was fifty-one years old at the time, and engaged in her Chiron Return.

We have pointed out that *chiropractic* is derived from the same root word as Chiron, meaning "to practice with the hands," but the connection goes much deeper than that and makes a very interesting story. A jack-of-all-trades named Daniel Palmer was experimenting with alternative methods of healing but having very little success in the business. It was almost by accident and certainly by whim that he first attempted popping the bones of one of his patients, thus virtually inventing modern chiropractic medicine as we know it. You have probably already guessed that Palmer was fifty-one when he made his unforeseen breakthrough!

The alchemists attempted to turn base metal into gold; at fifty-one, it is possible to achieve an alchemical process in one's own body or consciousness as one breaks beyond the self-imposed limits of Saturn and reaches towards a Chirotic understanding.

DREAMWORK AND ACTIVE IMAGINATION

In order to experience important archetypal dreams that carried messages from powerful dream figures, the ancient Greeks went to the temples of Aesculapius to practice "dream incubation." Since Chiron was the teacher and mentor of Aesculapius, he is in some sense an archetype of the dream, the dreamer, and the dreaming process altogether. There are many contemporary ways and means to "incubate" such important archetypal or planetary dreams, some of which have been examined in chapter 4 of this book.

Chiron may appear in dreams in a variety of ways, for he is teacher, mentor, healer, and shaman. In terms of contemporary society, he may even appear as a nurse, massage therapist, or a medicine man or woman, but the themes of healing and teaching are the ones that remain constant. The dream figure may have some physical disability, for as we have seen, Chiron is the wounded healer. Sometimes he or she may even manifest the classically Chirotic "wound" in the thigh, and thus may be limping or carrying a walking stick. It is unlikely that a Chiron archetype would show up in youthful guise—a youthful shamanic figure is more often a Mercury type. Remembering that the Chiron Return occurs when we are fifty-one, we should not be surprised to find the Chiron dream figure in her or his late forties or early fifties.

This age factor is, of course, astrological rather than mythological; it is based upon the symbolism of the Chiron of contemporary astrology rather than upon the centaur king of ancient Greek legend. But while we are considering the possibility of contemporary astrological influences on our dreams, it is worth examining the symbolism of the key. Chiron is astrologically regarded as the "key" to bridging Saturn and Uranus, and the glyph used to represent this planetoid is shaped like a key (⚷), so if a dream figure hands you a key (especially if the key is on an ornately decorative key chain), it may well be a Chiron figure. He or she may be silent, but it will be clear that an important message is being transmitted. He or she may be pointing the way to a sacred mountain or a cave or even a bottle of blended herbs in an herbal shop or a warm bathing pool. This type of figure is very likely to show up in the dreams of someone who is suffering a physical illness or in the process of undergoing therapies of the psyche; it is especially prone to turn up in the dreams of those who are close to dying. Chiron set himself apart from others by choosing to die consciously, and there may be a message about conscious transformational life/death/rebirth processes here. Chiron also figures prominently in the psyches of people who are involved in assisted suicides or those who have died and come back.

PLANETARY REMEDIES

Some of the recently discovered planets, as well as the major asteroids, have no "traditional" attributions or correspondences, and it is sometimes necessary to create them. Our example planet of Chiron is in this category, since it was discovered in 1977 and therefore completely absent from the old medieval repertoire. However, the staff of Aesculapius (as distinct from the caduceus of Hermes) may be taken as a Chirotic symbol, since Aesculapius was the student of Chiron. Also, the astrological symbol for Chiron resembles a key, and Chiron may act as a spiritual key to open the passage between Saturn and Uranus. Therefore a golden key may be said to serve as an amulet or talisman for Chiron.

If Chiron is out of balance in your horoscope, it will be clearly and immediately apparent. Chiron, after all, is the "wounded healer," and if you have Chiron problems, your own individual wound will become somehow quite visible and obvious. If it is a physical problem—Chiron quite often symbolizes physical ailments—it is helpful to remember that Chiron himself was a master herbalist, and that Chirotic ailments are usually amenable to natural remedies.

Chiron lived in a cave where he communed with the infinite in perfect solitude. To go on a retreat or a meditative journey can be a very effective way of dealing with Chiron problems. In times of stress or confusion, retreat to your cave.

Chiron was the teacher of Aesculapius, and as we have seen in chapter 4, the healing temples of Aesculapius made abundant use of dreams and dream therapy. If a problem arises in your life that is clearly related to Chiron, you may well find the answer to your dilemma in the form of a dream.

INVOCATION AND AWARENESS

You might choose to call upon or invoke Chiron when you are attempting to eliminate some lifelong behavior pattern that has served to weaken you or keep you addicted or enslaved in some way. Such an addiction may not be limited to substance or alcohol abuse: it could involve eating disorders, chronic self-deception, sexual addiction, or family re-patterning.

When empowered, Chiron is a guide, a shaman, a bridge between two worlds, an enlightened teacher. When powerless, the shaman suffers from the wound that he, the healer, cannot heal; thus Chiron is a slave to weakness or addiction, feeling helpless or hopeless to do anything about it or bring about change. Invoke Chiron's energy when you feel wounded, when you seek the healing of some chronic condition, or when you are feeling like you don't fit into the standard operating system of the rest of the world. Handicaps can be turned into strengths. The sacred wound or fatal flaw within ourselves is always healed by helping others to heal their wounds. Many therapists, healers, teachers, and astrologers have Chiron placed prominently in their charts. In terms of our contemporary society, you may be meeting with Chiron whenever you have a session with an acupuncturist or chiropractor, or when you attend a Native American sweat lodge. You will certainly encounter him whenever you visit a hospice, and your friendly local ecological activist, who loves the wild places, may very well be a Chirotic personality as well.

CHAPTER 20

URANUS
MAKER OF WORLDS

ASTROLOGY AND MYTH

Uranus is the original Sky Father—that's what his Greek name, Ouranos, means. He was the primal shaper who molded the universe and put it in order. In Greek mythology, this intensely creative partner of the Earth Mother Gaia appears only briefly in Hesiod's poem *The Theogony*. Grown tyrannical and therefore slain by his son Cronus (see Saturn), he disappears "in the first act." But he leaves an indelible impression upon myth as the originator of all creative thought and an indelible impression upon astrology as the namesake of the planet Uranus.

Indeed, the planet Uranus is strongly associated with our creativity, and like the original Sky Father, it tends to be a wild, ungovernable force of nature, a law unto itself. It was the discovery of Uranus in 1781 by William Herschel that upset an astrological worldview that had prevailed for some 2,500 years. The old-fashioned astrological mandala was an elegant creation, with the Sun and Moon ruling the quintessential "day" and "night" houses of Leo and Cancer, while the other five planets alternated with a day and night house each, thus taking care of the remaining ten signs in an orderly fashion. Uranus overturned the apple cart and threw perfect order into perfect chaos. This is what Uranus loves best.

In the late eighteenth century, when Uranus was discovered, it was quickly assigned to Aquarius for rulership. Similarly, in the nineteenth century, Neptune was discovered and given to Pisces, while in the twentieth century, Pluto was discovered and given to Scorpio for rulership. While these three planets' mythological archetypes may indeed resemble the natures of the signs they are said to rule, there are many followers of traditional astrology (and Hindu astrology as well) who do not believe these three planets should be given any rulership at all. Many Hindu astrologers exclude them completely from their charts, while Western traditional astrology uses them in houses but assigns them no particular dignity as far as signs go.

This is not to say that astrologers have been unhappy about the situation. In fact, most of them feel that the art of astrology itself is governed by Uranus, and that they (the astrologers) are basically Uranian in temperament. In the old days, astrology was "ruled" by Mercury, but one could say that Uranus is simply a higher, more empowered form of Mercury.

However, what may be even more important than these outer planets' correlation to the signs they are said to rule is their influence upon the prevailing events and characteristic temperament of the era in which they were discovered. After all, it isn't every day a new planet is discovered, and before Uranus it hadn't really happened at all. It was the late eighteenth century when Uranus was first seen through the eyes of a very Uranian invention, the telescope—without it, Uranus would have been impossible to detect. (Even more Uranian are the astronomical computers that now track and find not just new planets, but also new solar systems and galaxies!)

The late eighteenth century saw itself as a time of enlightenment, an age of reason, and a time when the cry of freedom was heard around the world. In fact, Immanuel Kant's *Critique of Pure Reason* was published in the very same year as the discovery of Uranus. The American Revolution was in full swing, and only a decade later came the French Revolution, where the cry of "Liberty, Equality, Fraternity" was the overwhelming *vox populi,* consistent with the Uranian temperament. European feudalism was being shoved aside to make way for the coming Industrial Revolution, where thousands fled small villages, abandoned the fields, and made their way to the cities where gigantic factories would now swallow up the masses. In the 100 years following the discovery of Uranus, so much new technology and machinery would be invented that the world was to take on a decidedly different look and sound. In fact, this era brought forth so many new ideas, free thinkers, inventions, and new ways of life that it has been pegged as one of the most important historical periods of change for that entire millennium.

These dimensions of the planetary archetype of Uranus are nowhere to be found in the myth of Uranus. For example, astrologers ordinarily associate the planet Uranus—and its sign Aquarius—with the passionate love of freedom and strong sense of humanitarianism so characteristic of the time of its discovery. It is difficult to perceive any of this in the cranky old sky god of the *Theogony*. The "creativity" inherent in both planet and sign is not so much the primal world-shaping of the sky god as it is an inventive, sudden, eccentric thing. Where does all this come from?

Philosopher Richard Tarnas has suggested that the planet Uranus is actually "carrying" one of the most important archetypes of Western civilization—that of Prometheus.[1] As we have seen, archetypes tend to float around in the collective mind until, when they are needed, they erupt into the light of day. We have given examples of this relating to the asteroids. The same thing might be said of Uranus. He "carries" the archetype of Prometheus in much the same way that Chiron "carries" Aesculapius or Neptune "carries" Dionysus. These important archetypes needed to make themselves known in the world again, and of course they needed to find their appropriate reflection in the sky as well. In its endless quest for scientific achievement, personal self-reflection, and restless ambition, Western civilization itself seems to be dancing to the tune of old Prometheus.

Prometheus was one of the Titans, the ancient race of earlier gods that was replaced by the Olympians. Though most of the Titans were imprisoned under the earth for rebelling against Zeus and the gang (see Saturn), Prometheus made his peace with the new guard—at least for a while. Prometheus became the creator of humankind; he fashioned us out of clay and blew his breath into us. (Uranus rules Aquarius, a "humanitarian" sign and an "air"—i.e., breath—sign.) He always had a weakness for the strange species he had created. At that time, we mortals were shivering in the dark, unable even to light our houses or cook our food. Only the gods possessed light and fire. Prometheus did the unthinkable—he stole the sacred fire from the gods. Climbing Mt. Olympus, he waited until the chariot of the Sun came by, then caught a spark of its divine fire in a fennel stalk. (The Sun rules Leo, which is the opposite of Aquarius, so we can see that Uranus and the Sun don't always get along.)

Prometheus gave fire to humankind, but the gods were not pleased. The gods, especially Zeus, were angered by what they interpreted as a rebellious act by Prometheus. By this time Zeus had become supreme ruler of the gods and man. It was unthinkable that a Titan—an older god who held a rather low-ranking position in the hierarchical scheme of the Olympians—would dare to act on his own accord without the approval of Zeus. Prometheus stole Zeus' fire, in effect. The gods chained him to a mountaintop and set an eagle to the task of tearing out his liver every day. Being immortal, Prometheus recovered daily. But it was lonely and painful up there. (He was eventually released—see Chiron.)

Thus we see how the child who steals his father's fire or takes a situation into his own hands—whether it brings chaos or enlightenment—will often suffer as a result. Both our archetypes for the planet Uranus were punished for their acts. Uranus had his genitals severed, thus removing and cutting off any further procreative power. Prometheus was exiled into isolation and had his liver torn apart daily. Uranian individuals may experience guilt, remorse, or the sharp and painful severing of ties to family and loved ones because they defied tradition and authority, acting on their own behalf.

In effect, Prometheus' act of stealing fire was no different from the Mercurial act of stealing Apollo's cattle. But Mercury outwitted and charmed the gods, thereby escaping punishment. Prometheus was not so lucky. His act of defiance cost him greatly, but made him the archetype of all those who are sacrificed for the good of the whole. Prometheus was willing to take the personal risk inherent in the act in order to ultimately benefit humanity. Many scientists, inventors, explorers, and pioneers of all kinds, especially leaders in New Age philosophies, can and do identify with seemingly outside forces guiding them or driving them to their ultimate destinies.

Let's not forget that the Promethean archetype carries with it the gift of prophecy. The Greek playwright Aeschylus, in his drama *Prometheus Bound*, repeatedly emphasizes Prometheus' forethought and prophetic knowledge. As the child of an oracular goddess named Themis, Prometheus can discern both past and future. Aeschylus presents him as an isolated force and as a suffering champion of man. But isn't that really what Uranus as an archetypal energy is all about? Uranians possess the sometimes courageous, sometimes self-righteous "knowing" that comes from a highly intuitive and spontaneous will that allows neither gods nor hierarchies to interfere with their plans to enact what is "right." Ask any true Uranians if there are forces in their lives that can keep them from living exactly as they please!

Of course, as is often the case, the "pure" archetype doesn't always have full rein. There are bound to be squares and such to Uranus from planets like Jupiter or Saturn that result in the individual making certain compromises along the way. Actually, the difficult aspects to Uranus from those two planets—Jupiter or Saturn—may often be experienced as the most difficult, because it was both Zeus (Jupiter) and Cronus (Saturn) who exacted some form of punishment on our friends Prometheus and Uranus. In one case, one might sacrifice Jupiter's domain, giving up a life of wealth and privilege in order to live one's own life, or in Saturn's case, never becoming society's responsible member of family, church, or society. But the inner fire never dies out. In principle and in truth, Uranian minds are always abuzz with the way things "should be." We astrologers are always fond of mentioning to Uranian types that they were probably born about fifty years ahead of their time, and that the world will one day catch up with the way they personally think (a comment that usually brings us a delighted and strong affirmation).

It is easy to fall in love with a Uranian, and people (especially women) often do. With his charismatic charm, his apparent visionary qualities, and the excitement that so often follows him around, who wouldn't be charmed? But be careful. Uranians are not known for their ability to stick around and become a permanent part of the family for very long. One aspect of the sky god Uranus is the embodiment of the original father who poured his seed upon fruitful Gaia and therefore became the prolific progenitor of many subsequent races and generations. This is also, however, an archetype of the original absent father, because with the one exception of being there for procreational purposes, he was nowhere near mother and children again.

Uranians are good at procreating new worlds and visionary ideas, but not especially good at long-term commitment—and yet Uranians do often wind up married and having families. The key to survival there is to let them have their space when they need it, and ordinary patterns of marriage and family may be completely overthrown in favor of a new form that usually turns out to be much more workable and greatly to the benefit of everyone involved. Don't try to predict the behavior of Uranians. You can't possibly know what they will do next because they don't know either. No matter how well you think you know them, they'll surprise you in the end.

So it is with our Uranian friends and family members. They may always seem like the oddballs in their group. In fact, this apparent difference separates them from the masses at a fairly young age, an age that is often too young for those affected to handle the stamp of "outsider" or alien being imposed upon them. But that is the power and strength inherent in the Uranian nature. When they finally begin to accept this "black sheep" quality about themselves, and see themselves as being different because of their visionary nature and their (actually) very enlightened manner of *not* identifying with society's clones like the whiter sheep, their inspired work and untold life adventures may begin in earnest.

The planet Uranus, like Prometheus, is the divine rebel. Uranus marches to the beat of a different drummer. He constantly reinvents himself and the world around him. Eccentric, empowered, and completely ungovernable, Uranus is the spirit of creativity itself. Uranus overturned the ordered world of astrology in much the same way that Prometheus shook up the orderly world of the gods.

DREAMWORK AND ACTIVE IMAGINATION

In one sense, Uranus is the archetypal sky god, a principle of the air, a mate to Gaia. In astrology, Uranus is connected to the sign Aquarius and to a group consciousness. If a dream begins something like this: "I was in a group of people in a large stadium," or "I was attending a conference," or "We were all gathered together in the neighborhood park or at city hall," then we are dealing with Uranian or Aquarian concepts.

Anything that stands out by virtue of its distinctiveness is likewise Uranian. It's the separate and the unique. It may be an aberration—a jewel among thorns. Flying is Uranian. So is the computer, a new archetype showing up in dreams. Uranus represents anything beyond the limits of time and space or Saturn's realm. Once we could see Uranus by the ingenious invention of the telescope, we learned there was a bigger universe out there than what was represented by the boundaries of physical time and space (Saturn). Computer networks, satellites, radio waves, wave patterns, UFOs, aliens, lightning, and aircraft all come under Uranus, and these objects are consistently showing up in people's dreams. And what do they represent? An ability to communicate (send and receive messages) much more efficiently (to the masses) than our messenger god Mercury, who is quick at sending individual messages. Uranian messages go out to and from the collective and often transcend physical reality.

However, in dreams Uranus may also resemble the Mercury archetype at times—after all, many astrologers refer to Uranus as the "higher octave" of Mercury. The same trickster qualities may be characteristic of both planets, and Uranus, like Mercury, tends to linger at the dark crossroads of our imagination. But there are differences. As one of the inner, personal planets, Mercury is more likely to be represented in the dream by someone we know, someone who is simply playing a Mercurial role. As an outer planet, connected with the world of the deeper archetypes, Uranus is more likely to be a pure dream figure, mysterious, unknown, magical.

Uranus is also infinitely more disruptive. If Mercury gives a mysterious smile while delivering a message, Uranus will laugh wildly while blowing up the entire post office. In fact, this quality of disruption is almost the trademark of Uranus. Look for someone whose role in a dream is quite simply to trash your ordinary reality. Uranus is the great awakener. Most awakenings are good; some are not. If such a dream leaves you feeling uneasy, guilty, and frightened, you may be dealing with Pluto rather than Uranus, and you need to go back over your dream journal to look for more clues. But if the figure who trashes your everyday concepts leaves you feeling just the least bit exhilarated, inspired, or filled with laughter and purpose, you have received a visit from Prometheus, the bringer of light.

PLANETARY REMEDIES

There are two basic reasons to seek healing for a planet that has gone out of balance: first, because the planet has become too weak, and second, because the planet has become too strong. In the case of Uranus, it's easy to tell the difference. If Uranus is weak, you won't feel very creative. You will be reluctant or downright afraid to express your individuality, and consequently you will be a dedicated follower of rules. If Uranus is too strong, you will be charged with electricity—so much so that you seem to rub everyone the wrong way, like getting a shock from the carpet. You will be just packed with creative and original ideas, but your mind will be racing too fast to do anything about it. Instead of being inventive, you will simply be fried. In this situation, Gaia as a mate to Uranus may be helpful. A connection to Earth or Mother Nature is an extremely helpful antidote to help release cyber-tension.

People who spend hours everyday staring at computer screens need to relieve themselves by spending time outdoors. Walk the dog, go for a bike ride, walk in a park or by a body of water, hug a tree—in short, anything that gets you out of your head and back in your body, feet touching the earth. Don't be surprised if, in a few years' time, a new type of illness or bodily disorder begins to spread like wildfire. It will be called something like "cyber-syndrome fatigue." People plugged to their computers all day, everyday, will begin to collapse while bodily functions seem to not work properly. Medical experts will first seem puzzled by it all and may try to dismiss it entirely until it reaches epidemic proportions.

The best thing to do is limit the stimuli flowing into your brain. Spend less time on the Internet; cyberspace tends to increase Uranian nervous energy without placing it in balance or turning it towards the creative. Even though Uranus gifts us with high-tech information, it is sometimes useful to access less information rather than more. Don't try to read a magazine and watch TV at the same time. Turn off all the gadgets. Meditate or take a walk in the woods. Do simple things. Chop wood and carry water. When the Uranian energy swirl finally slows down, that Promethean creativity will be free to emerge.

INVOCATION AND AWARENESS

As we have observed in relation to other planetary archetypes: "Be careful what you ask for; you just might get it." This is something to keep in mind with Uranus, the great trickster. In the common planetary attributions of the Tarot, Uranus is the Fool, a card that implies taking a giant leap into the unknown.

But there may very well be reasons to invoke this kind of energy; for example, when you are afraid of (a) being in a group or a crowd, (b) being isolated and alienated from everyone else, or (c) making changes and breaking away from established patterns and routines that no longer serve you. Uranus is evolutionary in nature as well as revolutionary. A relationship doesn't need to end when both parties are evolving, growing, and changing at a similar pace.

A job may reward you in monetary terms, either now via a paycheck and medical benefits, or with the promise of a retirement plan thirty years from now. But that is clearly Saturn's realm. Uranus is more interested in how it stimulates and inspires one, both mentally and physically. If you are going through the robotic motions of reporting to your job each day without any heart connection (the Sun), then you are in danger of suppressing Uranian energy. This is dangerous to do with Uranus because when it opposes its own birth position in the horoscope (the "life begins at forty" transit), you may be in for quite a shock.

Uranus is the divine fool, the one who "shakes the tree." When sudden twists and turns appear on the road, go with them instead of becoming agitated or stressed, because Uranus is usually looking down from a lofty perch, smiling on the sidelines. This is the time to invoke its presence and see where the path leads. Some good altar images of Uranus might be a picture of the court jester, your favorite alchemist or wizard or space alien, or your astrological chart (defining your own uniqueness). Animals, birds, and even mechanical objects such as aircraft or UFOs that symbolize flight and freedom would also be appropriate ways of invoking Uranus. Best of all is anything that smiles at us while reminding us not to get too caught up in the serious drama of it all.

---

1. Tarnas, Richard, "Prometheus The Awakener: An Essay on the Archetypal Meaning of the Planet Uranus," in *Spring* (Audio & Journal, 1995).

CHAPTER 21

NEPTUNE
ECSTASY AND DREAMS

ASTROLOGY AND MYTH

In mythology, Neptune or Poseidon is the god of the waters, and especially of the ocean. In this planet's dreamlike, misty silences and its visionary images, we do in fact gaze into the "waters" of our very being—the vast collective unconscious that is so often symbolized by an ocean. Since Neptune's discovery in 1846, it has been given rulership over Pisces, the twelfth sign of the zodiac.

Because Pisces is a water sign and is said to rule the vast ocean—the ocean that surrounds and nurtures the earth as well as the vast ocean of our unconscious—the planet Neptune is a fitting symbol. But what, really, does Neptune represent? As we shall see, Dionysus is one mythological archetype for our planet Neptune, but his predecessor is the god Poseidon (Latin: Neptune), who, in the Olympian system of rulerships given in the *Astronomica* of Manilius, was also given Pisces as his domain.[1] Yet another predecessor of the Neptunian archetype is the Babylonian god Ea or Enki, a god of the waters who is often depicted wearing fish skins.

The Greek Poseidon came to rule the sea in a "luck of the draw" sort of way. Once the gods defeated the Titans, Zeus freed his siblings from the belly of their father, Cronus (see Saturn), and the three brothers drew lots to assign rulership of the world. Zeus was given the realm of the sky, Hades the realm of the dead (the underworld), and Poseidon the charge of the seas. We must remember that Greece is a nation surrounded by the sea on three sides and comprised largely of small islands. Land and sea weave together throughout the Greek world, and in Plato's account of the sunken island/continent of Atlantis (in the *Critias*), Poseidon is said to have been its supreme ruler.[2] This legend predates Greek civilization by several millennia, so the association of Poseidon/Neptune to this oceanic realm is well etched in our predecessors' psyches. Many Neptunians can relate to the need to be in, on, or near the water for much of their lives.

Though Poseidon's home was beneath the waters, temples were erected to him at points where ships would come and go, and where offerings could be left to ensure safe passage through the unpredictable seas. Sailors that neglected to honor him in this way were often found high and dry, with no wind at all with which to sail, or crashed upon a barren rocky shore due to heavy storms and fog at sea (which the ancients interpreted as Poseidon's wrath). Odysseus (Ulysses) is probably the most renowned example of this.

Poseidon was originally a god of horses and a god of earthquakes as well, and neither horses nor earthquakes suggest that he was mild and dreamy, nor ineffective at dealing with worldly issues—yet these aspects have often been attributed to the nature of Poseidon or Neptune. The individual dominated or strongly influenced by this planet tends to be a dreamer—a dancer, a musician, a mystic, or sometimes just a hopeless drunk. Such individuals owe but little to the archetype of Neptune. As with Uranus, we must look beyond the names that the astronomers have chosen for the outer planets and examine the planet's very nature to determine its true archetype, and as Liz Greene has noted, the true archetype for this planet is Dionysus.[3]

Many of us know Dionysus primarily as a god of wine, reflecting his Roman equivalent, the god Bacchus. While it is true that alcoholism is strongly associated with the planet Neptune, it should also be pointed out that, to the Greeks, Dionysus was primarily a god of ecstasy. Roaming the world like some primal wild man, accompanied by nature spirits, animals, and wild women, he dances his way into a mystical state of consciousness. The word *ecstasy* literally means "to stand outside oneself"; the planet Neptune often transports us to a realm beyond the ordinary, a true ecstatic state that may indeed be achieved through drugs and alcohol, but that in its more positive manifestation is achieved through true mystical or poetic vision.

In myth, the god Dionysus is called a "god of women." The son of one of Zeus' consorts, he was hidden away in a cave of nymphs to keep him safe from the vindictive jealousy of Hera; hence he was raised as a woman by a tribe of nymphs. Emerging into manhood, he began his rambling through the world, inciting people to wild ecstasy wherever he went. Women were very sensitive to his influence and prone to fall into states of mystical ecstasy in his presence. Because of this, they left their homes and their families to romp for days at a time with the wild tribe of Dionysus. In regard to the actual cult of the god in ancient Greece, there is some evidence that women did indeed temporarily abandon their "duties" in order to take part in the ecstatic, orgiastic festivals dedicated to Dionysus. This was dangerous to the structure of patriarchal Greek society—women who claimed their own sexuality, neglected their "wifely obligations," and reached states of mystical ecstasy simply could not be tolerated. So the cult of Dionysus was frequently outlawed in the ancient world. Nevertheless, attempts to suppress it were usually unsuccessful.

Dionysus himself is associated in myth with one particular woman—Ariadne. It seems clear that Ariadne was once a goddess in her own right, for her name means "The Most High Holy One," and it is found on extremely ancient Cretan tablets; but in mythological stories handed down to us from a later period, she is portrayed as a mortal, a princess of Crete, the daughter of King Minos. Theseus was the Greek hero sent to Crete to slay the minotaur, a beast who was a man with the head of a bull. This minotaur was said to be trapped within the underground labyrinth of the palace of Knossos. Theseus was successful at achieving his aim, but this was due in large part to Ariadne's help and guidance. Ariadne fell in love with Theseus and helped him to topple the empire of her own father, Minos. By steadfastly holding the thread that would guide him out of the labyrinth, she allowed him to emerge after slaying the beast.

Some versions of the story claim that Theseus abandoned Ariadne on the island of Naxos. Her passionate mourning and weeping was so intense that it attracted the attention of Dionysus, who made her his bride and enshrined her among the immortal stars as the Corona Borealis. But in other versions of the story, Dionysus seems to have had his eye on Ariadne all along. In these versions, Theseus sent Ariadne on to Naxos ahead of him, fully intending to meet her there and make her his bride. But the god Dionysus came to Theseus in a dream, instructing him not to go to Naxos. Theseus had no choice but to obey direct orders from a god, and he never made the journey. Dionysus came to Naxos and claimed Ariadne as his own. They were wed in a sacred ceremony on Mount Olympus to the joy of all onlookers.

That Ariadne was a very ancient goddess is clear from the Cretan inscriptions. Some mythologists have suspected that she is the Goddess of the Labyrinth of Life, the leader of the circular dance that winds us in and out of experience and consciousness. As such, she and Dionysus constitute an immortal Shiva/Shakti pair, the mystical and erotic dancers who energize the cosmos.

Within the story of Ariadne, we have many Neptunian themes—the labyrinth, the visionary guidance out of the darkness, the hopeless love, the abandonment and subsequent grief, and the eventual union with the divine. Women who have a strong Neptunian theme in their birth charts often embody certain elements (if not all) of the Ariadne myth. They are passionate lovers, but often prone to fall victim to romantic illusions (Neptune is a planet of illusion). Like Ariadne on Naxos, they may even indulge themselves in a certain amount of romantic hysteria. But of all feminine archetypes, they are among the ones most likely to transform their emotions through mystical experience—though this will usually not be an ascetic or purely "spiritual" form of mysticism, but something more ecstatic and sensual. In fact, it is this desire to join with the "other," with the "beloved," that keeps the Neptunian in a lifelong search—as it is their way to the divine.

There is, of course, a downside to the Dionysian ecstasy. As we have noted, the planet Neptune is often associated with alcoholism, and the same could be said of drugs or any other temporary escape from "reality" (though the true Neptunian would probably argue, in her or his mystical fashion, that reality itself is just one more illusion). Mystical states of consciousness may be just as much of an addiction as anything else; the Neptunian is often dependent upon experiences of ecstasy in order to feel good about the world—and sometimes even to cope with it at all.

For the world may seem a dark and ugly place to the true Neptunian. The dream is always preferable. Hence Neptunian types may not only annoy us with their chronic avoidance of "reality" and its issues, but they may also seem childlike—or downright childish. Their artistic dreams and romantic illusions often serve as escape valves from the responsibilities of adult life; Neptunians may remain eternal children all their lives. This doesn't always take the form of alcohol, drugs, or dreams—individuals who like to "renounce the world" to lead an ascetic or "purely spiritual life" in some ashram or commune are generally Neptunians. Others might simply construct a fairy-tale existence around themselves and live in that bubble throughout life, preferring to keep the outside world at a distance.

At their best, however, Neptunians may inspire all of us. Their ability to stand outside themselves and thus enter into states of ecstasy is a true gift that has given the world much of its best poetry, music, dancing, painting, and mysticism. But perhaps we can see in Neptune a duality that is also apparent in its Piscean rulership—as Pisces itself depicts two fish swimming in opposite directions. With one fish swimming towards the heavenly realm and the other fish swimming along the material plane, it is no wonder that a dual nature emerges, and that both Poseidon and Dionysus may be found upon deeper examination. It is not uncommon for the Piscean or Neptunian to appear soft and dreamy on the surface, but also to have powerful urges, passions, and feelings buried within, which, when immersed in such deep water, have a hard time surfacing.

Regardless of what Greek Poseidon or Dionysus or Roman Neptune embodied in the ancient world, what may be more important is to observe the influence of this archetype over the last 2,000 years, especially now, as we draw towards the close of the Piscean Age. The last 2,000 years have been "ruled" by Neptune as the planetary lord of Pisces. Pisces embodies a deep mysticism, an awareness of suffering (whether from personal experience or empathy with others), compassionate action, and some degree of self-sacrifice. The god of this age has been the Christ figure, whose emblem is a fish and who embodies all these qualities. The mystical side of Christ has been centered around a vessel called the Grail cup, or this quest for the Holy Grail, with wine being one of the primary substances of the sacrament. (In this context, it is interesting to remember that early Christians "borrowed" much of their ritual and theology—including the sacred wine—from the cult of that other Neptunian deity, Dionysus.)

It is interesting to note the kind of relationship that Dionysus and Apollo had with one another (see the chapter on the Sun), because in Neptunian types we may often find a question about loss of personal identity, while the Sun represents the exact opposite—strong identification with the self. Both were gods of the theater and drama, and this is where the mask comes in. Actors will identify with both gods. They don their mask and costume, play the role, and then go back to being themselves. But many actors have admittedly been drawn to the theater as a means to better discover themselves through the characters they portray.

Because Neptune is such a slow-moving planet, its effects on a person's life may last for up to three years when it is transiting an important point in one's chart. Obviously, some of the more important transits of Neptune will be to the Sun, the Moon, and the four cardinal points (angles) of the chart. The Sun represents one of the strongest factors in building our sense of personal identity. When Neptune is transiting a person's Sun, a sudden loss of personal identity may occur. Their inner urges and impulses begin to pull them away from present-day reality. They long to be somewhere else and even *be* someone else. They are susceptible to unusual (even alien) forces that are attempting to make contact with them. The pull is strong—similar to that of the ocean's tides. Once swept away, they can never fully go back to shore and exist as they previously did.

This oceanic pull is not unlike that exerted by the Sirens of myth. These beautifully seductive female creatures resided on rocks in the ocean and sang harmonious melodies to approaching ships (which suggests that they were basically Neptunian). The sailors could not help but be seduced by such beauty and sweetness, but once they followed the Sirens' song, they sank to their deaths (or perhaps to a new life beneath the sea—but in any case were never heard from on earth again). This myth describes an internal process in which your previous identity is washed away with the tide, and, afterward, you will most likely not be able to identify with your former personality. How we respond to these Neptune transits is most important, because on the surface things really *could* stay the same in our lives—but there are beautiful sirens singing or whispering in our ears, beckoning us to another realm.

With Neptune, our otherworldly longings are heightened during the period of transit, and they often lure us away from the substance of our lives. So it is not uncommon for the corporate executive to walk away and write the book that she or he has always wanted to write, or sail around the world, or enter into a committed spiritual path, or fall madly in love with someone who seems seductively dangerous, but so intriguingly intoxicating that one can hardly resist. Mysticism and fantasy have a way of becoming more real than reality at such times, and suddenly one feels like Alice in Wonderland. Once the Neptune transit is over, the heightened sensations and longings one felt may dissipate, and life might even resume as "normal" once again. At most, it is possible to fully integrate into one's life the undersea treasures that Neptune has brought, or at the least have the effects linger as sweet nostalgia whenever the Sirens' song is played and you are transported right back to their world.

DREAMWORK AND ACTIVE IMAGINATION

Neptune not only appears in dreams—Neptune is the Lord of Dreams. Neptune is anything that allows us to lay aside rational thought and receive information through image, symbol, sound, and sensation. What, then, could be more Neptunian than the act of dreaming? Dreaming takes us immediately into a world wherein all perception is governed by Neptune's rules.

All the same, there are some characters in this Neptunian realm who may themselves function as Neptune's special agents. The mysterious gentleman or lady who draws you into a dance, the wizard or benign sorceress, the vaguely sensual but at the same time mystical figure who beckons, entices, enchants, and allures you—all these dream figures are archetypes of Neptune.

Poseidon's attribute, without which he is rarely seen, is his trident. It's not just a pitchfork! In the famous contest to name the city of Athens, Poseidon competed with Athene. He struck his trident on the rocky promontory and out poured a spring of running water. Was this a magical tool that enabled the user to find water? It is not unlike divining rods that achieve the same end. And indeed, "divining" is another Neptunian talent—people who have prophetic dreams and can see the future are said to be receiving divine revelations or visitations. When they do so, they are in Neptune's realm.

Dreams involving bodies of water, especially the ocean, will be related to Neptune. And let's not forget the creatures that live in the sea. In fairy tale and myth over the millennia, some sea creatures have been depicted in human form—mermaids, sea goddesses, and gods. Dolphins, with magical powers that transported young heroes and heroines to safety, also feature prominently. (Dionysus has a special affinity for dolphins.) These are all images that may well appear in dreams, but there is also a darker, more foreboding side to the sea that can emerge. Because the sea truly represents an ocean of the unconscious, fears and anxieties may also emerge beneath the deep, and Hollywood has profited greatly from this motif.

PLANETARY REMEDIES

There may be some exceedingly practical, earthbound souls who need more Neptune in their lives—who never rhapsodize about the flowers, or dance alone in woodland spaces. But it is very unlikely that any of them are reading this book!

Most of you stargazers have too much Neptune rather than too little. While it's only healthy to allow the Dionysiac ecstasy its rightful place in our lives, many of us spend far too much time in the cosmos and not enough time on earth. Dionysus needs some grounding. Saturn may actually prove a healthy antidote for such sensitive souls; refer to his chapter for suggestions on how to increase his power. When attempting to leave Neptune behind and return to earth, remember to pay all the bills and do all the chores before allowing yourself to frolic in ecstasy. Needless to say, indulgence in drugs or alcohol is a classic Neptunian symptom, best avoided by those who want to decrease this planet's bewildering power.

Neptune is one planet who thrives on meditation and other consciousness techniques. If it is really too strong in your chart, then forego recourse to psychics, channelers, and so on. For those of you who feel too earth-centered—mired in the mud of reality—there are always ways to bring Neptune into your life and float free of the doldrums (and no, we don't mean drinking yourself unconscious!). Ariadne and Dionysus were the rulers of the dance, and dancers tend to have a strong Neptune. If you need some positive Neptune in your life, go dancing. And of course no one can dance without music to dance to. Listening to music is another quintessentially Neptunian activity.

Ariadne was the mistress of the labyrinth; you could say that a journey with Neptune might be compared to walking through a labyrinth. And in fact, labyrinths are currently cropping up everywhere we look these days, having become a modern metaphor for how we walk through the spiral of life and achieve consciousness. Various New Age centers, retreats, and even conventional churches now feature labyrinths.

Sometimes they refer to these labyrinths as mazes, but this is not precisely correct. In a labyrinth, you can only go along a certain path, which if continuously followed, eventually leads you to the center, whereas a maze is a tangled mess that can have you forever going in circles. Therefore, labyrinths present us with a spiral rather than a linear approach to life. There are some who thrive by dancing the spiral and others who have difficulty accepting the sudden, abrupt turns. Ariadne, as the goddess who led Theseus out of the labyrinth, may similarly lead us out of our own labyrinths. These personal labyrinths may show up as tangled webs or circular paths or patterns that keep endlessly repeating, rendering us unable to see the patterns of our lives. By providing pattern recognition, we may sometimes become free of complexes. Walking a labyrinth is a marvelous "planetary remedy" for Neptunian confusion.[4]

INVOCATION AND AWARENESS

Becoming aware of Neptune is easy enough—we live in a society permeated by this planet's influence. Rock 'n' roll may have some Mars present in its grinding beat, but the fantasies it evokes for us are classically Neptunian. In fact, much if not all music is Neptunian in that it has the ability to shut off the thinking mind while transporting us to a feeling state. Even sports (another seemingly Martian province) can sometimes be Neptunian—at least if we're talking about Olympic figure skaters and gymnasts whose grace is more balletic than athletic.

Let us not forget the movies. We sit in the dark while dreamlike images float across our consciousness—what could be more infinitely Neptunian than that? And many film stars—especially those who really and truly embody the archetypes of our culture—have strong Neptunes in their birth charts.

Let us not forget Ariadne, either. She is the goddess to invoke when we need to climb out of our own tangled webs; she serves as a guide. Some may see her as a spirit guide; others as an angelic presence. One would certainly want to invoke her presence when one is feeling lost, trapped, confused, or disabled in some way. Ariadne guided Theseus in much the same way that Athene, the goddess of wisdom, helped guide and counsel the heroes of the great epics. But the primary difference between them has to do with the planes of consciousness upon which they exist. Ariadne is associated with the light that penetrates the dark unconscious reaches of the psyche and helps us abandon fears and complexes that have a disabling effect upon us. Athene speaks to our minds; Ariadne reaches us in our souls.

So Neptune is everywhere. Invoke this energy into your life through dreaming, dancing, listening to music, or writing poetry whenever you feel too deeply bound to the sad old world and in need of release.

But be careful. Neptune is nothing if not addictive.

---

1. Manilius, Marcus, *The Five Books of Manilius* (1697; reprint, Washington, D.C.: American Federation of Astrologers, 1953).

2. Plato, *Timaeus and Critias* (Harmondsworth, England: Penguin, 1971).

3. Greene, Liz, *The Astrology of Fate* (York Beach, ME: Samuel Weiser, Inc., 1984).

4. Artress, Dr. Lauren, *Walking a Sacred Path: Rediscovering the Labyrinth As a Sacred Tool* (Atlanta, GA: Riverbend Books, 1996).

CHAPTER 22

PLUTO
LORD OF THE UNDERWORLD

ASTROLOGY AND MYTH

The dark lord of the underworld was originally a lady. In Sumerian myth, the land of the dead is ruled by the fearsome Ereshkigal, whose hair is entwined with snakes and whose mouth drips with maggots. This Sumerian or Babylonian goddess somewhat resembles the Greek Medusa, the terrifying Gorgon with snakes in her hair, whose very glance turned people to stone. And, in fact, they are archetypally the same.

Ereshkigal, however, is best known as the tormentor of Inanna or Ishtar, the goddess of the planet Venus. Ishtar had ventured into the underworld in search of her dead lover, but the goddess of love fared rather poorly in the world of the dead, for Ereshkigal did not take to her kindly, and hung her on a meat hook in the deepest part of hell. The astrological correlate is that Venus-Pluto connections in a birth chart are frequently very difficult for reasons that we shall explore in this chapter.

Ereshkigal was eventually dethroned by Nergal, the fierce and violent god associated with the planet Mars, who stormed the land of the dead after having conquered as much as he could conquer among the lands of the living. However, an uneasy compromise was hammered out between the two of them, and ultimately Nergal and Ereshkigal ruled the underworld together as its lord and lady. One suspects the two of them were well matched.

This double rulership of the land of the dead was embodied in Greek mythology as well. When Zeus apportioned the three worlds among himself and his brothers, he gave the heavens to himself, the earth and sea to Poseidon, and the underworld to Hades, whose Roman name is Pluto. The myths seldom endow him with much character or personality, though this "silence" itself may be regarded as significant. Plutonian individuals, especially men, tend to be deeply introverted. Let us remember that this deity spends all his time with the ghosts of the dead, who never speak aloud or with their own voices. Hence the Plutonian individual may be more concerned with his visions and his intuitive feelings than he is with outer events. Homer refers to Hades the figure and Hades the place as the land of the shades. And indeed, one can immediately sense the shadowy and deep parts of an individual who is heavily Plutonian in nature.

This is not to say, however, that Pluto is always a pure introvert. Some may be familiar with the word *plutocrat*, which signifies "one who rules through wealth." The word plutocrat is derived from Pluto and has astrological significance. In ancient times, wealth was measured in terms of actual minerals extracted from the earth. Since the world beneath the earth was Pluto's realm, he was in some sense the god of wealth.[1] And even though the modern world recognizes paper (or even credit) as a monetary standard, those who control the wealth still tend to be Plutonian in essence. The tycoon on the ninety-ninth floor, the corporate raider, the billionaire recluse—all these individuals are strongly marked by the archetype of Pluto, and generally have a strong Pluto position in the natal horoscope. But as we all know, wealth may corrupt, and the corporate raider may be only one step away from the crime boss or Mafia don. These men, too—the lords of the criminal "underworld"—tend to have a strong Pluto influence in their charts.

As we have noted, the underworld lord was originally a lady, and Ereshkigal and Nergal ruled the realms of the dead in partnership. In Greek mythology as well, Hades or Pluto is best known as part of a marriage partnership, and the throne in the darkness is a double throne. In fact, the best known tale involving the god Hades is the one that concerns his winning of a bride.

Hades came roaring out of the underworld in his dark chariot and seized Persephone, the virgin daughter of the earth goddess Demeter, as she was romping in a field of flowers. Persephone's mother grieved so hard that she created the first winter, as related in our chapter on Ceres. Meanwhile, Persephone's stay in the underworld was becoming something of a transformative experience for her. It is said that she ate of some otherworldly pomegranate seeds while she was in Pluto's realm. Those who remember their folklore and fairy tale will remember that those who visit an elvish banquet or "fairy feast" and who eat of the food there must remain—perhaps returning to their own world a hundred years hence, to discover that everyone they know is dead. Thus Persephone likewise became a more or less permanent inhabitant of the underworld. After she had eaten of the pomegranate seeds, Zeus and the Olympian court decreed that she must now remain in the underworld for half the year, and the other half on earth with her mother—thus the seasons, winter (the underworld) and summer (the upper world). Persephone accepted her new role as the Queen of the Dead. Nothing in mythology suggests that she and her husband were unhappy with each other.

Persephone's eating of the pomegranate seeds suggests something not unlike Eve's eating the fruit from the Tree of Knowledge. This act gave the young goddess a wisdom and maturity she had not possessed before. It is one thing to gain the knowledge of our bright, sunlit—but in other ways perfectly ordinary—world. It is quite another thing to learn to navigate through the darkness of the soul, our own inner realm of the dead. Indeed, Persephone's role in actual Greek religion was a most important one, for she was one of the principal deities of the cult of Orpheus, a Greek mystery school that concerned itself with navigating through the realms of the dead (like the shaman Orpheus) and reaching a happy state of existence in the afterlife. To the Orphics, Persephone was the "Queen of Shades," the Goddess, all-knowing and all-wise. And in fact a woman with a strong, positive Pluto in her birth chart may very well become a contemporary Queen of Shadows, a wise woman who understands birth, death, and the lore of the three worlds. She frequently has strong psychic abilities, though it must be admitted that her relationships are often obsessive or overly intense—after all, she unconsciously seeks out the King of the Dead!

Pluto's connections in a birth chart are often rather difficult, to say the least. Aspects between Venus and Pluto in a birth chart are particularly challenging; in a woman's chart especially, they may show a strong connection with the Persephone archetype and may tend to symbolize the themes of violation, bondage, and obsession in relationships that we have already noted. While Venus-Pluto contacts are difficult, Moon-Pluto connections, with their associations of broken mother/child relationships and the theme of the Underworld Mother, are sometimes infinitely more so! Aspects between the Moon and Pluto can indicate a number of problems. There may be a strong feeling of abandonment, so that the native seeks out co-dependent relationships based on need and a false sense of loyalty. There may be attempts (often passive-aggressive and frequently quite unconscious) to control other people psychologically, or the native may, in turn, find herself or himself constantly attracting people who play such control games with others. There is frequently a tendency to "consume" other people emotionally—"smother love" instead of "mother love." One way or another, Pluto and the Moon are prone to find themselves at odds with each other in the birth chart, and in the lives of those who have Moon-Pluto connections therein.

If we should doubt the connection of this archetype with the Terrible Mother archetype (the evil stepmother or witch of fairy tales), let us note that the name Persephone means "she who is to be feared." The Queen of Shadows is not just a sweet-faced maiden playing in a field of flowers, nor the beautiful but rather introverted Goddess of the Dead—she is also a close relation to fearsome Ereshkigal, to Medusa, or to the darker forms of Kali. She should be treated with respect!

Still, as problematic as all this might sound for a person whose Pluto is overly stated in the birth chart, let's not forget that Pluto, along with Scorpio (the sign it rules), is all about transformation. In therapeutic, astrological, and psychological circles, one may encounter this type of Pluto person rather frequently—one who is continually transforming the emotional effects of many of life's earlier traumas. The Pluto/Scorpio type is continually reinventing himself or herself. The descent to the underworld carries with it a seasonal, cyclical rhythm. This is always followed by an ascent back to the upper world. To the people who repeat that cycle numerous times throughout their lives, there is an experience of freshness and renewal about it, as if an unconscious but powerfully enacted fate were forcing them every so often to purge their former self and begin anew.

This process does not occur quickly for most. It often takes the better part of one's life—at least the middle third—to achieve that goal. Look to the major transits of Pluto in one's life for clues as to when the periods of greatest transformation might occur. For those born with Pluto in Leo (1939 to 1957) and for those born with Pluto in Virgo (1957 to 1972), Pluto's transiting square to its original birth position occurs at about age forty. It is also worthwhile to check Pluto's transit to personal planets such as the Sun and Moon, and to important astrological points such as the Ascendant, for those periods will indicate the most profound of life's changes, and for these dates one must consult the horoscope.

Let us not forget that Pluto and its sign Scorpio typically accept the darker, shadowy projections of the realm of death that much of Western society finds uncomfortable and tries to forestall if not outright totally deny—whether psychological or physical. Pluto rules that realm proudly, with the silent understanding that all of us will visit him sooner or later.

DREAMWORK AND ACTIVE IMAGINATION

Some of the early Jungian psychologists who explored women's psyches (notably Esther Harding) have drawn attention to the archetype of the Demon Lover who appears in both dreams and fairy tales.[2] He is mysterious, both fascinating and dangerous at the same time. He is sometimes actually invisible and may first appear in the dreams of women simply as a symbol, a horse, or a bird. Ultimately he is deeply erotic, and his function as a woman's archetype is to awaken the deepest levels of sensuality. He is the unseen lover who seizes you from behind, who "takes you" in the dark.

The Demon Lover archetype appears in hundreds of cheap Gothic novels, much as he appears in women's dreams. He is the handsome but brooding man in black who is a renegade or piratical duke, count, or whatever, and typically an inveterate womanizer as well. The heroine's initial contacts with him are usually sharp and acrimonious, combative in nature. This, of course, is because he is her masculine Shadow. But as we have seen in some of our other chapters, it is the despised Shadow who opens our inner doorways to wholeness, to healing. Thus, by the end of the book, the Demon Lover will inevitably "ravish" the novel's heroine in bodice-ripping prose and then win her heart . . . thus the archetype of Pluto as he appears in pulp fiction.

Pluto, like the Gothic Demon Lover, is a mystery man, and the dark colors of these fictional bad boys may remind us of Pluto's association with the land of the dead. The god Hades or Pluto sometimes wears a helmet of invisibility, so we may understand why he often appears as an anonymous figure in dreams, and of course, he is a ravisher, as every young Persephone knows full well. One moment you are playing innocently in a field of flowers; the next moment you are the Queen of Shades, with all the requisite wisdom, sorrow, and intuition implied in that archetype. How did you get there? The Demon Lover carried you away, opened the dark Plutonian depths of your soul, and let you take a look—that's how.

Pluto also carries associations with the Underworld Mother, and this planetary archetype frequently appears in the dreams of men. Whenever there are issues of control, psychological dependence, and negative mother images generally, look for Pluto. One of the authors is familiar with a series of dreams from a male client that embodied the Plutonian mother in all its gruesome detail. The man's elderly mother appeared to him in a dream with her eyes blazing with hatred, vermin and vomit spewing from her mouth as she cursed him and set his house on fire. The individual felt that his mother was still attempting to control his life by acting as a "helpless victim" in need of his constant attention, and his dream certainly brought out that feeling. The mother's birth chart revealed a Sun-Pluto conjunction in Cancer with the Moon in Scorpio.

According to Artemidorus, this client's dream would certainly be a "bad" one, for he claims that a dream of Hades or Persephone in a "threatening" aspect tends to awaken our deepest fears. At the same time, however, Artemidorus seems to indicate that these two archetypes are generally experienced in their more positive mode. And in that case, they symbolize fearlessness rather than fear. After all, as he points out, those who live in the kingdom of the shades no longer have anything to fear.[3] Therefore, we may say that a Demon Lover or Shadowy Man who is well-disposed towards the dreamer, or a strange and mystic woman who proves helpful in a dream, indicate that we are facing our own inner process of transformation in a positive way.

Artemidorus also notes Pluto's traditional association with wealth by asserting that a positive experience of either Hades or Persephone is favorable for all financial matters. Remembering how often the Persephone archetype symbolizes the female mystic, we should not be surprised to learn from the old dream master that these archetypes may also prove favorable for "mystic and arcane practices."[4]

Some may suggest that the widow, all dressed in black, might be another Plutonian dream figure. That can certainly be true, but as we have offered other archetypes in the form of asteroids in this book, we believe this figure might be even more closely associated with the true nature of Ceres/Demeter (see chapter 12) as when she was in mourning for her lost daughter.

PLANETARY REMEDIES

In general, Pluto is an archetype that most of us would prefer to minimize rather than strengthen. The authors have certainly met individuals who claim to enjoy and even seek out "inner transformation," and who are consequently ready to leap right into their private underworld—but the practice isn't really recommended. We all experience plenty of transformation in our lives, and we are all forced to deal with our inner darkness at one time or another, to gaze through the mirror into our personal "kingdom of ghosts." There is very little point in trying to elicit such an experience in our lives, and a lot of common sense in simply taking it as it comes.

There are times, however, when the intensity of transformation may become too much for us, the speed of inner change too great to bear. At these times, we may wish to "propitiate" Pluto. To propitiate a difficult planet is very different than increasing the power of a helpful planet. It is a process of honoring the difficulty, of showing respect to its power and thereby avoiding its more destructive side—by way of analogy, we may deeply respect the power and majesty of a hurricane, but we may not wish to stand directly in its path.

One of the best ways of propitiating Pluto—of harmonizing its energies so that they work with more grace and balance in our own lives and charts—is to actually make ourselves aware of our own mortality. This can take many different forms, from simply studying (for example) Tibetan traditions about death and dying, and facing the issues that such a study raises, all the way to volunteering time at a hospice or other facility where one actually works with and interacts with the terminally ill or the dying.

INVOCATION AND AWARENESS

Just as we would seldom wish to increase the power of Pluto in our lives, so would we seldom wish to "invoke" him into our lives, or ask him to visit us with his wild gusts of transformative energy. Some women may find the Persephone archetype an attractive one, especially if they sincerely seek the deep wisdom of the "underworld," but we should remember that Persephone is not quite the sweet-natured Queen of Shadows that she appears to be, and that her archetype has powerful affinities with demonic feminine potencies like Medusa or the Terrible Mother. Best to leave well enough alone.

We may, however, find it helpful to become more aware of Hades and Persephone in our lives, which is something much different than actually "invoking" them. To become aware of these archetypes is to become aware of our own "shadow," of everything that lies hidden in our own private underworld. This includes our fears. When we have just witnessed a terrifying experience such as terrorism of any kind, or if we have just awakened from a dream where we have been terrorized in some way, invoking Pluto in a propitious way may be appropriate—as in a guardian or shamanic presence to guide us through this realm. This simply requires a deep and sometimes even brutal honesty regarding our own failings and weaknesses.

Every time we look into the mirror of our souls, and see some darkness there, we have become aware of Hades and Persephone in our lives, and we are ready to reap the benefits of their wisdom. Let us remember that consciousness of our own Shadow is the beginning of healing and (that Plutonian word again) *transformation,* and that Ishtar's journey into the realm of Nergal and Ereshkigal ended with her assuming the mantle of the Queen of Heaven. We all have the potential to do the same.

---

1. In ancient Hellenistic astrology, as well as in contemporary Vedic astrology, the Second House of the horoscope is a house of death as well as a house of wealth. This double signification may reflect the mythic connection described here.

2. Harding, M. Esther, *The Way of All Women* (New York: Harper & Row, 1975).

3. Artemidorus, *The Interpretation of Dreams: Oneirocritica,* trans. by Robert J. White (Park Ridge, NJ: Noyes Press, 1975).

4. Ibid.

APPENDIX I
THE MINOR ASTEROIDS

As proponents of asteroids insist, the yummy details and specifics that asteroids can add to the stories of one's life bring in subtle nuances that the planetary picture alone may not always provide. Since we are working with astrology as a mythic and archetypal language, let's use these minor bodies for amplification.

In reading the stories of some of these asteroids, you may recognize an obvious and immediate correlation to some of the planets, and this is as it should be. Eros and Psyche may be regarded as extensions of the love planet Venus, Pandora relates to Mercury and Uranus, Pan to Saturn, and so on. We leave it to you to determine just which myths or asteroids you want to delve into more deeply. If Venus plays a strong part in your chart, take a look at the love asteroids—Eros, Amor, Cupid, and Sappho. If Saturn plays a strong role in your life, it might be helpful to examine Vesta and/or Pan. Sadly (or happily for the reader), we will have to let the other 5,000+ asteroids go unmentioned for the present, but they are researchable and readily available in customized ephemerides. In other words, if you have a personal affinity to Merlin and Morgana or to Isis and Osiris, there is plenty of information to help you dig further.

HEPHAESTUS

Hephaestus' father was Zeus and his mother was Hera. How much more can a child ask than to be born of the king and queen of the gods? But if the king and queen do nothing but quarrel with each other, we might not envy his wealth and position so much. To make matters worse, he was not an especially attractive fellow. His mother—who, as we have seen, required nothing short of perfection from her children—was so annoyed about his ugliness at birth that she tossed the infant right off of Olympus. He fell to earth, landing on one of the Greek islands. The injuries he sustained as a result left him wounded; he was physically lame and walked with a limp, and was also psychologically introverted and frequently morose. He became the gifted craftsman and blacksmith of the gods who turned his inner demons into beautiful works of art.

Though rejected by both parents, fate stepped in. After he fell to earth, he was rescued by female nymphs who loved and cared for him. This may remind us of Dionysus (see Neptune), who was also raised by friendly nymphs devoted to preserving him from Hera's all-too-common wrath.

While Dionysus actually grew up disguised as a woman, Hephaestus did not, but because of the overwhelming presence of females in his young life, he grew to be quite enamored of them.

Both Dionysus and Hephaestus embody the feminine in a powerful way, even though they are men. But they are not men who are homosexually driven. They are typically men who love and adore women and express it through their being—in Dionysus' case through music and dance, and in Hephaestus' case through sculpting, jewelry making, or metal-working. He is the brooding creative artist, unlovely and inarticulate, who worships life, beauty, and women through his art. Despite his physical strength and power (he is typically depicted as a man of extraordinary muscle), he is not a "traditional" man, geared to the domains of Mars, Jupiter, Mercury, or Saturn. As the "Dionysian" personality is geared to Neptune, so Hephaestus is often hard-wired to more feminine archetypes, often symbolized in the horoscope by the planet Venus. After all, Venus is one of the principal indicators of the way in which a man relates to the feminine, and she is also the eternal patroness of the arts, so we should not be surprised to find her prominent in the horoscopes of these quiet, creative men who are enthralled in a beautiful but dangerous spiritual bondage to the anima.

It may take the strong guiding influence of a mother, foster-mother, grandmother, or older sister to nurture a young Hephaestus-type male and encourage his natural tendencies to flower. Or he may well require only the presence of a lover to whom he can devote his talent. Unfortunately, the blossoming of his talent is likely to be the only fortunate element in his love life. Most women seek him out as friend or a confidant rather than a lover. In his heart, Hephaestus is already enthralled with the most desirable goddess of all—Venus/Aphrodite.

Aphrodite was, in fact, his wife, bestowed upon him by father Zeus in a moment more touching than wise. While Hephaestus worshipped Aphrodite as much as every other man, he could not truly possess her. She is a wild force of nature that cannot be tamed. Aphrodite is the archetype of the woman who is sexually free, choosing her own lovers and living by no law save her own. In the myths, she ignores her brooding, silent husband altogether, indulging herself in countless affairs without the least regard for his feelings. Still he continued to love her, despite the sheer humiliation of it all.

Gifted, talented men who fall hopelessly in love with beautiful women are no strangers to the Hephaestus mythos. Modern-day men who play out this archetype may be the master craftsmen who sit at their computers or are engaged for hours on end in business meetings or some other such project that gets the focus of their attention. The beautiful Venuses to whom they are married are going to grow bored quite quickly and will let their imaginations and fantasies begin to wander. For an example, see our analysis of the relationship between the sparkling but flighty Lotte Lenya and the gifted but introverted Kurt Weill, as described in chapter 2 of this book. Venus needs to be adored! Whether the women involved in such relationships will actualize their fantasies or not depends upon their individual horoscopes, but it is a story to watch for in any case.

The cure for this dilemma would appear to be simple. Pay more attention to your partner! One woman recently observed and commented to a Hephaestian male whose marriage was clearly on the rocks, "Why don't you try watering and tending to your wife even half as much as you do your garden and plants?" But some Hephaestus men were born to create rather than relate. Their true brides are their poems, their symphonies, their paintings, their businesses. And some Venus women will never be able to receive enough adoration—even if they function as Goddesses to the multitudes.

The drama goes on.

PAN

Pan is a force of nature. More than that—it might almost be said that Pan is nature itself. His name simply means "all." Thus everything that exists arises from the vast matrix of primal, uncontrolled nature, and the humble goat god of Greek myth is a kind of raw metaphor for life itself. Half man and half goat, living in the woods like a savage, indulging himself in lusty sexuality and playing his syrinx or pan pipes for the sheer joy of listening to himself, Pan is beyond boundaries, beyond limits, beyond law.

As such, Pan represents an energy that humans have a hard time controlling, try as they might. We could actually perceive Pan as a kind of shadow figure to Saturn and Capricorn. As we mentioned in the chapter on Saturn, Pan was famous (or perhaps we should say notorious) for surprising travelers in the woods with a great shout, a great roar that instilled "panic" in his auditors. This panic aptly illustrates the fear and dissociation that many people feel when forced to deal with Pan's wildness, his raw energy. As archetypal psychologists have been quick to point out, those who suffer from panic attacks are those who have failed to integrate their own wildness into the fabric of their ordinary, decent, "respectable" lives. They don't know how to deal with Pan.

And how could they? Since the end of antiquity, Western civilization has had nothing but trouble trying to deal with Pan and his fierce magic. His cloven hooves and goatish horns formed part of the medieval image of the devil. The medieval church, with its hatred of human sexuality, recoiled from the raw nakedness and freely expressed sexual delight that Pan enjoys quite openly and publicly, actually delighting in the shock effect that it produces in those who suddenly encounter him and are startled by his tauntings. Pan, because he is part goat and lives in the woods, is portrayed naked, but his nakedness is quite different from that of, say, Chiron, who also lives in the woods and is part horse. Pan's naked body is almost always depicted engaging with nature in a sexual and erotic way.

In Aleister Crowley's Tarot deck, Pan is the image chosen to portray the devil. But if the god Pan does represent a wild and freely expressed nakedness, he may always be relegated to the outer fringes of society, as there is really no place in the context of a "civilized" social structure where Pan can be allowed to exist. However, in the human condition, one must find a place for Pan's expression, because the more suppressed the energy is, the more one needs to release it in some constructive way, which may be why there are so many panic complexes and conditions that ail our society.

A common dream for both men and women is being naked, fully exposed in public, to the shock and humiliation—if not sheer panic—of the dreamer. One young woman dreamed she was dancing naked, and, becoming fully entranced by the music, danced freely and pleasurably. Suddenly she noticed a long dark hallway, at the end of which was standing her mother, staring at her in disbelief. Her immediate thought was, "I must go cover myself immediately." But instead, she looked directly at her mother and smiled, continuing to dance. For the dreamer this was a huge leap, because this sort of thing was particularly out of character for her, due in large part to the influence of her mother. She had embraced Pan.

Asteroid #4450 is named Pan, discovered on September 25, 1987, at Palomar Observatory. There is a readily available customized ephemeris that can be obtained to chart his position in any horoscope.

PANDORA

Pandora was the first mortal woman and was created by the smith god Hephaestus under orders from Zeus. She was given many gifts and great beauty, and she was bestowed upon the Titan Epimetheus (Hindsight), brother of Prometheus (Foresight—see Uranus). Epimetheus had been given a special box and warned by Zeus not to open it. Human nature is curious, if nothing else, so how long did Zeus really believe that it would take before someone would open that box? It was a trick designed by Zeus in one of his less benevolent moments to punish mankind. He was in a chronic fit of anger over the fact that Prometheus had stolen fire from the gods and thus "enlightened" humankind. Zeus wanted to bring the arrogant mortals down a bit and keep the gods in control. Pandora, of course, opened the box, thus unleashing a host of plagues and diseases that flew forth and descended upon humankind. But there was one thing left inside, placed there by the wise and kind Prometheus—hope.

Pandora's story shares some interesting similarities with the Biblical Eve. Both were warned by the supreme deity (Eve by Yahweh, Pandora by Zeus) not to commit a certain act. Neither one obeyed. Consequently, the blame was placed upon them for the "fall" of humankind. In Eve's case, the fall of mankind ensued from her act of tasting the forbidden fruit—assuming, of course, that we really have "fallen," for early Christian Gnostics saw our taste of the forbidden fruit as a good thing. In the case of the apple, the serpent, and the tree, all of these symbols can be seen as relating to the sexual act. Once the fruit was tasted, Adam and Eve then became like God, as the serpent promised they would. They now knew the pleasure of the sexual act and gained the knowledge of reproduction. Furthermore, the serpent and the tree, as we have mentioned in other chapters (Mercury, Chiron, Lilith, Vesta), give us the knowledge of the kundalini and the opportunity to reach an enlightened god-like state. This was threatening enough to punish those who got too close to it. The box of Pandora can be thought of similarly, in that it can relate to female genitalia (the yoni)—one of the greater mysteries of life. (We discuss this in more detail in our chapter on Lilith.)

Though Pandora was created as a woman, her psychology was really that of a child or an adolescent—besides which, as the first woman, she had no precedent, no history in which she could learn or be coached from her elders about the consequences of her actions. Children will always attempt to open the box. Some are punished for such a deed, others are mildly reprimanded, and others are excused as just being children. Human nature has a hard time allowing the sealed box to exist without finding out what's inside. Perhaps these are the images of Pandora that will come through the dream process. The dream may not be about a box, per se, but similar elements may be visualized, such as opening a closet, a cabinet, or a drawer to encounter thousands of stored items (complexes, demons) that come tumbling out. There is also a good chance it may relate to sexual awakening, which to a child or adolescent is certainly a forbidden fruit that must not be tasted or a box that must not be opened. It involves entering an unknown realm, driven by the curiosity to know more. Pursuing unknown realms eventually leads to enlightenment of some kind. Though this enlightenment comes with a price, it still leads down a path that must be pursued.

Pandora is asteroid #55 and was discovered on September 10, 1858.

PSYCHE AND EROS

Eros, the god of love—what could possibly evoke more images and feelings of passion than his name? He is the god of "erotic" sensation and fantasy—that indefinable quality in the heart that poets, playwrights, and troubadours have fervently sought for some 900 years of Western history. Eros—variously known as Amor and Cupid (the Roman names)—is that youthful trickster god that shoots arrows of romantic love into his victims' hearts, rendering them senselessly and hopelessly lovesick, and thus unable to think or act rationally. Let's not forget that Eros is the child of Aphrodite (see Venus) and has within his domain the ability to perform whatever the goddess of love wishes.

The full story of Eros and Psyche has enjoyed expert psychological interpretation in Erich Neumann's *Amor and Psyche*, which is a retelling of the poet Lucius Apuleius' story from the fifth century.[1] Though Amor and Cupid are used interchangeably in the stories of this god down through the ages, we will be herein using the name of the original god, Eros. Briefly recounted here, the story goes something like this . . .

Psyche is the beautiful daughter of a prominent human family. So beautiful is she that men from near and far come to worship before her as if she were the goddess of love herself. This serves only to infuriate the real goddess of love, Aphrodite, who flies into a jealous rage and immediately calls for her death. Her family, not wishing to offend the gods, resolves the issue by bringing her as an offering (or sacrifice) to them. She is taken to the sea and blindfolded, as it is there that she will be met by a deep sea monster who will escort her to her death. Meanwhile, Psyche has been told that she is being taken there to be met by her handsome young bridegroom.

At the fated time and place, the love god Eros flies by. Spotting her exquisite beauty, he is momentarily awestruck and "accidentally" wounds himself with one of his own love arrows. Quickly he shuttles her away from her rock in the ocean and off to his own secret hiding place, a beautiful palace in the clouds. Psyche has already fallen deeply in love with her rescuer, but as she passes her time away in Eros' palace, she is still prohibited from knowing his identity. He comes to her only at night and only in the dark. This state of affairs continues for a while until her jealous sisters pay her a visit and instruct her to light a lamp once he is asleep and thus learn his true nature. The young, innocent, and inexperienced Psyche (much like Pandora) complies. That night, she lights the lamp from the darkened corridor and finally gazes upon her beloved. So awestruck is she by his beauty and sweetness that she accidentally spills the oil from the lamp. It lands upon Eros' shoulder. He awakens and immediately takes flight.

The word psyche means "soul," and thus one of the mysteries enacted in this story is the meeting—for the first time—of love (Eros) and soul (Psyche). A mere glimpse of that kind of love is so frightening that most mere mortals can't sustain it. Awkward and nervous actions conspire to give us a momentary glance and then quickly remove it from our sight until such time as it can be handled. Fate would eventually reunite the two lovers, but only after much conscious effort and focus towards that end on the part of young Psyche, who is required to endure many trials and challenges before Eros can be hers once again.

Notice how accidents and fated encounters play a big part in this story. The two protagonists fall in love before they really know each other, but, more importantly, before they really know themselves. Separation forces growth, personal change, and maturation for both parties. This story is played out constantly in human life. Love's search for soul and soul's search for love is the theme often portrayed in the epics and plays of yesterday as well as the films of today.

The search for a soul mate is a question that almost always comes up in astrological consultations. "When will I find my soul mate?" or even, "Do I have a soul mate?" How would one answer that question from an astrological chart? We have talked about the role of Venus and Mars in matters of seduction and romantic attraction, much like two teenaged lovers meeting and relating for the first time. We have spoken of Juno and Jupiter as the archetypal pair of marriage, even if it is often the marriage of status for power, prestige, or political gain. But what of soul mates? Here we may look to the story of Eros and Psyche, one of the most engaging myths about the workings of love on Mount Olympus.

There are three asteroids named for this little guy as well as an asteroid named Psyche. All have implications for how fate has woven the symbolism of love and soul into the context of our lives through these astronomical placements. Amor is Asteroid #1221, discovered on March 12, 1932. Cupid is Asteroid #763, discovered on September 25, 1913, and Eros is Asteroid #433, discovered on August 13, 1898. Psyche is Asteroid #16, discovered on March 17, 1852.

---

1. Neumann, Erich, *Amor and Psyche,* translated from the German by Ralph Manheim (Princeton, NJ: Princeton University Press, 1971).

APPENDIX II
PLANETARY ARCHETYPES

In this book, we have offered ideas and techniques to stimulate your thinking about working with the experiential part of the archetypes in discussion. We listed certain planetary archetypes whose universal meanings may be translated in countless ways. With space limitations being what they are, it is impossible here to convey these archetypes in the myriad ways they could potentially manifest, but the ones we presented may serve to stimulate your thinking. The planets we included fall into three major categories:

1. *The Inner Planets*—Includes the Sun and Moon, which for convenience' sake are referred to as "planets," as well as all planets leading up to the asteroid belt.
2. *The Asteroids*—Includes asteroids or other celestial bodies that have been named for mythological principles and that carry archetypal energy.
3. *The Planets Beyond*—Includes everything beyond the asteroid belt, including Jupiter, Saturn, Chiron, and the outer planets, Uranus, Neptune, and Pluto.

When we present these ideas in workshops and classes, audience members tend to offer impressive feedback on how these images are visited upon them. And, of course, you, the reader, will have come up with images of your own from studying your birth chart or transits, and especially if you are an artist, an intuitive, or a dreamer, and have a well-developed (active) imagination. If you have experienced a dream or an archetypal image that appeared to you, we would be happy to hear from you regarding this. Please feel free to share it here. You may also include your birth data or specify a significant chart pattern. Furthermore, if you are so inclined to share it with others, please sign the permission release and let us know. We will be glad to include it in upcoming articles, books, or classroom experiences.

Date of Birth: _____

Exact Time of Birth: _____

Place of Birth: _____

Dream or Experience: _____

_____
_____
_____
_____
_____
_____
_____
_____
_____
_____
_____
_____
_____
_____
_____
_____
_____
_____

I, the undersigned, grant the authors of *Mythic Astrology Applied* to use this story. I understand that my identity will be kept confidential.

_____

Signature

_____

Date

BIBLIOGRAPHY

Apuleius, Lucius. *The Golden Ass.* Translated by Robert Graves. Harmondsworth, England: Penguin Books, 1972.

Artemidorus. *The Interpretation of Dreams: Oneirocritica.* Translated by Robert J. White. Park Ridge, NJ: Noyes Press, 1975.

Artress, Dr. Lauren. *Walking a Sacred Path: Rediscovering the Labyrinth As a Sacred Tool.* Atlanta, GA: Riverbend Books, 1996.

Bach, Eleanor, and George Climlas. *Ephemerides of the Asteroids: Ceres, Pallas, Juno, Vesta, 1900–2000.* New York: Celestial Communications, 1973.

Baigent, Michael. *The Omens of Babylon: Astrology and Ancient Mesopotamia.* London: Penguin-Arkana, 1994.

Baigent, Michael, Richard Leigh, and Henry Lincoln. *Holy Blood, Holy Grail.* New York: Dell Publishing, 1982.

Bell, Robert E. *Women of Classical Mythology, A Biographical Dictionary.* London: Oxford Univ. Press, 1993.

Boer, Charles, trans. "The Homeric Hymn to Hestia." *The Homeric Hymns.* Dallas, TX: Spring Publications, 1979.

Bolen, Jean Shinoda. *Gods in Everyman.* New York: Harper & Row, 1989.

———. *Goddesses in Everywoman.* New York: Harper & Row, 1984.

———. *The Millionth Circle.* Berkeley, CA: Conari, 2000.

Bottero, Jean. *Mesopotamia: Writing, Reasoning, and the Gods.* Chicago, IL: Univ. of Chicago, 1992.

Brown, Dan. *The Da Vinci Code.* New York: Doubleday, 2003.

Campbell, Joseph, and Bill Moyers. *The Power of Myth.* New York: Doubleday, 1988.

Campion, Nick. *Book of World Horoscopes.* England: Aquarian Press, 1988.

Cox Miller, Patricia. "Euripides, Iphigenia at Aulis." Quoted in *Dreams in Late Antiquity.* Princeton, NJ: Princeton Univ. Press, 1994.

Crane, Joseph. *A Practical Guide to Traditional Astrology.* Reston, VA: ARHAT, 1997.

deGravelaine, Joëlle. *Lilith: Der Schwartz Monde.* Wettswil, Switzerland: Edition Astro Data, 1990. Translation of the original French *Le Retoil de Lilith.*

Dodds, E. R. *The Greeks and the Irrational.* Boston: Beacon Press, 1957.

Dossey, Larry. *Reinventing Medicine.* San Francisco, CA: Harper Collins, 1999.

Downing, Christine. *The Goddess: Mythological Images of the Feminine.* New York: Crossroad Press, 1981.

Ficino, Marsilio. *The Book of Life.* Translated by Charles Boer. Irving, TX: Spring Publications, 1980.

Gardner, Laurence. *Genesis of the Grail Kings.* Boston, MA: Element Books, 2000.

George, Demetra, and Douglas Bloch. *Asteroid Goddesses.* San Diego, CA: ACS Publications, 1986.

George, Demetra. *Mysteries of the Dark Moon.* San Francisco, CA: Harper, 1992.

Gimbutas, Marija. *The Civilization of the Goddess.* San Francisco, CA: Harper, 1991.

Gleadow, Rupert. *The Origin of the Zodiac.* New York: Castle Books, 1968.

Goldstein-Jacobson, Ivy. *Dark Moon Lilith in Astrology.* Alhambra, CA: Frank Severy.

Graves, Robert. *Greek Myths.* New York: Penguin, 1984.

Greene, Liz. *The Astrology of Fate.* York Beach, ME: Samuel Weiser, Inc., 1984.

Greenbaum, Dorian. *Late Classical Astrology: Paulus Alexandrinus and Olympiodorus.* Reston, VA: ARHAT, 2001.

Greenbaum, Dorian, and Vettius Valens. *The Anthology.* Translated by R. Schmidt. 3 vols. Berkeley Springs, WV: Golden Hind Press, 1994.

Guttman, Ariel, and Kenneth Johnson. *Mythic Astrology: Archetypal Powers in the Horoscope.* St. Paul, MN: Llewellyn Publications, 1993.

Hancock, Graham, and Santha Faiia. *Heaven's Mirror.* New York: Three Rivers Press, 1998.

Hand, Robert. *Night & Day: Planetary Sect in Astrology.* Reston, VA: ARHAT, 1995.

Harding, M. Esther. *The Way of All Women.* New York: Harper & Row, 1975.

Hillman, James. *A Blue Fire.* New York: Perennial, 1991.

———. *The Dream and the Underworld.* New York: Harper & Row, 1979.

———. *The Force of Character and the Lasting Life.* New York: Random House, 1999.

———. *Pan and the Nightmare.* New York: Spring Publications, 1972.

Homer. *The Odyssey of Homer.* Translated by Richmond Lattimore. Bk. 19. New York: Harper Collins, 1975.

Jay, Delphine. *Interpreting Lilith.* Tempe, AZ: American Federation of Astrologers, 1981.

Johnsen, Linda. "Dealing with Disaster: The Vedic Approach." *The Mountain Astrologer* June/July 1997.

Jung, Carl. *Memories, Dreams, Reflections.* Edited by Aniela Jaffé. Translated by Richard and Clara Winston. 1963. Reprint, New York: Vintage Books, 1989.

Kerenyi, C. *Eleusis: Archetypal Image of Mother and Daughter.* Translated by Ralph Manheim. New York: Shocken Books, 1977.

Kirksey, Barbara. "Hestia: A Background of Psychological Focusing." *Facing the Gods.* Edited by James Hillman. Dallas: Spring Publications, 1980.

Lattimore, Richmond, trans. *The Iliad of Homer.* Vol. 5, bk. 4. Chicago: Univ. of Chicago Press, 1951.

Lemesurier, Peter. *The Healing of the Gods: The Magic of Symbols and the Practice of Theotherapy.* Element Books, 1988.

Lovelock, James. *Gaia: A New Look at Life on Earth.* London: Oxford Univ. Press, 1982.

Manilius, Marcus. *The Five Books of Manilius.* 1697. Reprint, Washington, D.C.: American Federation of Astrologers, 1953.

Meier, C. A. *Ancient Incubation and Modern Psychotherapy.* Translated by Monica Curtis. Evanston, IL: Northwestern Univ. Press, 1967.

Moore, Thomas. *Care of the Soul.* New York: Harper Collins, 1992.

———. *Soul Mates.* New York: Harper Perennial, 1994.

Neumann, Erich. *Amor and Psyche.* Translated by Ralph Manheim. Princeton, NJ: Princeton Univ. Press, 1971.

Parman, Susan. *Dreams and Culture.* New York: Praeger, 1991.

Perera, Sylvia Brinton. *Descent to the Goddess.* Toronto: Inner City Books, 1981.

Plato. *Timaeus and Critias.* Harmondsworth, England: Penguin, 1971.

———. "Phaedrus." *The Works of Plato.* New York: Modern Library, 1956; 263–332.

Ptolemy. *Tetrabiblos.* Edited and translated into English by F. E. Robbins. Cambridge, MA: Harvard Univ. Press, 1940.

Robinson, James M., ed. *The Nag Hammadi Library.* San Francisco, CA: Harper, 1990.

Rudhyar, Dane. *An Astrological Mandala: The Cycle of Transformations and Its 360 Phases.* New York: Vintage Books, 1974.

Sagan, Carl. *Cosmos.* New York: Random House, 1980.

Sandars, N. K., trans. *The Epic of Gilgamesh.* London: Penguin, 1988.

Santa Fe New Mexican, "Man Sinks into Mother's Grave," Sunday ed., May 21, 1995.

Schwartz, Jacob, Ph.D. *Asteroid Name Encyclopedia.* St. Paul, MN: Llewellyn Publications, 1995.

Shaw, Miranda. *Passionate Enlightenment: Women in Tantric Buddhism.* Princeton, NJ: Princeton Univ. Press, 1994.

Sitchin, Zecharia. *Divine Encounters.* New York: Avon Books, 1995.

———. *The Twelfth Planet.* Santa Fe, NM: Bear & Co., 1991.

Starck, Marcia, and Gynne Stern. *The Dark Goddess: Dancing with the Shadow.* Freedom, CA: Crossing Press, 1993.

Stevens, Anthony. *Ariadne's Clue: A Guide to the Symbols of Humankind.* Princeton, NJ: Princeton Univ. Press, 1999.

———. *Private Myths: Dreams and Dreaming.* London: Penguin Books, 1996.

———. *The Two Million Year Old Self.* Texas A & M Univ. Press, 1993.

Sullivan, Erin. *Retrograde Planets.* Arkana/Penguin, 1992.

Tarnas, Richard. "Prometheus The Awakener: An Essay on the Archetypal Meaning of the Planet Uranus." *Spring*, 1995.

Valens, Vettius. *The Anthology.* Translated by R. Schmidt. 3 vols. Berkeley Springs, WV: Golden Hind Press, 1994.

Wolff, Toni. *Structural Forms of the Feminine Psyche.* Translated by Paul Wazlawik. Zurich: Carl Jung Institute, 1956.

Woolger, Roger and Jennifer. *The Goddess Within.* New York: Fawcett, 1989.

INDEX

Abraham, 206
Achilles, 23, 60, 243
Actaeon, 99
Adam, 205–207, 291
Adonis, 26, 120
Aeschylus, 256
Aesculapius, 60–61, 63, 73, 241, 243, 245–249, 255
Agamemnon, 23
alchemy, alchemists, 13, 48, 86, 88, 107, 112–113, 119, 190, 237, 247, 261
Amalthea, 219, 233
Amaterasu, 81
America, Americans, 9, 138, 175
American Beauty, 188
Amor and Psyche, 292, 294
Anath, 206
Anchises, 118
anima, 12, 141–142, 288
anima mundi, 122, 131
animus, 12, 141–142, 176
Anthony, Susan B., 175
Anu, 5–6, 220
Aphrodite, 5, 8–9, 11, 25–26, 38, 47, 99, 105, 117–119, 121–125, 138, 140, 155, 183–185, 196–197, 200, 222, 288, 292–293
Apollo, 9, 38, 60–63, 82–85, 87, 95, 106–110, 129, 131, 153, 174–175, 222, 226, 245, 256, 269
Apuleius, Lucius, 96, 292
Aquarius, 8, 34–36, 38, 41, 48, 175, 180, 231, 233, 253–255, 258
archetypes, 8, 12–16, 18, 23, 25–30, 34, 37, 39–41, 47–48, 52–54, 60–61, 65, 68–69, 71, 73–75, 82, 86–87, 89, 96, 98, 101, 105, 107, 111–114, 119, 121–125, 130, 133, 137–141, 144–145, 151–152, 158, 166–168, 173–175, 178–180, 185, 187–190, 197–198, 200, 205, 208–212, 222, 232–233, 235, 237, 244–245, 247, 253–258, 260, 265–266, 268–269, 271, 273, 278–283, 288–289, 295, 297
Ares, 9, 137–138, 173
Ariadne, 153, 212, 267–268, 272–273
Aries, 18, 69, 132–133, 138
Artemidorus, 67–68, 76, 87–88, 98–99, 110–111, 122–124, 126, 133, 167, 178, 189, 199, 236, 282, 284
Artemis, 9, 47, 95, 98–99, 142, 159, 185, 200
Arthur, 117
Ashtaroth, 118
Ashtoreth, 206
Ashurbanipal, 6
Asklepios, 60, 245
Assyria, 6
Astarte, 118
astrology
   Babylonian, 7, 93, 137, 219
   Chinese, 117
   Hellenistic, 137, 222, 284
   Hindu, 46, 85, 87, 93–94, 97, 253
   medieval, 67, 94, 187, 199, 224, 233, 236
   Vedic, 100, 284
   Western, 8, 45, 93, 117, 132, 232
Astronomica, 102, 114, 265, 273
astronomy, 67, 93, 109, 243
Atharva Veda, 67

Athene, 9, 13, 63, 95, 119, 143, 151–155, 157, 159, 171, 173–180, 185, 200, 205–206, 209, 220–221, 271, 273
Athens, 173–174, 220, 271
Atlantis, 158, 265
Avebury, 93

Babylon, 5–6, 18, 45, 105–106, 117–118, 137, 183, 206, 220
Bacchus, 266
Beltane, 158
Benigni, Roberto, 139
Bening, Annette, 188
Bergen, Candice, 153
Berlin, 25, 31
Bible, The, 8, 59
Bolen, Jean Shinoda, 13, 19, 40, 119, 126, 152, 159
Bond, James, 139
Botticelli, 45–46, 121
Brando, Marlon, 111
Brazil, 9
Brecht, Bertolt, 25
Buddha, 122
Buddhism, 126

Campbell, Joseph, 12–13, 121
Cancer, 98, 130, 165–167, 224, 231, 235, 253, 282
Candlemas, 158
Candomble, 24
Capricorn, 5, 39, 41, 48, 70, 98, 132, 198, 231, 233, 235, 289
Celts, Celtic, etc., 9, 12, 64, 81, 158
Centaurs, 60–61, 243–244, 246–247
Centaurus, 61, 244

Ceres, 9, 52, 54, 133, 151, 154–155, 158–159, 161, 163–169, 175, 186, 197, 278, 282
Chan, Jackie, 139
Chaos, 14, 129–130, 205, 219–220, 253, 255
Chi Kung, 144
China, 10, 183
Chiron, 60–62, 112, 205, 208, 241, 243–249, 255, 290–291, 297
Christ, 13, 83, 130, 269
Christianity, 11, 14, 81, 96
Chthon, 61
Cleopatra, 122
Clinton, Hillary Rodham, 153, 155–157, 159, 177
collective unconscious, 11–12, 24, 34–35, 265
Corona Borealis, 267
Coronis, 60
Cos, 61–62
Crete, 61, 153, 174, 219, 267
Critias, 265, 273
Critique of Pure Reason, 254
Cronus, 9, 37, 130, 173–174, 195, 198, 219–220, 231–232, 236, 243, 253, 256, 265
Crouching Tiger, Hidden Dragon, 178
Crowley, Aleister, 290
Cumae, 195
Cupid, 287, 292, 294
Cybele, 95
Cyprus, 118

daimon, 17
Dakinis, 122
Dark Lover, 65

Day of the Dead, 158
de Medici, Lorenzo, 45
Dean, James, 111
Delos, 95
Delphi, 61–62, 83–85, 131, 153, 173, 195, 222
Demeter, 9, 47, 98, 133, 154–155, 159, 163–167, 185, 200, 278, 282
Demon Lover, 281–282
Dia de los Muertos, 158
Diana, Princess, 87
Dionysus, 38, 40, 60, 85, 163, 166–167, 185, 255, 265–269, 271–272, 287–288
Divine Child, 12, 48, 164, 167, 185
Dodona, 222, 225
Dossey, Larry, 59

Ea, 265
Earth Goddess, 61, 94–95, 101, 129, 131, 168, 278
Eastwood, Clint, 139
Egypt, 7, 45, 59, 61, 81, 96, 107
Eleanor of Aquitaine, 175
Eleusis, 164, 166, 169
Emerald Tablet of Hermes, 48, 113
Enki, 6, 220, 265
Enlil, 5–6, 206, 220
Enuma Anu Enlil, 6
Ephesus, 67
Epidaurus, 61–62, 71
Epimetheus, 289
Ereshkigal, 120, 137, 277–278, 280, 284
Eros, 183, 196, 287, 292–294
Euripides, 61, 76
Europa, 219

Europe, Europeans, 45, 64, 93–94, 130, 134, 174–175, 196, 208
Eurydice, 109
Eve, 279, 291

Fates, 98–99, 221
Father Time, 232
Ficino, Marsilio, 45–46, 48, 50, 53, 55, 88–89, 100, 121, 124, 226
Fonda, Jane, 153
Freud, Sigmund, 11–12, 14, 16, 31–38, 68
Freya, 121

Gaia, 9, 17, 83, 94, 101, 127, 129–134, 153, 158–159, 163, 168, 185, 195, 222, 231, 253, 257–259
Gaia Hypothesis, 129
Galen, 67
Gardner, Laurence, 206
Gawain and the Green Knight, 81
Gemini, 18, 31, 36, 95, 109–110, 209
George, Demetra, 208
Germany, 25, 30
Gilgamesh, 8, 19, 206
Gimbutas, Marija, 130, 134, 174
Gnostic Gospels, 207
Gnosticism, Gnostics, 291
Gods
  Babylonian, 265, 277
  Greek, 13, 53, 96, 152, 174, 219
  Olympian, 5, 138, 174
Goddessess
  Greek, 13, 96, 152
  Hindu, 96
  Olympian, 174
  Tantric, 122, 124
Golden Ass, The, 96, 102

Goldstein-Jacobson, Ivy, 208, 213
Graves, Robert, 102, 174, 196
Great Mother, 70, 93–94, 163
Greece, Greeks, 5, 8, 10, 13, 23, 26, 38, 40, 46, 54, 59, 61, 64, 68, 76, 82, 93, 98, 106, 117–118, 129, 137–138, 151–154, 173–174, 183, 190, 195, 200, 206, 219, 222, 231, 233, 243, 247, 265–266
Greene, Liz, 266
Gudea, 65–67, 69
Guinevere, 117, 158

Hagar, 206
Halloween, 158
Harding, Esther, 281
Harran, 113
Hecate, 96–97, 99, 102
Helios, 82
Hephaestus, 26, 29, 119, 174, 185, 188, 287–289, 291
Hera, 9, 26, 95, 117, 154–157, 183–188, 190, 200, 220–222, 224, 266, 289
Heracles, 186
Heraclitus, 17
Hercules, 82, 243
Hermes, 9, 48, 63, 70, 96, 105–109, 111, 113, 119, 129, 173, 197, 248
Hermetic philosophy, Hermetic sciences, Hermetics, 53, 107, 119
Herschel, William, 253
Hesiod, 129–131, 152, 173, 177, 253
Hestia, 9, 154–155, 195–201

Hillman, James, 13–15, 17, 19, 45, 86, 90, 108, 114, 201, 238–239
Hinduism, 14
Hippocrates, 61, 245
Hitler, 25
Holst, Gustav, 226
Homer, 8, 23, 65, 76, 108, 121, 178, 191, 225, 277
Horus, 96, 98
Hyperboreans, 85

Iasion, 163
Icarus, 158
Ice Age, 93, 102
Iceland, 121
Iliad, 8, 23, 64, 173, 186, 191
Inanna, 6, 117, 206, 277
India, 7, 45, 48, 50, 52–53, 64, 67, 84, 107, 124, 140, 183, 234, 237
individuation, 24, 34, 36
Io, 185
Ishkur, 6
Ishtar, 7–8, 93, 117–118, 120, 183, 277, 284
Isis, 95–96, 98, 158, 206, 289

Japan, 9, 81
Jay, Delphine, 209
Jesus, 81, 83, 96, 98, 207
Joan of Arc, 175
Jove, 9, 223, 227
Judaism, 205–206
Jung, Carl, 11–16, 31, 34–38, 41, 47, 68–69, 159
Juno, 9, 26, 40, 117, 126, 142, 151, 154–159, 175–176, 181, 183–191, 205, 220, 222, 294

Kabbalah, Kabbalists, 53, 73, 196, 205, 207–209, 211
Kali, 96, 206, 280
Kant, Immanuel, 254
Kerouac, Jack, 111
Khidr, 112
Kishar, 65
Knossos, 267
Kowal, Charles, 246
Kübler-Ross, Elisabeth, 245–246
kundalini, 107, 112, 119, 197, 200, 208, 291

Lagash, 65
Lake Tritonis, 174
Lammas, 158
Lancelot, 117
Lee, Bruce, 139
Lenya, Lotte, 25–29, 31, 40, 289
Leo, 8, 34–36, 38, 84, 157, 208, 224, 231, 253, 255, 280
Leone, Sergio, 139
Leto, 95
Levadia, 62
Libra, 52, 132–133
Libya, 174
Life Is Beautiful, 139
Lilith, 30–31, 96, 158, 176, 186, 196–197, 200, 203, 205–213, 291
Llew, 81
Loth, 81
Love, Courtney, 209
Lovelock, James, 129
Lugh, 81
Luna, 7, 9

Madonna (pop singer), 209, 211
Madonna (religious figure), 121, 153, 197
mania, 38
Manilius, Marcus, 95, 102, 110, 114, 138, 165, 265, 273
mantra, 45, 52–53
Marduk, 6–7, 158, 219–220, 231
Margolis, Lynn, 129
Mary Magdalene, 121, 207
Matrix, The, 139, 289
McLachlan, Sarah, 210
Medea, 207
Medusa, 153, 176–178, 206, 277, 280, 283
Meier, C. A., 71
Mentor, 11, 36, 178–180, 247
Merlin, 12, 107, 236, 289
Mesopotamia, 18, 126, 130, 219, 231
Metis, 152, 173–174
Michelangelo, 45
Middle Ages, 107, 120–122, 175, 183
Milky Way, 81
Minerva, 175
Minoans, 61
Minos, King, 219, 267
Mithras, 81
Mnemosyne, 113
Monroe, Marilyn, 40, 122
Montana, 179
Moore, Thomas, 17, 45
Morgana, 289
Morrison, Jim, 40–41
Mother Earth, 127, 129–134, 163, 166, 195
Mother Goddess, 93–94, 96, 130, 155, 159, 163

Moyers, Bill, 13, 19
Mt. Olympus, 23, 29, 225, 255
Mt. Pelion, 243
Muses, 38
Mysteries of the Dark Moon, 209, 213
Nabu, 6–7, 105

Nag Hammadi Library, 207, 212
Nannar, 6
Nanshe, 65–66
Naxos, 267–268
Neanderthals, 93
Near East, 118, 130, 153, 196, 207
Neith, 153
Neolithic, 93, 130
Nergal, 6–7, 137, 277–278, 284
Neumann, Erich, 292, 294
New York, 19, 40–41, 73, 76, 90, 102, 114, 126, 159, 169, 175, 180, 201, 212, 239, 284
Newman, Paul, 106
Nibiru, 219
Nietzsche, Friedrich, 85
Nindub, 66
Ningirsu, 66
Ningishzidda, 66
Ninhursag, 6
Ninib, 231–232, 238
Ninurta, 6–7, 66, 231
Nisaba, 66
North Node, 209

Odin, 107–108, 112
Odysseus, 178, 265
Odyssey, 8, 64, 76, 173, 178
Old Testament, 59, 205
On the Road, 111, 260

Onassis, Jacqueline, 156
Oneirocritica, 67, 76, 126, 284
Ophiuchus, 61, 63, 245
Orpheus, 47, 109, 279
Orphic hymns, 53
Ortygia, 95
Osiris, 289
Ouranos, 9, 37, 118, 130, 253

Paganism, 84, 119
Pallas, 9, 35, 151–152, 154–155, 158–159, 163, 171, 173–180, 186, 205, 209
Palmer, Daniel, 247
Pan, 13, 39, 158, 184, 219, 233, 238–239, 287, 289–291
Pandora, 289, 291–292
Paphos, 118
Paris, 40, 65
Parthenon, 173
Paul of Alexandria, 222
Pausanias, 67
Perera, Sylvia Brinton, 120, 126
Persephone, 60, 70, 98, 159, 163–168, 185, 278–284
Persia, 7
Phaedrus, 38, 41
Philostratus, 67
Phoenicia, Phoenicians, 118, 219
Pisces, 30–31, 98, 123, 130, 138, 166–167, 222, 224, 253, 265, 268–269
Plato, 12, 14, 38–39, 41, 45, 265, 273
Poseidon, 9, 163, 220, 265–266, 268–269, 271, 277
Priapus, 184
Prometheus Bound, 256

Prometheus, 37, 60, 244, 254–259, 261, 291
Psyche, 11, 13, 15–16, 23, 35, 60, 69, 75, 87, 138, 143, 158–159, 248, 273, 289, 292–293
Ptolemy, 67, 76
Pythia, 131, 153
Python, 83, 131, 153
Pythoness, 84

Queen Elizabeth I, 175
Queen of Sheba, 206

Rambo, 139
Red Sea, 206
Redford, Robert, 106
Remus, 137
Renaissance, 17, 40, 45, 48–49, 67, 88, 100, 107, 120–121
Reno, Janet, 177
Rohini, 82
Romans, 8, 10, 137, 175, 183
Rome, 8, 10, 26, 40, 137, 163, 183–184, 195, 200, 206
Romeo and Juliet, 122
Romulus, 137
Russia, 113

Sabaeans, 113
Sagan, Carl, 118, 126
Sagittarius, 28–29, 31, 61, 95, 222, 224, 244
Samhain, 158
Sanger, Margaret, 175
Santa Claus, 108
Santa Fe, 70, 76, 159
Sappho, 289

Schwartz, Jacob, 159
Schwarzenegger, Arnold, 139
Scorpio, 8, 32–33, 61, 98, 132, 134, 138, 141, 157, 253, 280, 282
sect, planetary, 7, 19, 84, 94, 110, 114, 145
Selene, 95, 99
Self, 13–14, 16, 25, 34, 76, 88, 109, 269, 280
Semele, 185
Shakespeare, William, 101, 121
Shakti, 119–120, 267
Shamash, 7, 81, 93
Shekinah, 196, 207–208
Shintoism, 81
Simon Magus, 207
Sin (deity), 7, 93, 102
Sitchin, Zechariah, 76, 157, 159
Sol, 7, 9
Solomon, 206
Sophia, 207
South Node, 157, 209
Spacey, Kevin, 188
Spica, 96
St. Nicholas, 108, 113
Stallone, Sylvester, 139
Sting, The, 106
Stonehenge, 93
Sturluson, Snorri, 121
Sufis, 112
Sumer, 5–6, 8, 59, 105–106, 117, 206
Surya, 82

T'ai Chi, 144
Talmud, 205
Tammuz, 120
Tantra, Tantrics, 122, 124, 126

Tarnas, Richard, 254, 261
Tarot, 224, 260, 290
Tartarus, 232, 236
Taurus, 6, 8, 17–18, 32, 36, 52, 98, 132–133, 166, 219
Telemachus, 178
Terminator, The, 139
Terra, 9
Terrible Mother, 280, 283
Tetrabiblos, 67, 76
Thatcher, Margaret, 177
Themis, 62, 256
Theogony, 129–130, 253–254
Theseus, 153, 219, 267, 272–273
Thessaly, 60
Threepenny Opera, The, 27, 29
Tiamat, 219
Tibet, 122
Titans, 130, 173, 236, 255, 265
Tree of Life, 196, 208
Triptolemus, 164, 166
Trophonius, 62
Typhon, 220

Ulysses, 265
United States, 138, 157, 179–180, 210, 227
Utnapishtim, 8
Utu, 6

Valens, Vettius, 95, 102, 222, 227
Vedanta, 64
Vesta, 9, 52, 87, 151, 154–155, 158–159, 175, 186, 193, 195–201, 289, 291

Vestal Virgins, 195
Virgo, 96, 98, 110, 130, 132, 134, 165–167, 186, 280
Voudoun, 24
Vulcan, 26–27, 29–31, 119, 188

Wayne, John, 138
Weill, Kurt, 25, 27, 30–31, 289
Weimar Republic, 25
Winfrey, Oprah, 153
Wise Old Crone, 97
Wise Old Man, 12, 48, 65, 107–108, 112, 235–236
Wise Old Woman, 65, 107, 112
Woden, 107
Wolff, Toni, 158–159
Wyoming, 179

Xena, 175, 178

Yahweh, 205–206, 291
yoga, 45, 50, 53, 107, 199

Zen, 9
Zeus, 5, 8–9, 26, 53, 82–83, 85, 95, 105–106, 119, 129, 152–154, 156–157, 163, 173–176, 183–190, 219–222, 224–225, 231–232, 255–256, 265–266, 277–278, 287–288, 291
Zipporah, 206

About the authors ...

Arielle Guttman has been involved with the study of astrology since 1977. In 1980 she founded an astrological consulting firm, Astro Originals, through which astrological seminars, personal and business consulting, astrological teaching and lecturing are conducted. For several years she has been involved with asteroid research, and by including those asteroids in her astrological work, has found a growing interest in this, "the feminine" aspects of astrology. She has lectured for numerous astrological organizations and conferences, both in the United States and in Europe. She is the author of *Astro-Compatibility,* and co-author of *Mythic Astrology Applied* and *The Astro Carto Graphy Book of Maps.*

Kenneth Johnson holds a degree in Religious Studies from California State University Fullerton. His emphasis has been in the study of mythology and this interest is reflected in his writing and his astrological practice. Kenneth discovered astrology while traveling in Europe during the summer of 1973. He studied in Amsterdam and London before returning to the United States and developing a practice which focuses on archetypal themes and personal mythologies. In addition to his astrological interests, Kenneth is also a musical theater librettist and a member of the Dramatists Guild.

Be sure to also purchase Guttman and Johnson's companion edition, *Mythic Astrology,* available from Echo Point Books

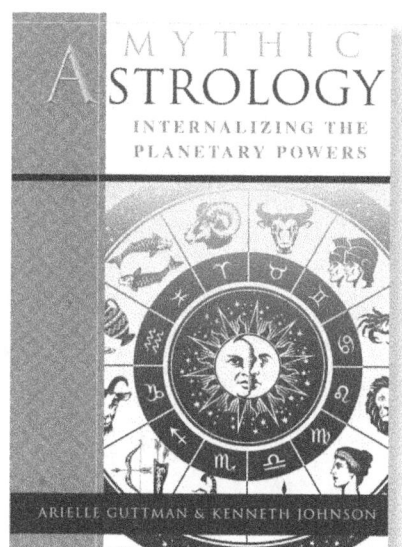

Mythic Astrology

Discover a whole new side of astrological wisdom: mythic astrology, the application of ancient myth to personal self-discovery. *Mythic Astrology* introduces you to the age-old symbolic connections between celestial factors, mythological figures, and the archetypes which govern our inner and outer lives.

PAPERBACK ISBN 978-1-63561-853-2

Our books may be ordered from any bookstore or online purveyor of books, or directly through our Web site, www.echopointbooks.com. Or visit our retail store, located in Brattleboro, Vermont.

www.ingramcontent.com/pod-product-compliance
Lightning Source LLC
Chambersburg PA
CBHW080531170426
43195CB00016B/2528